CONTENTS

KU-647-521

0149058

D623
2860
VOB (Eng)

MANAGING
MULTIMEDIA

CA

CAN

2 8

Don

0201877392

MANAGING
MULTIMEDIA

ELAINE ENGLAND • ANDY FINNEY

ADDISON-WESLEY

HARLOW, ENGLAND • READING, MASSACHUSETTS • MENLO PARK, CALIFORNIA • NEW YORK
DON MILLS, ONTARIO • AMSTERDAM • BONN • SYDNEY • SINGAPORE
TOKYO • MADRID • SAN JUAN • MILAN • MEXICO CITY • SEOUL • TAIPEI

Cover designed by Designers and Partners Ltd, Oxford
and printed by The Riverside Printing Co. (Reading) Ltd.
Typeset by Scribe Design, Gillingham, Kent
Illustrations by Gary Weston

Printed in Great Britain at The University Press, Cambridge

First printed 1996

ISBN 0-201-87739-2

British Library Cataloguing in Publication Data
A catalogue record for this book is available from the British Library.

Library of Congress Cataloging in Publication Data applied for.

INTRODUCTION

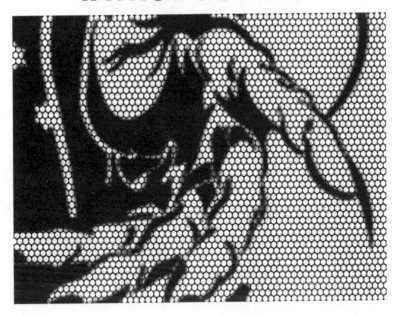

How to use the book and CD-ROM

Who is it for?

This book is useful for anyone studying or practising multimedia. It addresses the multimedia management role of head of a project. There are a variety of titles that are used to denote this – Producer, Managing Editor, Analyst or Senior Software Engineer – for example. The term Project Manager is used here because it is a neutral term which does not betray any media origins since multimedia is produced from a fusion of talents across several media.

Project management theory and practice also offers insights to help keep control of projects. Multimedia projects are notoriously difficult to keep within time and budget because there are so many variables. This book analyses all the variables within multimedia projects from clients to techniques, team members to applying project management principles.

Because the book follows the life cycle of a project, it broadens the understanding of the multimedia context for those with a single specialism such as programming or graphics, while giving a practical business and management slant for others.

It will prove useful for those commissioning multimedia as the clients' roles and responsibilities are defined in parallel with the project manager's. It clearly identifies the phases of a project and acts as an introduction to the process. It can act as a reference for those new to multimedia.

The structure of the book

The chapters are organized around the development of a project from initiation to completion. Administration, management and production processes are interweaved reflecting the way they happen during a project. Because some phases occur simultaneously, the linear nature of the chapters misrepresents the overall process to an extent. However, we have tried to cover all the phases for developing a team-based, client-driven, commercial project which uses the equivalent of some original video footage, a range of audio assets, and commercially sourced and in-house produced graphics.

We used this type of project as the default because it has the greatest number of tasks and resources. Other multimedia projects – non-commercial and non-team based – would need many but not all of the aspects covered here. Multimedia games and entertainment titles sometimes have a different development cycle if they are truly market-driven. This market-driven model is mentioned as a point of comparison to client-centred projects but is not explained in detail. Research and international projects have more phases, and are referred to when appropriate.

The major differences between non-commercial and commercial projects are the amount and type of rights clearances that are needed, as well as the smaller production scale where fewer staff are used in audio, video and graphics production. If you are working on these types of projects you may not have as many administrative and legal aspects to cover, but many will be the same, just needed on a smaller scale.

The glossary will serve as a ready reference for any terms that need further explanation. We have tried to make it as comprehensive as possible and it is also included on the CD.

The structure of the chapters

Chapters 1 and 2 give the background knowledge for the topics of multimedia, projects and multimedia project management. These will provide a common base of understanding between us.

Icon of Project manager's responsibilities.

From Chapter 3, we follow the development of a project. Each chapter begins with a resumé of the project manager's responsibilities.

These will prepare you for the concepts that will be covered, and help focus your interpretation of them to the role outlined. During the book, the complete range of responsibilities builds up into the equivalent of a job description. If you are reading the book for a general purpose, then you can skip the resumés and read the chapters for salient information.

Icon of Theory into Practice.

During the chapters you will find suggested tasks. These are to help you transfer the principles into practical activities of relevance to your own situation. Because there are so many types of multimedia projects, we have tried to stick to principles which can be applied across the greatest variety of projects. But, the principles will only serve you for your own situation if you take the time and effort to apply them. The theory into practice tasks can help you build up project-specific sets of reference materials that suit the range and type of projects you develop.

Icon of Refer to CD.

Where appropriate during the chapters you will be referred to the CD for information which is represented better in an electronic form, as well as for practical exercises on visual and audio examples.

Icon of Summary.

Each chapter has a summary. These reinforce the main points covered in the chapter but can also be used as a quick reference when you are developing a project and reach the phase being discussed. Some people prefer to read the summaries prior to reading a chapter to decide if it has direct relevance for them. Others read them first to preview the chapter, to prepare them for it.

Icon of Recommended reading.

Where possible we have included recommended reading at the end of chapters but quite a few of the aspects covered here have relied on practical experience and represent the authors' interpretation of that experience rather than insights from defined theory.

The structure of the CD-ROM

The CD with this book aims to be both a companion and an extension of the book itself and is a mixed mode disc combining digital audio and data.

The structure of the CD-ROM corresponds to the chapters in the book and you can find the examples and exercises that are referenced during the text in the book. With these, we have tried to overcome the static and monochrome limitations of the printed page with colour illustrations, some audio, video and animation and hyperlinks. There is also an electronic, searchable copy of the glossary. Along with this there are a variety of demonstration software packages. These include examples of the kind of software that is commonly used in multimedia production and will give a good introduction to some of the tools that you will use as you produce your applications. They will help you to extend your understanding of the principles covered in the chapters dealing with audio, video and graphics.

As well as CD-ROM data this disc contains a few CD-Audio tracks, which can be played on any compact disc player as well as on most CD-ROM drives. These are examples for Chapters 8 and 13 and they start with Track 2 of the disc. Please do not try to play Track 1 of the disc since this contains CD-ROM data and, if you hear it at all, it may damage your equipment.

The CD-ROM is based around an HTML document which can be read with the same software you would use to surf the World Wide Web on the Internet. We have done this to allow the greatest access to the disc. In case you are not a Web surfer, Web browsers for PC/Windows 95 and Apple Macintosh are included on the disc itself. This disc is in a standard format, called ISO 9660, which can be read on a wide range of computers, including PC and Macintosh. Most of the material can be used with other platforms, as can the HTML document, since the files are stored, where possible, in standard formats.

The most up-to-date information on the CD can be found in the ReadMe file on the CD-ROM itself. This is a text file and can be read with any word processor and is the best point for you to start. To start to explore the CD itself you use your browser to open the document called simply START.HTM and then follow the links.

Acknowledgements

Many thanks to all those who gave their time and expertise to comment on the drafts and helped shape the book:

Judith Aston, Lecturer in Multimedia Production, Faculty of Art, Media and Design, University of the West of England, Bristol, UK.

Chris Barlas, Chairman, Authors Licensing & Collecting Society, UK.

Jardine Barrington Cook, Logica, UK.

Birte Christensen-Dalsgaard, UNI.C, Danish Computing Centre for Research and Education, Aärhus, Denmark.

Mark Dillon, Director, On-Line Services, GTE Entertainment, USA.

Mike Philips, MediaLab Arts Course, School of Computing, University of Plymouth, UK.

Malcolm Roberts, Senior Manager, Bank of Montreal Institute for Learning, Scarborough, Ontario, Canada.

Gisella Rosano, Designer/Developer, Bank of Montreal Institute for Learning, Scarborough, Ontario, Canada.

William S. Strong, Partner, Kotin Crabtree & Strong Attorneys at Law, Boston, USA.

Charles Walker, Partner, Walker Tomaszewski Solicitors, London, UK.

We both recognize that many of our past and present colleagues have contributed to the span of experience covered here and thank you all – too numerous to name individually.

Finally we also recognize the debt to all the pioneers who persevered against the odds and kept the faith that multimedia would be mainstream. You were right.

Elaine England
Andy Finney
March 1996

CHAPTER 1

THE BACKGROUND: MULTIMEDIA AND PROJECTS

What is multimedia?

'Oh yes, we're a multimedia company. We sell books and videos.'

The very word multimedia sometimes has some people reaching for their guns. It even makes one television executive put his wallet away. But just what is multimedia?

Let us hope that the foggy confusions about multiple media (presumably what the quote above really meant) and mixed media ('art work with bits of raffia in it') are behind us. The French may still refer to media integration, which has no small merit; but let's blow away some of that fog and see what is revealed.

Someone asked the comp.multimedia discussion group on the Internet the question recently. What is the definition of multimedia? The most succinct reply was this, from the English consultant Tony Feldman:

> Multimedia is the seamless integration of text, sound, images of all kinds and control software within a single digital information environment.

Historically, multimedia – and by this we usually mean interactive multimedia – is descended from computer-based training (CBT) by way of interactive video. It was relatively simple to extrapolate the simple teletype interaction that a computer operator might have with a mainframe machine, in the days when all programmers wore white coats, to programming the computer to ask meaningful questions and collate the results.

At the time that videodisc arrived on the scene almost every computer was controlled by typing esoteric commands onto a keyboard and reading the results as text on a screen. The teletype may have been long gone but the computer monitor was still functioning like one.

Videodisc appeared on the scene at about the same time that computer displays were becoming more visual and people, rather than corporations, were able to buy them and put them on their desks. It was logical to use a computer, following the CBT model, to control a videodisc player and so add pictures and sound. By taking the videodisc output and electronically combining it with the computer's display on a single screen, Interactive Video was defined.

Good interactive video using videodiscs is only now being surpassed by all-digital multimedia. The use of time-based media like movies and sound places demands on the performance of a computer system that can be expensive and difficult to deal with. However, worldwide research into compression of all forms of media for use in computer-based systems is giving us more and more tools to use (even play with) in multimedia. Most importantly, by taking all the media from the digital domain, the scope for manipulation and integration is significantly greater than before.

The use of the word 'seamless' in this context is important from an artistic as well as a technical perspective. The viewer (or user if you like) of a computer should be as cushioned from the technology as possible and the designer should be able to choose the best medium to get across the particular message. It is often said that a good interactive video or multimedia program is very much like a television programme that is under your control.

In fact multimedia has a chameleon-like ability to pretend to be many things. In designing an application you have the freedom to use so many disparate media types and techniques that a television programme is only one option. Sound and pictures can help to attract your viewer to the humblest of menus and make the most tedious of help screens interesting.

The disciplines of multimedia are as diverse as the media types. Familiarity and even expertise is required in the facets of television and radio production as well as a facility with computer software. You need to forget the notion that specialism is more important than all-round ability, because the skills you need to master when making multimedia are very broad. They will include project management and cost control, computer system architecture and logic, video and audio editing, text and image manipulation ... at least. Add to this the need to be able to integrate the disparate elements in a meaningful and appropriate way.

Of course there is a downside to this integration. Computer projects are notoriously difficult to scope and budget, and to people coming into multimedia from an audio/visual background this is often a difficult problem. The custom and practice in professional audio and video is to design and write your programme and hire in specialist facilities by the hour to turn your ideas into technical reality. It ought to be like that in multimedia; but here the situation is more complex. It is analogous to building the videotape recorder at the same time as editing the tape. Coupled with this there is a common lack of knowledge of just what can be achieved with the technology (and this applies to developers as well as clients) as more and more is achieved with gradually changing computers and other equipment. Software techniques change too, and even fashions of tools with which to build the final application.

For people with a computing background there is the difficulty of scoping and specifying the way in which the application is to work in the knowledge that the content is usually more important than the computer program that controls and displays it. The software team leader will often be reporting to someone who does not share his or her intricate knowledge of the computer and may find it hard to believe that superficially simple things can be difficult and yet seemingly complicated changes in structure can be achieved by quickly changing a few things in the code.

For end users, whether they are in a classroom, in the home or at work, multimedia improves the flow of ideas and information. It is a rich canvas on which to communicate, but this richness brings with it complexities and challenges and quite often the only way to see what can be done is to try it.

What is a multimedia project?

Varieties of projects

As we've noted, a project in multimedia means any series of tasks that deliver a combination of media that has a computer component integrating these together. There are hardware-oriented multimedia projects where the aim might be to specify, introduce and integrate a delivery platform, such as video-conferencing with a tailored user front-end, into an organization. There are software development projects which combine media components into an application to run on a delivery platform. The delivery platform will be one that can support an interactive combination of video, graphics, animation, sound and text. This could include anything from a floppy disk to video on demand.

This book will concentrate on client-centred software development projects that need a team to work together to achieve the project. This type of project covers the majority of circumstances that will be met in project management and production. This is the reason for the focus. There are multimedia professionals who carry out all aspects of a project alone so they will not need the staff-management aspects covered here. However, the principal stages of a multimedia project are the same. Managing the project cycle and handling clients need the same skills whether working alone or as a team.

Varieties of clients

A project begins with a definition stage between the initiator of the project and production personnel. This relationship is easy to define when an external client initiates the process and seeks someone to produce the application. But, in some circumstances, the initiators can be people from within the same organization and in this case they are known as internal clients. It will help if you consider that a client is anyone who has the authority to control time and budget considerations and has the right to sanction design decisions. This definition covers both internal and external clients.

In this type of project, the production personnel will be working to organization or management requirements. This might happen in a multimedia games company where the ideas for a game can originate within the company itself, for example. The process of developing a project is in principle the same for external and internal clients except that the contractual agreements will probably, but not always, be more straightforward for internal clients if they exist at all. A lot depends on the company's structure whether formal agreements are needed between departments where budget transfer is concerned. You will still need to establish ways of working together though and the project will need to run to time and budget constraints.

When a multimedia company is trying to win business, it might approach another company and begin initiating a project. In this case, the initiation process is different from the one that will be described here because there is a demonstration and persuasion process. This forms part of sales and marketing management and will not be covered here.

Market-driven projects are initiated through analysis of a particular market – entertainment, for example – where the needs and wishes of prospective customers are monitored as well as the style and sales of competitors' products. The information is used to help make decisions on which applications to develop and what features to use within them. The company has to find a sponsor, investment, or invest its own money to develop the titles. Little market analysis is done within multimedia at present because the market sectors are still emerging and unstable so there is a lot of creative guesswork. This type of development will not be covered in detail here but it will warrant more attention as market sectors and platforms stabilize.

So, there are diverse projects and ways of classifying projects within the multimedia business but they all share some of the characteristics that are explored in the main chapters.

The client-centred multimedia project cycle: Overview

During the definition stage you are trying to get an understanding of what the clients want and to match their needs to a multimedia solution. This often needs to be carried out quickly so you work from assumptions rather than facts. We refer to this as 'scoping the project'. Your clients may be external clients from another company or internal clients from within your own organization. Clients are the people who hold the authority to start or stop the project and can authorize the money to be spent on it.

Once you have scoped the needs of the application and have a time-scale, you can begin to work out the costs so that you can formulate a proposal to the clients. The proposal indicates the range and scope of the work you will produce according to the time and cost you define.

When the clients accept the proposal, the project explodes into activity with several layers of operations happening simultaneously. In the book we will cover one strand or one major part of a strand at a time, but the project cycle diagram demonstrates the true nature of the process.

You need to establish how you will work with the clients because you will depend on them at certain points to give you assets or decisions to allow you to continue the work according to schedule. While you are establishing the ways of working and the legal aspects of the contracts, work starts on the project development. The details of the content, platform, media and techniques to be used, interface and interactive design are firmed up and production gets under way.

The production could not happen without personnel, so assembling the team by recruitment or use of internal staff is also happening in parallel at this time. While the production team are working together, the management aspects of teamwork come into play.

Of course, the actual asset production work – audio, video, graphics, text – which leads to integration of the assets gets under way. Coupled with asset production is the administration of the rights in the materials used. This is not a trivial task because of the lack of consensus of how to treat multimedia by those that hold or administer copyright.

Meanwhile, as asset production evolves, so does the testing to ensure that all the pieces will meet the specifications so that integration can take place as smoothly as possible. As the media components are integrated, the

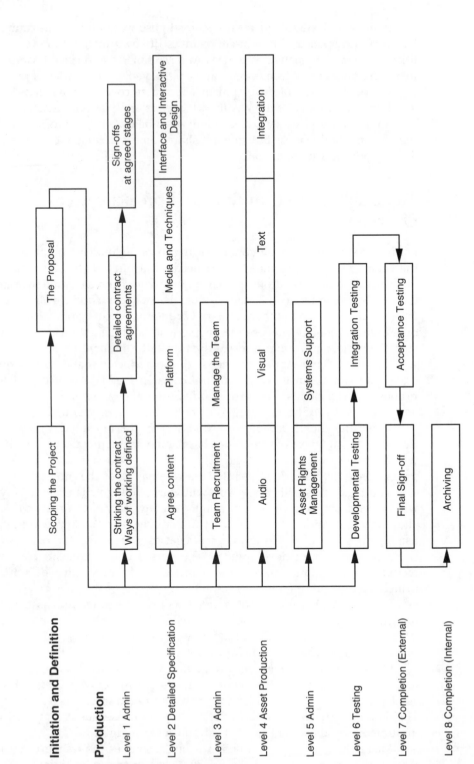

Initiation and Definition

Production

Level 1 Admin

Level 2 Detailed Specification

Level 3 Admin

Level 4 Asset Production

Level 5 Admin

Level 6 Testing

Level 7 Completion (External)

Level 8 Completion (Internal)

The client-centred multimedia project cycle.

code underlying integration needs to be tested thoroughly in a variety of circumstances on the equivalent of the final delivery platform, even if an authoring tool has been used. The development platform may well have been different and there are often adjustments that have to be made for the delivery platform to ensure the software operates according to specification.

The clients will be uneasy about giving final sign-off because they recognize that they lose any bargaining position they have at this point. You have to have an end point that is clear or the budget quickly turns into overspend. The precise terms for final sign-off need to be negotiated before the end of the project to help the process run smoothly.

Finally, it is tempting to consider final sign-off and delivery as the end of the project. For most it is, but many forget the importance of archiving the project in a systematic, well-documented way. If there is return business for upgrading the application, or reuse of assets needed for the same client in another project, you'll save time, confusion and money if it is easy to locate any asset, piece of code, or documentation that might be needed.

This then is the main model of multimedia project definition and production that will be expanded in the following chapters. There are many more stages that occur within each of the major ones identified here. These represent the tip of the iceberg, so to speak. The simultaneous nature of levels 1 to 6 should indicate the complexity of interaction that happens between the team members and the processes of production. This should also serve to demonstrate why project management principles need to be applied to help control the complex interaction.

Summary

- Multimedia is the seamless integration of text, sound, images of all kinds and control software within a single digital information environment.

- The skills needed to produce multimedia are diverse.

- Apart from competence in software and media design and production, cost control and staff-management skills are needed.

- A client is anyone that has the authority to control the time and budget, or sanction the design.

- A client-centred project follows stages of initiation and definition followed by production. The production phase has several levels which are interrelated. It is not a linear process.

Recommended reading

There is no specific support material recommended for this chapter. The definitions are based on experience.

CHAPTER 2

THE BACKGROUND: MULTIMEDIA PROJECT MANAGEMENT

Multimedia – industry fusion or confusion?

Because multimedia uses many skills and its people come from a variety of backgrounds, the multimedia environment does not have a single defined way of working. Multimedia companies tend to have a bias according to their origin and the background of their management. The bias will usually reflect video production, computing, publishing or interactive training/education. Functional specifications have to blend with storyboards and source code coexists with time code.

Each of these disciplines has different role names, phases of production, methods for documenting production, ways of working, organizational structures, and cultures. The individuals who work in the companies have their own specialisms. Some will recognize the environment they find themselves in but many will not. They will have to adapt to the new terminology and structure.

Communication across the disciplines is problematic. Imagine a person with a video producer's background being asked to produce a Functional

Table 2.1 Comparison of multimedia origins.

	Video production	Computing	Publishing	Interactive training/ Education
Roles	Executive Producer, Producer, Director, Production Assistant, Script writer,	Project Manager, Analyst, Programmer,	Commissioning Editor, Senior Editor, Editor, Author,	Training Analyst, Interactive Designer
	Video Graphics Artist	Computer Graphics Artist	Print Graphics Artist, Illustrator, Cartoonist	
Production phases	Commission, Research/script, Shoot, Offline edit, Online edit, Distribute	Analyse Prototype, Program, Test, Release	Commission, Research/write, Review, Re-write, Proof, Produce, Distribute	Analyse, Design, Prototype, Re-design, Produce, Test, Release, Evaluate
Documentation (client/ commissioner receives)	Storyboard, Script, Rewrites	Functional Specification, Technical Specification, Change Management Procedures	Proposal, Drafts, Re-drafts, Proofs	Proposal, Outline Design, Detailed Design, Sign-off Agreements

and Technical Specification or a programmer being asked to produce a storyboard, and assimilate time code data from an edit shot list. This happens.

Table 2.1 shows how each industry has developed its own way of producing a media product. Multimedia production cuts across these as it needs aspects from all for successful production.

Where does project management fit into this?

Although there are obvious differences, the industries share the production of media products. Their ways of working have evolved to suit the production methods for a particular media, market and distribution cycle, in some cases over many decades. We often imagine television to be a new medium, but it has been around for 40 years or more, and drew on practices from radio and the movie industry.

They are all team-based, complex activities with one role acting as the team leader/coordinator. They are all producing a particular end-product as the result of the team effort. Each product has unique properties. These aspects are characteristics of project management and they apply to multimedia management too.

A project manager is expected to produce a product by organizing and controlling resources according to planned expenditure, in a certain time frame and to a defined quality level. This fits the description of a person in charge of a multimedia project. For the purposes of this book the term project manager will be used to denote a person with this role irrespective of the specialist origins where the role might be called producer or designer.

Is multimedia project management the same as project management?

Although project management methods offer a good basis for multimedia project management, there are limitations and confusions that need to be recognized and considered. Some of these are inherent in project management methods and some occur because of the particular nature of multimedia.

Time, Cost, Quality triangle.

Limitations of project management methods

Traditional project management principles were derived from engineering projects where the link between time for production, the cost of the product and the quality of the end-product was established. The principles state that if any one of these factors is changed, the others are affected. Once a project has started, the project manager needs to monitor changes and assess the impact on the planned time, cost and quality of the product.

Some of these principles were used as the basis for the project management computer-based software packages that exist today. They provide a method to help define the breakdown of the project into tasks and the sequence of tasks that need to be performed according to a time line. This is called a Gantt chart. Some tools link the use of resource to the costs incurred and some attempt to link the dependence between tasks, time and resources.

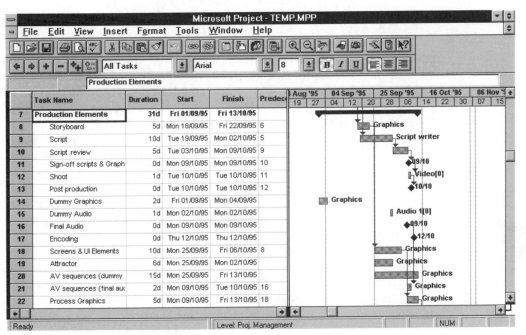

Gantt chart example. Screen shot reprinted with permission from Microsoft Corporation.

The definitions of tasks, sequence of production, resources needed and cost breakdown need to be done in some way as part of the multimedia project manager's role and are not straightforward.

Traditional project management methods tried to address the interrelation of the dependencies between tasks to the sequence of production and time. This was done using a technique called Network Analysis which was also known as Critical Path Analysis.

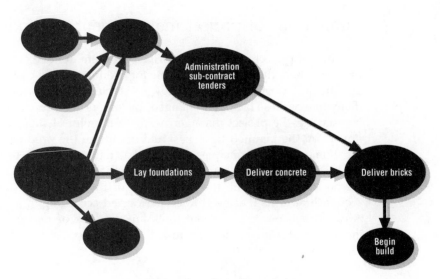

Network analysis: Example 1.

Network Analysis encouraged project managers to use a diagram to show the logical links between tasks, illustrating which ones would be in simultaneous development and which ones were dependent on others reaching a certain stage before work could begin. The critical path is derived from this analysis. It is the sequence of development of tasks that allows the optimum progress through the project.

For example, in a building project (Example 1) the delivery of ready-mixed, quick-setting concrete is dependent upon the foundations being ready to receive it. If there is a delay with the foundations, the delivery of the concrete has to be delayed. The one is critically dependent on the other. But in this case the opposite is not true because the digging doesn't have to stop if the concrete is going to be late. The subcontract tender process for the bricks doesn't have to stop if the foundations are delayed.

Sometimes, however, the dependency does work both ways. Sometimes dependency states change. Sometimes something that was not dependent can become dependent. Sometimes something that wasn't critical becomes critical. It begins to sound mysterious – it is, and there are no set rules for when or why things change their nature!

To give a multimedia example, your project may be going well and you had worked out the sequence of production with a good understanding of which parts could be under production simultaneously without affecting each other and which major parts needed to wait for several processes all to be complete.

Example 2 is for the purposes of demonstration and only represents a small part of the project. It addresses major parts of the project, not detailed processes.

It shows that while computing and graphics tasks begin as soon as one part of the content/script is agreed, audio and video production wait until all the relevant content is agreed. This is usual because audio and video

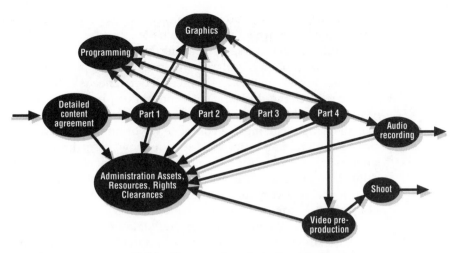

Multimedia network analysis: Example 2.

production is often better done in one phase than in pieces. You only want to hire a video crew or hire a videotape edit suite once for a defined time, for example, whereas your graphics and programming resources have a longer commitment to the project.

But consider this problem while looking at the diagram. You are likely to know how many voice-over artists are needed from the initial agreement of the structure of the application but not exactly how much or what they will say until the whole content has been agreed. The clients have specified that they want to use a particular artist in this project because his voice has become identified with their products through advertising. He is an actor as well as voice-over artist but is known best for minor character roles.

The project is almost halfway through the content stage. You have had to adjust the time-scale of developments because of hold-ups on sign-off of Part 1, but you are getting more confident that the next stages will run pretty smoothly. You decide to check out the availability of the artist with an indication of which month you'll need him and most likely which week. You find he'll be filming on location for two and a half months around then for a TV series. He can only manage to give you one or two days and these are a full month before your content should be finished *if nothing else affects its planned progress.* You can't afford to wait till he finishes his location shooting because the project release date is linked to a fixed conference day in your clients' organization and you've already lost a lot of contingency time. Although you try to influence the clients to change, they insist on using this artist.

Completing the audio script now becomes more critical than completing the rest of the content. This is an example of something becoming critical when it wasn't a problem. The network analysis would have to be reworked in a radical way to split out the way of working for achieving this. The voice-over date would be fixed and influence all the phases of production linked to it whatever else occurred in the project. Fixed dates and times have more effect on project development than anything else so the sooner they are identified, the better.

Some of the problems in using Network Analysis are evident in this example. Although popular during the 1980s, its popularity has waned. The first difficulty is met when the level of detail needs to be decided. It is possible to clutter the diagram with connections between tasks very easily. A large amount of space is needed to outline a complex project and relatively small changes can mean a complete reworking of the level of detail and the whole diagram as in the case shown above. Sometimes Network Analysis makes the process appear so complicated that there seems to be no clear development path. It is also difficult for others to grasp its meaning and relevance. It is very time consuming to maintain if the project environment is prone to as many changes as multimedia.

However, the impact of the fixed date for the voice-over and the consequent changes in use of resources, different priorities for completing tasks and dangers of not meeting the date need to be recorded in some way that all understand. At the moment this is usually done by word of mouth backed up by a written account if the project manager is experienced. The project management software tools can show fixed deadlines in the Gantt chart but the reasons behind the line-up of tasks is not clear and with so much going on all the time, it is sometimes easy to forget why you made a seemingly odd decision. This is why other documentation becomes important.

If we return to looking at project management methods and tools, the computer tools can prove useful in the planning stage of the project particularly if the clients help construct the schedule and agree to their time involvement on tasks. It also helps if they get an understanding of the process so that they can appreciate why you suggest certain solutions to problems that arise.

What is quality in multimedia?

The first limitation of conventional project management tools lies in the definition of quality. In engineering projects it is easier to specify quality in measurable terms: for example, the dimensions of the product, its durability, the physical mechanisms and how they operate, the components and so on. But in any media project how is quality defined in measurable terms?

Technical levels of quality like the audio being mono or stereo and encoded at a specific digital level can be defined clearly, but the quality of design is problematic. Without the definition, the impact of changes in time and cost on quality is very difficult to make a case for.

The tools do not help in defining the quality level that is agreed between client and producer. The link between time, cost and quality of product is not shown in any breakdown of tasks or the resource/cost schedule and this is a problem. The three are interrelated so that any change to any one will affect the others but a direct correlation does not

How do you measure multimedia quality?

exist. There is a tendency for project mnagers to overlook the impact of time and cost on quality because of this. Because the quality level is not specified as exactly in multimedia projects as it is in manufacturing projects, for example, it is even harder for project managers to define the impact because it is so intangible.

The different perspectives on the meaning of quality in multimedia were neatly described by Hanspeter Bürgin, the Coordinator for the inter-active media awards for the 5th World Conference for Banking and Finance, Basle 1995. The set of judges came from different backgrounds in interactive development and so looked for different features. The features were perfectly valid for each perspective but meant that it was difficult to get a consensus. So, the judges then reached agreement on a set of critieria before making their decisions.

This difference of perspective as to the nature of quality is similar to what happens within multimedia teams because the members come from different media backgrounds. It also occurs between developers and clients for the same reason. There can be a gap between the team's understanding of quality and that of their managements as well. So the definition of quality in multimedia is a major problem.

If we look back at Table 2.1, quality has been defined in different ways in the different disciplines. Video Production produces a storyboard and script for the client to agree content and visual treatment. Computing uses a functional specification to define how the application will operate and a prototype to show look and feel. Publishing uses editors and peer review processes to control the quality of work submitted. Interactive Training and Education uses the Outline and Detailed Design documents to agree the quality level of content and a prototype for the look and feel. In market-driven projects quality is assessed by whether the product is successful in the market. The production quality relies on the creativity of the develop-ment team.

This highlights some of the problems in defining quality in multimedia. There are some objective parameters for the technical aspects but many subjective aspects for design quality. Each project will define its own 'quality' priorities according to the subject and the target audience.

How then can the time, cost, quality equation work for multimedia? It can only work with a guiding principle defined as quality – one so general that it will operate for all multimedia projects. The principle needs to be viewed with the understanding that it is only acting as a control mechanism for time and cost.

For budgetary purposes then, the following definition of quality will be useful. Underlying all the processes is the definition and agreement of content and its treatment. The content means the information that is going to be presented and the treatment means which media and which techniques will be used and what it will look like.

Design quality for media projects = content and treatment agreement

How are time, cost and quality linked in multimedia?

Time, Cost, Quality triangle.

The relationship between time, cost and quality is far from linear. If we consider a classic request from a client in a less complicated process than multimedia and study the effects, it will give a clear indication of the relationship between time, cost and quality and demonstrate the principles that should be applied in multimedia.

'Oh! and there's just a small change ...'

You are a specialist furniture craftsman. A client has ordered an armchair in a particular style using particular materials, with a particular fabric and a particular fitting. You worked out the cost and delivery time accordingly to a formula taking into account the type and availability of the materials and the complexity of production.

However, after a week, the client changes his mind about the fabric. What are the implications to cost and time? The knock-on cost will depend on how far along production the original request has got.

■ Project Management Note 1. Change may have cost implications for administration and production.

The original fabric could be at any of the following stages at different times of the process. It could have been cut out, sewn, fitted. So the customer may well have to accept some charges and a changed delivery date. In this case the fabric had been cut and sewn so there is redundant work and materials and rework. You will have to start the production again.

■ Project management Note 2. Change may have time implications because of rework.

When you explain the time and cost knock-ons, the client insists that he really needs the chair in the original time. There may be no way that this can happen. You may not be able to achieve it as the time limit may now be too short. The new fabric choice is from a special supplier and is much more expensive than the original choice. When you contact them, they are out of stock. It will take time to order.

■ Project Management Note 3. Change may make the project impossible to achieve if it produces factors beyond your control. Also, there are some processes that cannot be speeded up.

If you make it into a special order where the workers will need to work overtime, more costs need to be passed to the customer.

■ Project Management Note 4. If time-scales are immovable but you have to absorb changes, the workload increases and causes extra cost.

Or, you might offer a standard fitted cover rather than a loose one as this takes less time but is of a different quality. Alternatively, you might suggest a different style and shape for the chair that is easier and faster to produce.

■ Project Management Note 5. The quality of the product is changed to meet the time constraint.

It has taken a few hours for you to assess the situation, time and cost implications and relay three alternatives to the client. You need a quick decision because your new time-scales and costs are based on starting immediately. Your client doesn't reply to your fax immediately. You phone his company the next day to be told he's out of the country on business for two days and isn't contactable! Your work's supervisor is reworking the production schedule and is on hold waiting for the decisions! The fabric supplier keeps phoning to ask if you're placing the order or not!

■ Project management Note 6. Never be fooled by 'it's just a small change'.

THEORY INTO PRACTICE 1

Look back at the example and substitute the following. It should give you an insight into the repercussions of change in a multimedia project.

The style of the chair (type of wood, springs and stuffing)	= content agreed
The shape of the chair	= structure agreed
The fabric	= treatment of content agreed (usually known as 'look and feel')

Even though there were only three quality variables here – style, shape and fabric – it is easy to understand how a relatively small change can have significant repercussions depending on when the change was requested, how far into production the product was and how quickly new decisions are agreed.

Multimedia has many levels of quality and variables within each of the production processes – video, audio, graphics, text, animation, content treatment. Each of these has several stages to production so any changes at any point can have upward, downward, backward, forward and diagonal effects.

The schedule and plan become difficult to change and update. You have to predict the time and cost implications of slippage and this means consulting members of the team who will be affected by the proposed change. You also have to balance what can be absorbed and what effect this has on any contingency you had allowed in time and cost.

You have to agree the change and the knock-ons with the clients. Then you have to communicate the changes and the impact to the whole team because they are making decisions based on the time they're allowed. A change a day is not uncommon so imagine the impact on your time from the administration of these changes.

So the main difficulties inherent in the use of the project management methods and tools are:

■ The quality level isn't specified within the existing methods in a such a way that the impact of changes on it is measurable. If there are changes, the project manager has to predict all the consequences and update the plan of time and costs accordingly. The tools are not dynamic enough in prediction of the impact on time, resource and cost in relation to quality level. The value of the Network Analysis technique from traditional methods is difficult to define. Its value even for traditional projects is questioned. But the importance of defining the dependencies and their changing states is right in principle but difficult in practice.

In the armchair example, the quality was agreed in detail before the project started. In multimedia applications, the quality levels are often not well defined because the client and producer have little common ground in communication. When the multimedia specialists try to explain, their language is incomprehensible to clients. The clients can't specify what they want because they are not sure what they can have to begin to match it to what they want. The producer cannot specify cost and time accurately until there is a clear specification so quite a lot of time needs to be spent to understand the scope of the project. It is because of this upfront effort that many companies ask for staged payments to make sure that their costs are covered even if the project never goes ahead.

■ If you start from a poor definition, the clients will make so many changes that the project will get out of control quickly. We will deal with how to get a good definition later. Even if you are market- not client-driven, if you don't have a good definition at the beginning, the product will evolve and take more time and effort to complete than might be necessary. Sometimes the time of release of a product to market is vital – in time for Christmas presents, for example, or the market characteristics have changed and it is no longer receptive to the style of product.

How the nature of multimedia affects the project management process

The time, cost and quality principles are important but do not translate directly to multimedia. They can be applied when a process is well defined and the clients understand their role in the development process. In the building example the clients and architects would have taken a long time to define the shape, structure and cost of the building before work commenced. The clients recognize that once the foundations have begun they cannot change the shape of the end-product. They may try to change the construction materials or some features of the building but the points at which they can no longer affect the process are clear. The structure of a multimedia project is not as readily recognizable but the consequences of changes to it past a certain point in production are as bad as changing the shape of a building under construction.

Partly this problem is due to the seemingly fluid nature of computer software. There is no definite relationship between elements of a program that comes near to the definite way a building sits on its foundations. This does not mean that such dependencies do not exist. Good programming practice can minimize problems due to change – object oriented programming being one element of this – but not remove it. For example, adding a section into a program where this requires another item to be added to a menu can be very problematic if the menu has been built up in a sophisticated visual style with many layers of video and stills.

Multimedia management is much more like managing innovation. The process and end-product are constructed according to unique circumstances. Each multimedia application is hand-crafted because the content is unique even if standard tools are used. The personal qualities of the project manager – leadership style, team management, client management, credibility – come to the fore more. Aspects related to general management like level of authority, level of control over resources and level of control over budget are connected to the structure of the organization the project manager works for. These can have a significant effect on projects, either aiding or hindering the project manager in project development.

Planning, monitoring and control of time, cost and quality are still prime factors in a project management role but because the whole environment is unstable and intangible, the complexity increases and the risks of failure are higher. The total organizational structure contributes to success or failure but often the project manager has to accept the blame unfairly for setbacks.

Successful managers of innovation try to control the project earlier in the process than traditional project managers since the earlier control is taken the sooner the risks for disrupted project progress decrease. The link between planning and control is stronger. Rather than just plan time, cost and quality, you need to anticipate risk areas and take measures to decrease the risks. This includes controlling the expectations of the clients, the development team and the company management. In market-driven projects, you try to minimize risks through market analysis, by having strong distribution channels and through marketing and advertising the product to give it the maximum chance for success. So to manage innovation, knowledge of likely risks and how to cover them is crucial.

These personal and managerial qualities, like the concept of quality level, are not as definable as time and cost. They have to be put in context, in the environment where the project manager needs to operate. It is easy to recognize that multimedia does not have one environment but is a hybrid because of the range of skills of the people involved and the different approaches taken depending on the bias of the company. (See Table 2.1)

Because of this, only a few of the basic principles will be put into a context here to demonstrate the extent to which a project's success can be affected by organizational structure, team leadership, and risk analysis. Each individual environment and mix of people needs assessment to reach a more detailed understanding.

Organizational structure effects

If you are a project manager working in an organization with a traditional hierarchical structure, certain characteristics may have a tendency to interfere with your ability to get on with the job. You will have been assigned a project team but some key members may continue to receive instructions and take their lead from their functional superiors. This is sometimes referred to as 'dotted line' responsibility because of the way it is shown on an organizational chart and is quite common in the technical side of media companies. An engineer working as part of a programme team will be responsible to the producer for his or her work on the project but also responsible to a senior engineer for technical standards.

In the case of multimedia the programmer may have a senior programmer and the graphics artist may have a senior graphics artist who set their standards of work and, in addition, will generally control their workload as well. They may be working for other project managers on other projects during the time-scale of your project. In this case, their seniors will control their time and effort on your project. You may find that your programmer cannot complete the task you need on time because another project has been given priority.

You end up fighting for resources without the authority to influence the situation. This shows a definite role conflict. You cannot be held responsible for your project slippage if you don't have control of their time. Control of time should be one of your biggest responsibilities. You might well be able to split their time but the manner and exact amount should be within your control according to your project demands. This type of conflict which interferes with project progress also applies to non-human resources. If your team members don't have access to the right equipment at the right time because others have been given priority, there are further hold-ups.

There is a need for shared resources in a business and the management will only be seen to be doing their job by trying to get the most from the least to increase margins. But there's a fine line between downtime costs when sharing resources and savings from labour and equipment charges.

It doesn't take long for a hierarchical allocation of resources to get abused by those best placed to do so in the organization. This is mainly because everyone's projects fall prey to shifts in expected workloads and all is fair in a hierarchical war depending on your rank!

If you are working in an organization where functional and project managers coexist, both roles need to be tightly defined. The functional manager's role needs to change to a more generalist role because the project manager's role is specifically tied to the project and is therefore specialist. The authority over people and equipment for the term of the project has to be established and it needs to rest with the project manager. If not, there is no real role for a manager of this type.

Any request for resource time or equipment that has been allocated to the project should go through the project manager. Otherwise, the programmer and graphics artist tend to agree to the extra work for the functional manager without being fully aware of the present status of the project. For example, they wouldn't know that you are trying to block a major change resulting from a phone call from the client at the moment they agree to extra work. You finish the phone call but have failed to block the change and need them to absorb the extra work on your project.

As the project manager's role is also to monitor the time and cost of the project, a functional structure may cause problems. Many multimedia organizations operate control over time and costs via time sheets. There needs to be some mechanism for monitoring time and translating it into real costs rather than projected costs and time sheets are a well-accepted practice. However, there are many debates about how much time can be allocated to projects against time used for organizational administration, general meetings and the like.

If the internal and external resources for your project fill in time sheets which go to the finance/account function then it is their responsibility to have up-to-date records of costs for you to keep track of how much you have left to spend. The project manager has to make many decisions of reallocation of budget and spend. If the accounts section is behind with inputting the hours from your project, you may not be able to get an accurate understanding of how much you have left.

You will find there are occasions when you need to know exactly how much you have left daily, especially as you get near the end of the project when spend becomes more critical. Confusion can arise if items of equipment or software form part of the budget costs, depending on how the invoices are dealt with. These invoices may go to the respective functional heads and then to accounts, and the first you know of them is a sudden drop in your actual budget. You may have been expecting them but sometimes the actual point when they are paid is important. You need to take the figure off your expected outlay of money and then you have a better understanding of exactly what you have left against the remainder of the expected outlay.

Accounts rarely keep project information at this detailed level. They don't need the information but you do. They have to reconcile the overall project payments to overall spend and reconcile it with the information from other expenses. They have different interests to serve in reporting the overall position to management.

The whole question of how the financial data for each project is kept and who needs what information when, is a real problem. But a project manager needs to have detailed breakdowns of projected cost and actual costs to use in negotiations with the client. You need to make decisions on how much might be absorbed for small changes for the client as gestures of good will and when to charge for other changes because there is a real danger of the project going over budget.

The structure of the organization will dictate who has what type of financial information, who can have access to which financial data and under what circumstances. If there is the equivalent of a project manager role in the organization, the financial structure should facilitate this role and its needs as well as the executive management information. Many multimedia organizations that have the equivalent of a project manager role do not organize their financial data to help the role. Without accurate records of cost, a project management role cannot be fulfilled.

It used to be the traditional project manager's responsibility to keep track of the budget and report on it, but the need for better up-to-date executive management information on the overall position of the company tends to centralize the financial data. Only a fully automatic system where time-sheet data is input regularly and collated with freelance and external project costs will fully serve the needs of a project-led company.

This is an area which needs to be worked out according to the company and employee needs, and will become more important as companies grow larger.

A hierarchical organization will tend to have strict control over who can spend money. If the project manager or equivalent does not have a good level of authority over spend, projects may get held up waiting for the correct authorization. It is right that there is control over spending but authority levels need to be allocated on criteria worked out by the management according to the company's needs.

THEORY INTO PRACTICE 2

Your programmer has met a problem that one piece of software will solve. The company doesn't own it. The technical director who must sanction software purchases is on leave, and the systems manager who acts as his unofficial deputy is on a stand at a conference for three days. You have a deadline in two days and don't have the authority to spend company money.

What would you do?

There are no wrong answers. Some might be better than others. Here are some replies from project managers. They might match yours and give you some new insights.

(1) Buy it myself and claim it back later on expenses.
(2) Never start a project unless you've agreed some authority to spend money unsanctioned.
(3) I used to buy things myself but it took so long and so much hassle to get repaid, I ended up out of pocket because I went overdrawn. They didn't care. Then they just expect you to do it all the time. It's in their interest, really. Now I just explain to the clients why I can't make the deadline – they have a go at the management who have a go at me but I'd get the software. One day they'll listen, I suppose.
(4) I'd find someone with some authority and get them to buy it. But it takes so much time to justify why you need it. They're always busy and blame you for not sorting something out sooner.

There are two points to note here. Project managers will only spend wisely within a defined level if they have good information on the present spend, otherwise they will be spending blind. So authority to spend should be linked to the responsibility to monitor the overall budget of the project to avoid this. Secondly, if project managers buy a piece of software they have a responsibility to ensure it is really necessary, the company doesn't have a copy, the licence agreement is recorded and filed according to company policy and the correct people are fully informed of what they have done. This will avoid others replicating the same spend later through lack of knowledge of the existence of the software.

An alternative organizational structure constructs a team for a particular project under the project manager's control. The core of the organization is organized to support and facilitate projects, general administration and general management. The project team may exist for only one project and then be disbanded or moved into other teams.

This is more like the model of video production. The producer recruits people and facilities according to budget and needs. He or she has authority to spend within budget but has to report back within the company on progress and spend.

Within this type of structure there is more flexibility which seems to be needed in creative projects but the organization has to work hard to facilitate, coordinate, record and communicate. There are central needs which have to be controlled – allocation of team space, meeting space, access to phones, network and so on. The larger the organization the harder it becomes and the informal ways need to become more formalized without becoming restrictive. This is the challenge for the management.

There is a further structure emerging as a model for project-run companies and it is based on a retail model where people are tasked to find business for the company. Their salaries tend to be linked to commission based on the amount of business they bring in. Their skills of persuasion and influence are important but there are dangers for the project manager and also the company under this structure. Because they need to win the business, they tend to offer too much on too little information and raise clients' expectations of what they will receive. One of the features of managing innovation was to control the expectations as early as possible. There is an inherent conflict between these roles.

Again the management needs to recognize this, then make decisions of how best to resolve it.

A project manager may move between several types of organizational structures if freelance. The strengths and limitations of the working environment affect the risks to projects so it is as well to become aware of them. You need to build in more contingency time for achieving tasks if the organization is chaotic!

The project manager as team leader

A multimedia team can vary in size and skills. Different projects need different teams to achieve them. The team may grow and shrink during the course of the project. Parts may be sub-contracted out if necessary.

Sometimes a team member may take on two roles – graphics and author-ing, for example. The team definition will begin from the definition of the major components of the project. Then those with skills that match the requirements will be allocated or recruited.

A typical team in terms of roles may have:

- a leader who might also use his or her specialism from a media background to contribute to part of the project development,
- someone who will agree the content and treatment with the client and the relevant members of the team,
- someone to produce the computer graphics,
- someone to program,
- someone to arrange and manage the audio and video production.

There are support roles that you'd expect to find as part of the organiza-tion structure such as technical support and secretarial/admin. There are often important support roles that the organization may need to employ if they don't have the skills in-house and the project needs them. Project/personal assistants, picture researchers, cartoonists, animators, rights clearer, video graphics artists, translators, specialist programmers, computing consultants and technical consultants are examples.

All the usual problems of personality conflict and professional conflict can happen in a team. But a leader of a multi-disciplined, professional project team made up of individual specialists also faces people used to making and taking decisions for themselves within their own specialisms.

The control of a creative, skilled group is not easy. In multimedia, they all have a relevant perspective on the way the content should be structured and treated. All the key people will have some training in their professional background to analyse and treat information within their discipline. This is a potential strength but also a potential weakness of the group. The project manager will have a bias from a background specialism which will be evident in the perspective of the treatment.

The first management decision of whether you will impose a general design solution on your team or involve them fully in the creative decisions is often made for you and outside your control. An initial specification might have defined the media mix in general terms because of the budget agreed up-front. For example, colleagues might have worked up the proposal for the clients because they had the time available. The budget might have been based on the cost of ten minutes of video for Windows, no video graphics, VGA graphics (approx. 100 screens), a few five-second low-level animations, 30 minutes of audio and so on. It is possible that neither you nor your team members had any involvement in the initial specification.

This type of specification acts as a constraint under which you have to try to work irrespective of whether the detailed examination of the content indicates a different media selection mix. Most projects can't get off the ground without such a high-level specification. If the detailed understand-ing of the content suggests a better media mix and you feel it is in every-one's interest to point out the improved benefits to the clients, the same conditions apply to your suggestions for changes to the program structure as to suggestions coming from the clients. You need to convince them to pay more or sacrifice some other aspects of the program.

This directive management approach to your team sounds harsh. However, if the time allowed for decisions at the beginning of a project is so compressed then this will be a set of circumstances where an initial directive stance may be appropriate. It does not mean that you continue to dictate solutions to the team. Wherever possible their input is needed to give a rounded product so your management style has to adapt to the changing circumstances of the project as explained in Chapter 12, Team Management Principles.

The main difficulty is to decide which parts of the content should be treated in which way. The decisions are often made quite early in relation to the budget agreed. Your team will have plenty of ideas on what will work more effectively. They have freedom of thought in relation to the top quality that they could attain in their specialist areas and are often frustrated by the decisions that have been made.

They are not subject to the constraints of time and cost in their thinking and, if they haven't experienced the difficult dynamics that occur between the company and the clients to reach enough of an agreement to proceed, they find it hard to compromise their enthusiasm and professional opinions. You need to make the reasons behind the decisions clear and focus them on tailoring their suggestions to improvements consistent within the time and costs that will serve the user best.

Some of the most difficult problems arise if your team members suggest ideas in front of clients. Once clients have been motivated by an idea that sounds good, you are in a vulnerable position. It is essential that you brief the team to make suggestions openly anytime except when in meetings with clients. In market-driven applications the working atmosphere is different. Creative brainstorming between the team members is common up front and during the production. Because all the decisions can be taken quickly and internally, more time is created for fine-tuning and experimentation. This can still get out of control so someone has to focus the team on the deadlines and call the tune of how much the changes are costing in terms of effort.

It also causes problems if your team members respond to clients' suggestions in meetings agreeing that they can do what is wanted. They will be concerned to demonstrate their technical and professional competence. But it is not what is possible that is the issue, it is what is possible in the constraints. The team members feel free of the constraints and will not make the wisest decisions. This is a common cause of tension between creative decisions makers and business decisions makers. The project manager has a foot in both camps!

You need to make the reasons clear and set ground rules for how team members communicate with clients. They should not make any agreements for changes unless they directly affect only the material they are working on and they can contain the changes to the next working deadline. You have to be kept informed of the changes if these are agreed independently with the client, on the phone for example. If they receive requests from the client that fall outside these parameters then they have to be referred to you. Some clients may play you and a team member off against each other in order to achieve a change in the design. In this case it is important that your team tell you of anything of this nature they discuss with the client.

When ideas are suggested by team members, your problem is to determine how much they can affect the decisions of quality level without incurring time and cost penalties. If you do not allow them to shape the program in some ways you run the risk of losing genuine improvements, their motivation, trust and respect. If you allow them to influence the structure but don't control them, then there is a big risk of overrun on time and costs. The dilemma is to tap into their appropriate strengths up to the level that can be contained within cost or budget or fight on their behalf to convince your management and the clients of the cost of the increase in quality.

If the project manager shares a discipline perspective with a team member the balance of power in decisions can easily be unbalanced. It is difficult to try to listen to suggestions objectively when your own discipline is driving your thinking in a different direction. So the split role of project manager and specialist complicates the job.

Sometimes the time-scale of the project is so tight that decisions have to be taken quickly and imposed on the team. Allow changes only for technical efficiency. The team will try to affect the structure and look and feel but in this case you should focus them on the shortness of time and make sure that what is specified is technically possible in the time.

On other occasions you need to offer a defined time to the team to talk through the outline structure agreed and ask for any suggestions for improvements. This team effort is valuable at the beginning stages of the project. It is important that you influence their decisions of which to implement according to time, cost, and benefit to the user. The time for suggestions has to have a limit because the later into a project changes occur, the more impact on the remaining time they have.

You need to consider if there may be hidden agendas. This is problematic if the suggestions are outside your own specialism. There may be personal motives driving the suggestions as the members of the team might want to create an opportunity to try out some of the latest techniques purely to have the experience which will keep them abreast of the latest advances in their area. These might not be in the project's scope or interest. This is a balancing act but you need to understand your team's motives and accommodate them within your constraints.

It is true that you cannot time creative ideas. Many good ones will occur during the project that will have to be rejected. As the detail of the content emerges, the conception of the best treatment will be affected. You do not want to discourage ideas. They are part of professional development and there's value in the team recognizing their worth. They will serve other projects because the factors that led up to the ideas will be recognized earlier in subsequent projects where it is easier to implement them.

Throughout the project, as team leader you have to represent the views of the users. They are the most important group but they have no representatives on the project. The project's success depends on the users' reaction. Your decisions on which changes have priority over others should try to serve the users above all others. There are many interests which drive the project in one direction or another. Often the clients will prevail even when they make decisions that are counter to professional advice because they are in a position to call the tune.

If user interface and cognition are not your strength, then identify the people in the team who have them. If necessary bounce the suggestions off other colleagues who have strengths in these areas to test them out. You need to ask all those who make suggestions for change, including yourself, to define the benefit to the user. It is surprising how often this will help the decision making.

This has been a rapid overview of some circumstances and how they can affect the management role of the project manager. The full chapter on team management, Chapter 12, examines some of the principles behind management styles. Consequently, the pressure, time and cost constraints on decision making are less evident there. However, a project manager is expected to employ the appropriate style for a given set of circumstances.

The role of the multimedia project manager

It should now be clear that the role needs to control the progress of the project against any detrimental influences to the time, cost and quality that can occur from the client, the place of work, the market forces and the team. The needs of the user should drive priorities and decisions during the course of design and production and that is true for both client-centred and market-driven projects.

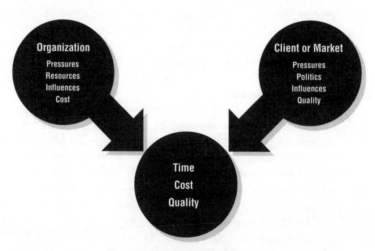

The role of the multimedia manager.

This is not a recognized definition within multimedia as it operates today. Project managers or the equivalent have usually evolved from specialist roles of computing, graphics, video production and interactive education and training. Most have received little or no exposure to general business and management principles. Any training is usually confined to professional development within their specialism. This is driven by the constant changes within the professional areas and the need to keep abreast of them. As the tools and standards become more stable, there may be more time to broaden the scope of their training.

Within the past few years, multimedia courses have been offered as specialist options at postgraduate level. Now they are beginning to be offered at undergraduate levels. Some of these include business and management options so the need is being recognized.

Summary

- Project management principles unite the disparate ways of working in multimedia development.
- Not all project management methods transfer well to multimedia development.
- Time, cost and quality principles are important but the overall concept of quality in multimedia is embryonic.
- Multimedia design quality = content and treatment agreement.
- The impact of changes on time, cost and quality can put the project at risk.
- Multimedia management shares similarities with the management of innovation.
- Anticipation of risk and measures of control are important.
- Organizational structure affects the project manager's role, responsibility, authority and control.
- The multimedia project manager has a difficult role as team leader because of the diverse, creative team.

Recommended reading

Block R. (1983). *The Politics of Projects*. New York: Yourdon Press Computing Series

Brooks F.P. Jr (1982). *The Mythical Man-Month. Essays on Software Engineering.* Reading, MA: Addison-Wesley

Chicken J. (1994). *Managing Risks and Decisions in Major Projects*. London: Chapman & Hall

Reiss G. (1992). *Project Management Demystified*. London: E. & F.N. Spon

Webb A. (1994). *Managing Innovative Projects*. London: Chapman & Hall

Young T.L. (1993). *Planning Projects*. London: The Industrial Society

CHAPTER 3

SCOPING A PROJECT

Project manager's responsibilities

- To ascertain the clients' brief
- To attune yourself to the clients and their culture
- To clarify unclear information
- To gather sufficient information to write a clear proposal
- To explain any queries the clients have

Your objectives

At the first meeting with the clients you are trying to decide if their brief is realistic in terms of the time for development, the expected use of media and the results needed from the project. You need to understand these in order to define the cost and quality level that can be produced in the available time and to define the number and type of resources you'll need for the project.

The way initial meetings are conducted varies from company to company and will to some extent depend on the way the initial approach by the client was handled (if the client is new) or the past history (if the client is an established customer). That will affect the number and type of people who would attend a meeting which could vary from a single person hosting an initial briefing to a full-scale meeting attended by representatives of the main disciplines involved: production and management, graphics and software.

Many companies rely on the experience of the person conducting the interview to ensure that relevant information is taken. There is no standard approach and this means that projects tend to evolve differently, displaying a variety of problems. This can often be traced back to the early meetings where some vital facts were missed, so it is important for more than one person to take notes and for any unclear points to be revisited. It might be useful to finish the meeting by confirming the action points for both sides, especially if the clients have to undertake some contributory work.

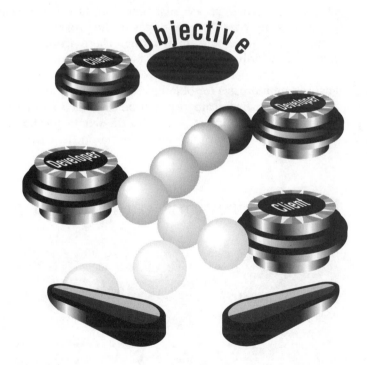

The fundamental requirement of such a meeting is for you as a developer to understand what the clients want. Unfortunately this is not necessarily as simple as it might seem because you and your clients will probably have different backgrounds and your clients may be unfamiliar with the strengths and weaknesses of multimedia. At its worst this results in the clients seeming not to know what they want. (This is a different problem to the situation where the clients genuinely do not know what they want. In this case you would hope that the clients would ask your advice.)

The training field has recognized this problem and has come up with an answer called Needs Analysis. Some trainers specialize in this and are called Training Analysts. Multimedia could learn a lot from the techniques to define and refine clients' wishes because it saves time later in the project. Trainers have had to invest in Needs Analysis because they are accountable not just for the transfer of information but also for proving that the learners have absorbed it. If there is no clear, agreed definition from clients of which knowledge and skills are important to transfer, trainers cannot devise tests to prove that the correct transfer has taken place.

A clear, agreed definition of what clients say they want at the beginning of a project is useful if they try to change the scope of the project as new information arrives or if new people are brought into the project and influence its direction. Without the definition the project can meander around and you won't have any recourse to ask for extra time or costs for the changes.

It would be good practice for companies to spend time collating the experience of their project managers/producers to produce clear, flexible guidelines and checklists for stages of the project which could serve as the company's defined way of working. There are drawbacks to using such guidelines rigidly and these will be pointed out.

This specimen questionnaire will provide you with a checklist and ensure a sound basis for obtaining the first level of information for a multimedia project. Each category will be explained so that it is clear why the information is important. A copy of the whole questionnaire is included at the end of the chapter and can be found on the CD.

Clients' previous multimedia experience

Project name/no:

Contact details
Client/Organization name:

Address:

Tel: Fax: Email:

Project contacts:
Name(s)   Positions

Direct line:

Previous multimedia experience

None   A little   Fair   Good   Experienced

Experience description

Products: Producer:

Prior experience affects everyone and clients are no exception. It sets up expectations which you need to understand. They may have had good and bad experiences. You can learn what they like and don't like in terms of ways of working as well as in interactivity. If they are return customers you need to find out as much as you can from the people who worked with them before. In fact you should have done this prior to the first meeting if it was recognized that they had been clients previously.

Even if they are previous clients it is still good practice to find out what they particularly liked and disliked the last time.

Type of project

Project type

Commercial	Corporate	Government
Presentation		Point of sale
Point of information		Training
Advertising		Education
Publishing (specify)		Research
Edutainment		
Entertainment		Other (specify)
Reference		

Often clients have no understanding of the different categories that exist to describe a multimedia project. It will help them and you to shape their ideas if you can begin to categorize the type of information that they want to communicate.

There are many differences between working on commercial, corporate, international and governmental projects. The scale is different. The components and resources needed are different. The budgets are handled and reported in different ways. The way information is structured will be affected by a company culture and image, or the specification that's worked out by the international partners in the case of, for example, a European Commission project. There will be conventions and controls in corporate work from other parts of the organization – corporate communications departments also known as 'Style Police', for example. The administration involved for an international project is far more than usual. You might be one of several project managers of various levels and with differing responsibilities in an international project.

We can look in some detail at different types of project.

Point of sale (POS)

These are retail projects where the application needs to sell products. These are often confused with Point of Information since the customer can usually get information on the products then request the sale. The deciding factor will be if the customer can commit to buying the articles on the spot in some way. The goods may be ordered by credit card for later delivery or, in some cases, can be supplied to the customer there and then.

POS systems are becoming more common and are growing in size and complexity. Retailers want to be able to take payment for the products as well as the requests to buy so the emphasis in these projects is moving towards having a payment system as part of the application and links to the companies' databases to check availability.

A related kind of multimedia is **Home Shopping** which is virtually the same as POS but, as you might imagine, the consumer uses the system from home. This will usually involve a communications link of some kind into the retailer's computer for ordering and some other functions, but often the audio-visual shopping information is held on a CD in the consumer's system. Faster communications links between the retailer and the consumer, such as video-on-demand capable links, lead to the consumer holding none of the sales information locally but accessing everything from the retailer down the line.

Point of information (POI)

There are a wide range of applications that fit this category, from tourist information systems to applications in museums that give specific information about exhibits. They are often intended for use by the general public. Some are based in receptions of large corporate organizations where a more specialist slant needs to be taken for the type of audience.

Kiosks, of which POS and POI are types, are a significant area for multimedia. The requirement for sophisticated and attractive user interfaces to encourage public use provide a good outlet for design skills. Since the kiosks are usually specially designed systems, the hardware configuration can be chosen so as to be best for the task with few constraints other than cost.

Multimedia presentation

This is a growing source of business in multimedia. Most presentations tend to be needed for large corporations whose executives need to project an internationally competitive company image. Multimedia fits perfectly into the kind of conference presentation where large audiences watch the speakers on a projection TV screen as well as in the flesh. The tools for computer-based presentations have made it possible for many to produce the lower-level forms of computer-based presentations, but when image, style and impact are important, the higher end of animation, video and video graphics, and sound are important.

These tend to be quick, high-pressured projects because there is a definite immovable deadline – the day of the internal or external presentation. Also, decisions to use the more complex high-production multimedia elements – like video graphics, animations or original video footage – are often taken late. The projects are of a shorter duration than many of the other projects and are usually meant to last for approximately 20–30 minutes. They can be an aid to a speaker who talks to and around the visuals but it is getting more common for them to form the basis of a stand-alone demonstrator for conference stands or general publicity as well. This would then give the project a dual status of presentation and Point of Information.

These are not easy projects but there is a tendency in the industry to give them less credence than the production of larger applications. The shorter time-scale increases the difficulty and the risks. They are harder to control and there is often no room for contingency. Also, since they often involve the projection of corporate image, the company's style guidelines have to be taken into account and this can often be a cause of frustration to the graphic designer.

Because they are high-profile, high-pressure projects, a strong, clear method of working and agreement procedures need to be established. Any delays are critical.

Training

Training applications can be either commercial or corporate. Some which start as a corporate product can later become commercial by virtue of being offered for sale outside their original target company. The training market has in the past been one of the strongest for multimedia development but the recession tempered training budgets and fewer applications have been produced. Several of the larger organizations produce their own applications. Others commission multimedia companies to produce them for in-house use. If the training application goes on general sale through training distributors then it is a commercial venture. It is important to remember that a change such as this may affect the rights bought for the original project.

Training has its own methods of working. There is a strong emphasis on defining the expected changes in the user's behaviour as a result of using an application. Data collection for evaluation might form part of the specification. There are differences between structuring information for learning and structuring it for information transfer which need to be addressed. The techniques for ensuring cognitive retention are different from designing for immediate reaction to strong visuals.

One of the major initiatives in training recently has been the move towards accrediting work done in the workplace. This has meant defining skills and competencies that underpin various roles in the workforce and then sorting them into hierarchical levels. Many vocational bodies have been involved in this definition and their own qualifications have been restructured accordingly. The trend to do more on-the-job and on-site training rather than send staff away on courses opens opportunities for multimedia developers.

Advertising

Advertising agencies are beginning to recognize the potential that multi-media might offer. Some are experimenting with prototypes but most of the interest is still at a strategic level in the companies. This sector is likely to grow but at the moment is still an unknown quantity. Besides the question of making ads interactive themselves, which is possibly another version of POI/POS, there is the potentially fascinating issue of how an interactive audience treats advertising. A video-on-demand audience might pay differential rates for viewing, depending on whether they wanted (or would tolerate) advertising or not.

Education

The use of technology is growing in schools and higher education. Government initiatives are helping to put hardware into schools (albeit in rather small quantities) and to give grants towards software development. The standardizing of curricula means that there is a potentially large market.

The popularity of the Internet as a multimedia information and reference source shared between millions of users was spawned through its use in universities. Although it started as a text-driven method of communication, it is changing rapidly into a distributed multimedia channel not only for higher education but for business as well.

Publishing

Traditional publishers (in this context record and audio-visual as well as book) have been watching the multimedia market for several years. Many of them have experimented with some projects and some have set up their own production facilities. It has been difficult to determine which of the technology platforms would win enough of a market to make it viable to publish interactive products. This still has not fully settled out but it is becoming clearer that the market will not be going away and it will continue to grow.

Some multimedia companies have set up their own publishing arms to try to reap the better returns that publishing could offer. It makes business sense to invest in your own productions if you will get a better ongoing return than from the profit made once on productions for a client. Ownership becomes an important issue. Audio-visual content development forms a major part of the cost of development. The ability to reuse such assets in other forms or as the basis for new development depends on ownership. If you do not own any, you have to start from scratch every time. This overlaps with rights management which will be covered later.

Many of the titles that are being published fall into a strange category called Edutainment. These are meant to attract the home owners of computers to buy for their children's general education but have enough general interest to be used in their own right by a wider age range. A worked example of an edutainment project scope is given in the next chapter. It is unusual in so far as it is client driven not market driven because the company is approached by the client to produce the title jointly.

Entertainment is another category that is aimed at the home and business markets. Games, quizzes, titles built around celebrities like pop stars or actors and even television soaps would be examples from this section.

Reference titles like atlases, road maps and encyclopaedias have made their mark and are popular development gambles with publishers.

International projects

These types of projects, particularly if they are government research related, demand a good deal more administration than others. There are many extra levels of communication and documentation that are built into the project plans to ensure that the progress of the project is monitored and recorded. These projects follow international project management principles and as such are well structured and defined. The projects start with a specification stage and then contracts and resources are allocated according to this.

In European Union funded research projects, for example, there is a process of external review where experts are called in at regular intervals to analyse and comment on progress. The companies that are partners in a European project are called a consortium. The funding and budgeting structures are very different from other multimedia projects because the Union funds up to 50% of the total budget with the Consortium members contributing the other 50% either in money, time equivalent or in the value of assets they bring to the project.

Developers are often subcontractors for the consortium members and can become dependent upon the cash flow arriving from the Commission before they then get paid in turn. The consortium will only get paid if the external reviewers agree that the project progress is achieving its aims as defined in the specification, called the Technical Annex. So the developers need to thoroughly understand what is necessary, to what standard and the milestone dates to ensure that everyone gets paid!

Major international projects like the European Union ones often break new ground so developers can find themselves working with untried technology and software. This undoubtedly makes the projects higher risk and contingency time has to increase because of the risks. This applies to any research project.

Technology doesn't stand still so there is constant prototyping and trialling of new technology platforms and tools. In tools development it is common for the software to be tested by people outside the company writing it. The final stage of this is beta testing and is where the writers think the software is finished and it is up to you to test this claim. There are very good reasons for wanting to build multimedia projects with beta versions of tools, not least because of the lead it might give you over your competitors. On the downside are the difficulties caused when the tools do not come up to expectations or when bugs are found. As a developer you may be the first person to really try to build an application with this new tool and it can be surprisingly easy to 'break' it.

Content (general statement)

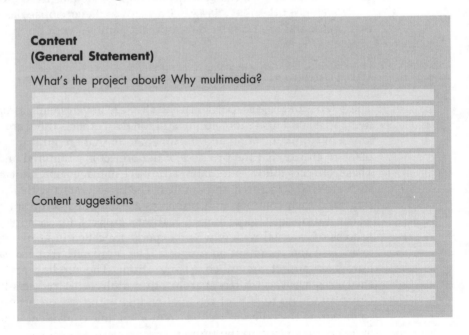

**Content
(General Statement)**

What's the project about? Why multimedia?

Content suggestions

During the discussion about the type of project it is likely that you will have got a reasonable idea about the general content as well. It should enable you to complete this section and perhaps some of the others without taking too much time. Use the information you have had to reiterate the ideas as you fill in the categories to check that you have fully understood what the clients have said.

Here is an imaginary example of what might be put in this category:

The project is to form part of the Centenary Celebrations of the museum. It will contain a brief history of its development from its founding till now. The local history connections with its original benefactor and architect together with its main achievements have been suggested as contributing to the content.

The audience/users

Audience/Users

Commercial		Corporate	
General public		In-house (all)	
Specific market		Exec	
Sectors (specify)		Managers	
		Sales force	
		Other	(specify)

The type of user will affect the style of the application more than any other factor but it is easy for the self-interests of those involved in the development to become the dominant interests. A lot more information about users will be needed from subsequent meetings.

The combination of the numbers and type of user will affect decisions about which platform and tools will be needed. It is no good producing an application which won't reach users because they haven't got access to it. Quite often clients have not considered in enough detail how the product will be used.

This information gives a good feel for the weighting of the project in terms of the size of the production team that will be needed. It is also very important to have this information early and in writing because clients have a habit of trying to extend their intended audience to cover more groups. You must resist this once you are past the early stages of the project.

It is easy to make the mistake of thinking that a change in the number of users will merely mean that extra copies of the application will be needed. If this really is the case, then it is no problem if the client agrees to the extra costs. However, it is rarely this straightforward. You need to recognize that any change in the size of audience may have an effect on the type of audience and so will have an impact on the range of content. This is not always evident when the change is requested but as the detailed design takes shape, the clients will most likely ask you to split the information into specific sections for the types of users or extend the original content to cover more useful information. So the interactive structure could be affected as well as the amount of material. Then the number of media components needed to serve the information would increase.

All these change the scope of the project. You end up having to go back to the beginning with any budget agreements or ask for sacrifices in the rest of the content for the program. Once clients have agreed content it is hard for them to agree to cuts. If you agreed to the extra users and later try to explain to the clients that they are expanding the structure and content so the costs need to be reworked, you run the risk that they'll say you should have warned them and that they won't accept the extra costs.

This is one case where you must make an agreement that if clients try to extend or alter the information later to suit the new users and it has an impact on the time and budget, they will bear extra costs or cut the material intended originally. You need to recognize the potential risk early and cover it.

We'll take an example from a corporate project to prove the point. If the intended audience was originally the non-management-level sales force and then it extended to include first-level management, it is easy to spot that different messages will be needed for management and non-management. It is harder to recognize the risk if the intended audience was originally executives and then it becomes top management. The difference in messages would depend on the company and its way of working.

Estimated number of systems/location

Estimated number of users (approx.)

1–100		5000–10 000	
100–500		Other	(specify)
500–1000			
1000–5000			

Estimated number of systems   **Location:**

The number of users need not reflect the number of systems needed. If the systems are going to be put in Open Learning Centres where a number of people will use the one system in rotation, then knowing the number of users does not help specify the number of systems or the locations where the maximum projected use will be found. Similarly, if a project is classified as a consumer title, which means for sale to the general public, then this question may be irrelevant other than as an estimate of market size. But if you need to clear rights in materials used, the numbers of users will be important for the costs. The location of use can also affect costs. If the market for use is international, the rights clearances go up. See the contract and rights management chapters (Chapters 5, 10 and 17) for more details.

Benefits/achievements wanted

Benefits/achievements wanted

Not applicable   (Reason)

The organization will benefit by/objectives/wants

1.
2.
3.
4.
5.
6.

The users will benefit by/objectives/needs

1.
2.
3.
4.
5.
6.

Often this section is one of the hardest to complete. If clients do not have a strong understanding of what they wish to achieve, they will keep changing the brief without even noticing it. As they move towards a stronger recognition during the project, they'll redefine what they want. This should be cautiously encouraged since, with careful handling, it will lead to a better result and one that the clients feel happier with. But remember the implications of late change.

It is worth putting in effort to get clear definitions and advisable to send the clients away to agree what they want for themselves and for the users. The definition takes quite a lot of discussion. It is easier for the clients to be general than specific so it takes skill to keep refining to clear statements. This is similar to the process of defining training objectives. The terminology you choose to use may depend on the clients. If they are used to formulating objectives then this might be the best term.

Without this definition you won't get a feel for how much content there might be or how you might begin to treat it to achieve the results. If there is more than one contact in the organization and they are divided in their vision of what each needs from the project, you will end up being pulled in different directions. You need a unified statement. The time spent working on this section pays dividends later. Do not proceed without it being completed satisfactorily.

The information defined now will affect how you devise your testing strategy during the next stages of the project. This is covered in detail in Chapter 18, Testing. The final sign-off will depend on you proving that you have achieved what has been specified. You will have to consider how you will demonstrate this in practice. If showing the benefits depends on feedback from the users, you might advise your clients that they should have a prototype field test to allow the users the chance to influence the design, or it might be advisable to allow for usability testing at the end of the project. Both these forms of testing are time intensive and costly. If there is a definite time span for the project, you will know if there is enough time to build in these tests. If not, and you explain their benefits to the clients, they will make the decision to include them or not. Your clients should make the decisions of which and how much testing they require so that they recognize and accept the subsequent risk of quality loss. Refer to Chapter 18, Testing, to understand your responsibilities for testing.

Content (existing assets)

Content (existing assets)				
Written			Contact:	
Video footage		Spec:	Contact:	
Graphics/Stills		Spec:	Contact:	
Audio		Spec:	Contact:	
Content expert(s)			Contact:	

Because the creation of assets is costly and time consuming, it is wise to see if there are any suitable existing materials that could be used. The script writer will welcome any written materials and access to content experts. Any audio/visual materials need to be of a certain quality to make it viable to reuse them so the technical specification of their type is needed here. This will help to gauge a rough cost of development. If there are no suitable materials they will all have to be created and this will affect both time of development and cost.

A good provision of material from the clients will affect the costing process. But, even if there are suitable existing materials they'll need to be reworked and integrated. Beware of clients overestimating the suitability of their existing material. Clients do not understand the various processes that are needed and often argue that with the provision of materials the cost of development should be much less than you submit. How you can deal with this will be covered in the next chapter. Check also that clients have the copyright for use in an electronic form for all the materials they will submit to you otherwise you could face a lengthy, costly clearance process or have to produce new assets. See the Contract 2 chapter (Chapter 10) for more on this.

Time for development

Time for development

Client expectation		(months)	start date
			end date
Any fixed dates			
(demos etc.)			
To be specified in proposal			

There is often a mismatch in expectations between clients and developers of the development time that is needed for a project. Clients do not usually appreciate the complexity of some of the processes involved. Their expectations may be impossible to achieve and the scope of the project may have to be reduced to meet a definite time-scale.

You need to understand any factors which are driving clients in their decisions on the time-scale to see if they might be negotiable. This is why any fixed dates become important. We've seen from a previous example how a fixed voice-over date had several knock-on implications. This is the right place to establish as much as you can about their needs for completion because this will help determine how much content and what media might be achievable. Be careful to check what deadlines really mean because you might find you lose a few days because of the need, for example, to ship the software to another country for a conference or to allow time for rehearsals.

Platform

Platform

Existing platform(s)	Specification:		Nos:
	Location:		

Client's suggestion	Specification:		Nos:
	Location:		
	Reasons:		
To be specified in proposal	Factors to consider:		

This can be complicated. If there is an existing platform which you are expected to use it could impose limitations on the media and quality it will allow. Also, it may not be suitable for the intended audience to access correctly. The combination of the specification, location and the numbers of machines are important to help identify how the existing platform can be best utilized or an alternative suggested.

Sometimes there is no existing platform but the client has a suggestion. This might happen when a competitor has used a platform and the client wants to compete with them. The reasons for the choice are important to see if there is room for negotiation because there are many factors which can drive a decision in both right and wrong directions.

Quite often clients expect you to suggest a platform based on the information that they have given about the users and content. It is a good idea to check if the organization has any strategic plans or directions for technology so you can integrate your decisions into them if possible. Beware of hidden agendas which can lead to clients seeming open to suggestion but really wanting you to suggest something specific.

Media mix

Media mix
Expected length of program/how long a user would take to complete (hrs/min)

Client's media expectations	None, wants suggestions		Text	%
	Video	%	Graphics	%
	Audio	%	Animation	%

The length of time for a user to complete a program, combined with the type of media, gives a good basis for costing. If clients have an idea of total time for a user to cover all the components, it provides a yardstick for how much of the space should be occupied and therefore how much of each medium might be possible. More often, clients expect you to specify how long it will be according to what is needed in the content. If clients do not give a figure, indicate that they don't know.

The same is true of media expectations. They may have impossible expectations because the amount of video may not fit on a compact disc. The content may not lend itself to the mix they suggest. However, their expectations can help shape the use of media and help with the costing. It is healthy to try to get clients to voice any expectations they may have because it gives you more information to work from to make decisions or to negotiate.

Most often clients will not have thought about the project in these terms but you should try to encourage them to answer the questions. The answers, whatever they are, give you an important starting point. Even if clients seem to have no idea, you can guide them by asking probing questions such as:

> Do you expect any video footage?
> Do you expect a lot of talking around one picture on the screen?
> Do you expect screens that change often?
> What do you think your audience will expect?

If clients really want to leave the decisions to you, then once you have an impression of the content and the audience, it will help for you to fill in the percentages and talk them through with the clients. You can use them to set up common expectations for the cost you quote.

This percentage chart also proves useful if later the clients start asking for an increase in the use of one type of media because during development they come to appreciate its potential. The percentage rating would help you win cost increases and de-scoping of other media because you could show that if one increases, others must decrease or the time must increase.

Budget

Budget

	£ approx
Budget Holder:	Position:
Tel:	
Cost to be proposed and negotiated	

In an ideal world (for the developer), projects would be scoped and specified and clients would then pay for work done on a time and materials basis. Unfortunately clients will usually want a fixed price up front and will not want to change that even if circumstances change. Doubly unfortunate is the difficulty of accurately costing any software project, let alone one with as many constituent parts as multimedia. For the sake of this discussion we will assume a fixed-quote budget.

This can turn into a see-saw battle. It is common for clients to withhold the budget sum they have because they know you will scope to the top budget figure. Many prefer you to draft a few alternatives with a range of costs so that they have an indication of the quality and cost. Then they can negotiate from a better position.

Quite a few clients will be inexperienced in the costs of multimedia projects and will expect you to be able to give them an estimate during the first meeting. This is unfair but it can help for you to have some examples of the range of costs that can be incurred for different length projects of different qualities to help them understand a top and bottom price.

You can't really work out an estimate unless they have specified a length to the program and expected percentages of media and you know the usual production charges per minute of your company and have a good guess at any extras like rights clearances costs. Even then, the considerations about the content, existing assets and platform will affect the costs and we have only gathered first-level information about these. You need to explain why it is difficult to cost and which factors affect the cost.

The clients may not necessarily be the budget holder. They may have to refer the decisions on in the organization and negotiate themselves. It is important to know if they have the authority to release the budget themselves because if their decisions can be changed then you have to take this into account for two reasons. The first is that you need to be talking directly to the top decision makers to keep the decision time and sign-off time as short as possible to avoid delays in the project, since end dates are rarely as flexible as start dates. Secondly, you need to find out if the budget holder will have any authority over the content before he or she releases the budget. You do not want to work for agreement with your clients then have their boss make changes.

Organizations work in different ways so you need to find out how their authorization to spend operates and what controls are in place to stop it. This can affect the turn-around time for decision making throughout the project and it will help to sort out your approach to this as early as possible.

THEORY INTO PRACTICE 3

Look back over the scoping questionnaire. Would you be confident in using it with clients? Can you give reasons why you need each category of information without looking at the text?

If you are not working with client-centred projects, what equivalent questions need to be answered to scope your project?

Post-meeting responsibilities

Clients may need to get back to you with some of the information you've requested – the benefits to the user, for example. Make sure you agree a time frame to receive the information. A lot of time can be wasted during these early stages which can affect the start and end date of the project and therefore what you can produce.

If they don't get back to you in the agreed time with the right information, take this as an indication of what they will be like to work with and make a mental note that if the project goes ahead, you will build in contingency time at points where the clients need to find information or give decisions. This may seem a harsh judgement, but you'll need to make many decisions on very limited information. You need to identify potential risk areas as one of your main responsibilities and start trying to minimize them. This type of decision making is characteristic of managing innovation.

You will have information to check out from the meeting as well. If the clients have given any contact numbers for further information you need to pursue these to firm up on facts. The clients may think there is little visual data available but the contact may be able to indicate that there is good source material of the right specification to help with the project.

Once the scoping questionnaire is complete, make a copy and send it through to the clients as a record of the meeting and the information given. Get into the habit of dating the documents for the day of their despatch as well as having the date of the original meeting. This can often prove important later in the project, particularly in corporate projects.

Organizations are changing their focus all the time and staff changes occur during projects so you can find yourself working with a new person who has a completely different perspective on what the organization wants in a particular area. From his or her perspective, the new person will be quite right to point out some fundamental changes he or she was aware of at a particular date, but you will be able to show that this was not the information you had. If he or she wants major changes then the project has to be re-scoped at the clients' expense.

Summary

- Establish the clients' expectations and needs for the project in detail, what assets they can bring to the project, the audience profile and the budget.
- Record the meeting clearly to form the basis of the proposal.
- Assess if the brief is realistic in development time, use of media and the clients' expected outcomes.
- Give clear requests for further information from the clients within a time frame.
- Follow up any information you need as soon as possible.
- Send a record of the meeting through to the clients.

Client-centred project scoping questionnaire

Project name/no:

Contact details

Client/Organization name:

Address:

Tel: Fax: Email:

Project contacts:

Name(s)   Positions

Direct line:

Previous multimedia experience

None   A little   Fair   Good   Experienced

Experience description

Products: Producer:

Project type

Commercial   Corporate   Government

Presentation   Point of sale

Point of information   Training

Advertising   Education

Publishing (specify)   Research

   Edutainment

   Entertainment   Other   (specify)

   Reference

Content
(General statement)

What's the project about? Why multimedia?

Content suggestions

Audience/Users

Commercial		Corporate	
General public	☐	In-house (all)	☐
Specific market	☐	Exec	☐
Sectors (specify)		Managers	☐
		Sales force	☐
		Other	☐ (specify)

Estimated number of users (approx.)

1–100	☐	5000–10 000	☐
100–500	☐	Other	☐ (specify)
500–1000	☐		
1000–5000	☐		

Estimated number
of systems   Location:

Benefits/achievements wanted

Not applicable ☐   (Reason) _____

The organization will benefit by/objectives/wants

1. _____
2. _____
3. _____
4. _____
5. _____
6. _____

The users will benefit by/objectives/needs

1. _____
2. _____
3. _____
4. _____
5. _____
6. _____

Content (existing assets)

Written ☐   Contact: _____
Video footage ☐   Spec: _____   Contact: _____
Graphics/Stills ☐ Spec: _____   Contact: _____
Audio ☐   Spec: _____   Contact: _____
Content expert(s) ☐   Contact: _____

Time for development

Client expectation _____ (months)   start date _____
                                         end date _____
Any fixed dates _____
(demos etc.) _____   _____
_____

To be specified in proposal _____

Platform

Existing platform(s) ☐ Specification: _____   Nos: _____
                                        _____
                        Location: _____
                                  _____
                                  _____

| Client's suggestion | | Specification: | | Nos: | |

Location:

Reasons:

To be specified
in proposal

Factors to consider:

Media mix

Expected length of program/how long a user would
take to complete (hrs/min)

Client's media expectations	None, wants suggestions		Text	%
	Video	%	Graphics	%
	Audio	%	Animation	%

Budget

£ approx

Budget Holder: Position:

Tel:

Cost to be proposed and negotiated

Recommended reading

As this chapter was based on experience, there is no reading material
recommended.

CHAPTER 4

THE PROPOSAL

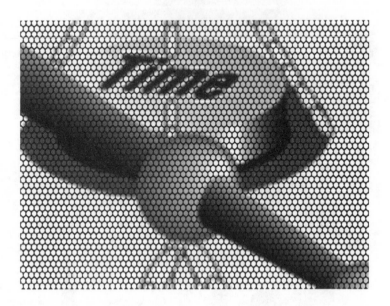

Project manager's responsibilities

- Given the brief, to offer a realistic, fair deal in the time-scale and budget for the client and the development team
- To make no false promises
- To make decisions based on the facts and your assessment of risks

The aim of the proposal

The proposal will summarize the development decisions and these will be based on the information you have received from the clients, your experience and the discussions you have had with colleagues about the possible alternatives for the treatment.

The aim is to give the clients a clear high-level understanding of the approach and platform that will be adopted and the reasoning behind this. The proposal should include a suggested schedule for development of the main stages and overall cost. The clients need enough information from the document to make a decision to continue or not. This will be based on how convincing and relevant your suggested treatment is for their needs.

They may have asked a few companies to propose for the project so your treatment may be in competition with others. This often leads to pressure to offer more than is salient and sets up risks for the development stages. You have to balance your responsibilities to the clients, your company and the development team.

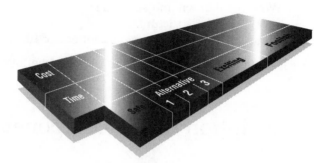

Offering alternatives.

One way to do this is to reach a decision on what would be safe to offer for the time and cost, and what would be foolish to offer for the time and cost but would be exciting and innovative. You can then work out a range of best alternatives which would allow some shift from the safe baseline, but not too much. This keeps the project challenging without making it impossible. You may even find that one or two additions need to be put forward with some extra cost tags, but it is good for the clients to be given some options to consider.

The main difficulty should be obvious. You have to commit the company and team to a plan of work for a cost which is almost certainly based on incomplete information. The complete understanding of the amount and nature of the content is unknown until later in development. You need to compensate for the unknown by building in contingency over the development stages. You can build this contingency into the overall cost, or you can include it on an item by item basis.

What it should contain

The proposal should not be a long document. It needs to make its impact quickly and clearly. You will not be able to go into great detail because so much of the content information is unstable. You should also indicate that the document, as its name implies, is suggestive not prescriptive. You will need to adjust some features as the amount and nature of the content becomes explicit, so you need to make sure that the clients understand this and that it may result in shifts in cost.

The proposal should cover the following:

General Introduction and Executive Summary
Statement of what the client wants from the application
Statement of what the user needs from the application
Description of the general treatment and reasons for choice
Variations on the treatment that are possible
Outline diagram of the proposed structure
Description of the human resources needed
Work breakdown and schedule
Cost/payment structure
Company statement of the limitations of the proposal.

Each of these will be explained in detail in the following section.

Description of the components

General Introduction and Executive Summary

This will collate some of the data from the scoping questionnaire: the definition of the type of project, its purpose, description of the numbers and type of audience. If the platform is fixed then this could be included here. Give the reasons that multimedia was chosen as the vehicle for delivery. It is worth considering whether there should be an executive summary at the beginning of the proposal. This becomes more useful as the length of the document increases and basically provides a resumé of the proposal. It is different from an introduction in that it will summarize the decisions and may even give a cost. The person who will find an executive summary useful is anyone you would expect to read the final part of the proposal – the budget – first.

Statement of what the client wants from the project

The statements that the clients have given at the first meeting need to be shaped into a sharp, business-focused account. It is helpful if you can use phrases and terminology that reflect the business area of the clients. If you have attuned yourself to their business approach during the first meeting you will find it easier to write to suit them. If you were not at the first meeting you need to debrief your colleagues carefully and ask them to read the proposal before sending it out. Some companies split the responsibility for the people who write proposals and the people who manage the development teams. There are pros and cons to either way but whatever situation you find yourself in, you have to work hard to understand the clients' business and to show that you understand it. This can be as simple as realizing that people from an audio-visual background often find the term 'user' rather unfriendly and might prefer to think about 'viewers'.

It is useful if you can explain some of the positive factors that multimedia will add to help them achieve their needs.

Statement of what the user needs from the application

The clients will have interpreted the needs of the users in the scoping questionnaire. You should reshape these but you can also add your experience of the users of an application from a professional point of view. It is important to state that their experience of the application must be the focus of concern for all. You can explain computer literacy levels and predict the level needed from the program to suit the users. If there are examples of attributes from similar programs that have appealed to this type of user, you should introduce these here.

Description of the general treatment and reasons for choice

It is impossible to predict the answers that different companies will give to the same request. It is like commissioning an advertisement. The general treatment might be the combination of ideas from several strands of experience within a company or it might be up to an individual to define an overall approach. The ideas should reflect the aims of the client and the needs of the users and it is important to explain why the suggested structure will achieve these.

You should discuss the main areas of content and indicate how they will be linked. A diagram, along the lines of a flow chart, would be useful here. The media selection for each area of content needs to be discussed and the reason for the choice of media explained. It helps at this stage to indicate the total number of minutes of material which will be in each section as this will later provide the editorial control over the amount of information contained in them.

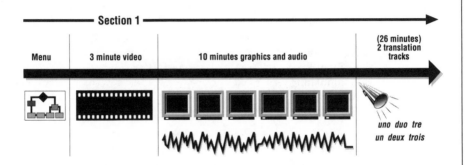

Content and media definition.

For example, if you promise 10 minutes total audio and graphics and three minutes of video in one section but as the detail comes to light it becomes clear that it will need 15 minutes of audio and graphics to do the topic justice, then you have the power to bargain for extra money for the extra time. Equally, if there is not enough to put in this section you might suggest cutting out the three minutes of video here but adding three more minutes in a better place.

	Area 1	Area 2	Cont.
Content areas suggested	Portrait and records of founder	Museum records of special exhibitions	
Wants and Needs			
Clients			
1. To inform about the history of the museum	✓	✓	
2. To be the centre point of a centenary exhibition			
3. To add a dimension to the exhibition			
4. To demonstrate the museum's contribution to the locality		✓	
5. To instil local pride	✓		
6. To encourage people to come			
Treatment	Graphics and audio: about one and a half minutes brief history – linear		
Users			
1. Ease of use	✓		
2. Attractive	✓		
3. Motivating			
4. Content brief but stimulating	✓		
5. Memorable			
6. Cater for all age ranges	Suit youth and adult		
Time			

Identify gaps in the content (museum POI example).

The process outlined below might help you in your decision making for proposal treatments. It presumes you have filled in the equivalent of a scoping questionnaire. The data used here is based on the museum example, found at the end of this chapter. You will need to refer to this in order to understand the incomplete chart (opposite) and the analysis here.

There were a couple of definite suggestions for content and an overall indication of what was wanted from the clients' and users' perspectives. So you can start by matching the suggested content against the needs to find out where the gaps are. Then it is easier to concentrate on filling the content gaps to fulfil all the needs. This type of exercise can focus creative brain-storming from your team to fulfil definite purposes rather than have complete free play with ideas. The aim is to suggest content and treatments which will cover all the wants and needs at some stage.

In the example, the clients made two content suggestions which are listed across the top. The first suggestion has been worked through the table for you with ticks and a suggested treatment. You and your team would need to decide if the content could match the 'wants' of the clients listed on the left. If the content can be valuable in fulfilling their wishes you need to suggest the treatment of the content which would suit these needs.

In the example the portrait and records of the founder certainly form part of the history of the museum and may help towards instilling local pride. The precise nature of the records and how they will be treated in detail could be focused this way if the script writer/researcher is told to do so.

Once you have started to show how the content might suit the purpose, you should begin to get a feel for the best media to use. As a portrait is static rather than video, and the records will be text based, it would seem a good idea to suggest that a treatment using graphics and audio might serve the purpose. This has been filled in on the chart as an example.

As you decide about the treatment, you should check the needs of the users as this can influence your decision. The account here needs to be brief, not just because it is a requirement for the user but because the generation of new graphics to fit with audio is time consuming and therefore costly.

A question of balance.

Again, the directions to the graphics artist and script writer could help to slant this section to be attractive and stimulating, so these could be ticked as responsibilities for the people who will produce the components. At this point you can suggest some timings and an overall duration for the section but these will change as you work out costs later.

So the decisions about treatment can be influenced and need a balance between the needs of the user, the type of materials available, the time to produce and an appreciation of the cost. It is this simultaneous weighing of several factors that makes multimedia decisions a complex skill.

Once the clients' suggestions have been accounted for, you will be able to see where there are gaps in the needs and wants. These will require content to fill them. This is the most creative aspect of the decision making and is where most of the risks are taken because assumptions have to be made on availability of material, suitability of treatment and reactions of the clients.

Remember to include online help and preference selection if these are appropriate. Help can either be general – ideally your functionality should be simple enough to require minimal extra help – or context specific. Preferences can be of varying complexity depending on the expectations of the user but, for the museum example, one consideration might be a choice of language.

Choose the media that you think would best suit the content you decide on. At this stage you should not worry too much about platform or media restraints. Add these onto the page or spreadsheet so that it is easy to change them later. It helps to differentiate the ones which originated with the clients so as to separate them from those suggested by your company members.

This won't be as easy as it sounds and it can help to brainstorm with colleagues. One category of content should serve more than one requirement, so that you keep control of the amount of material even at this stage.

When you've got a feel for the content range, you need to look at the expected media mix if the clients have stated one and check it off against the treatment you've suggested. The platform decisions can affect media decisions, so take this into account now, changing the treatment accordingly. But keep a record of what you had intended as you might find these can influence the clients later. If there isn't a platform stipulated, make your decision based on any strategy that the clients have indicated and the needs of the users. Indicate the reasons behind your choice of platform.

Put a total time on each category with each media component time broken down into constituent times. For example, you might have decided to set a scene with two minutes of video and then allow the user to choose between five points of view about this video. If each interview was one and a half minutes with audio over graphics, the total for that category would be nine and a half minutes.

Then cost out the media components. You need to refer to past experience – both your own and that of your colleagues – to do this. Different companies work in different ways for costings so you'll need to adjust this part accordingly. Some will give estimates based on the combined staff and production costs related to media components. For example, a company might have tables of costs per half hour of different video formats – full drama production on location, full drama production in studio, studio interviews, location interviews – and you can cost each type of video production according to your estimates. Another set of tables might list the digital conversion costs and so on, so you gradually apply the tables to the components you have suggested to arrive at the total estimate. It is important for the tables to be current in this case.

Internal	External	Time/weeks	Cost
Area 1			
Jake (graphics)		1	
Sue (")		1	
	Area 1		
	Phil (script)	¾	
	Phil (audio)	½	
Area 2			
		Total	

Rights clearances	
Category	**Cost**
Stills	
Music	
Voice-overs	
Video footage	
Total	

Identifying costs from staff, time and rights breakdown

Another way of costing starts with the staff and the time needed as shown. Apply internal and external costing rates according to the roles and general salary levels for the role. The time the staff will be needed depends on several factors – new material development, complexity of the graphics, use of animation and special techniques, and so on.

It helps if you look at the costs of a recent project to estimate an average time for production of graphics per day. This is an inaccurate rule of thumb since the difficulty of graphics production varies so much according to content, so take this inaccuracy into account in your estimate. Gradually build up the picture of how much time the content would take to research, process and produce.

Rights clearances can be very costly so they need to be considered here and refined later. Work to an estimate of how many voice-over artists you might need for what length of material. They are costed per hour even if there is only ten minutes' work. You also have to consider how much and what type of music – library, commissioned, recorded – as these have variable costs too. If you have to clear permissions from picture libraries or companies there will be costs attached. The same is true if you will be using existing footage from a film library. All these factors will affect the costs you need to build in to arrive at a realistic offer to the clients. See Chapters 10 and 17 on Contract Issues 2, and Rights, Copyright and Other Intellectual Property, for more detailed information on rights.

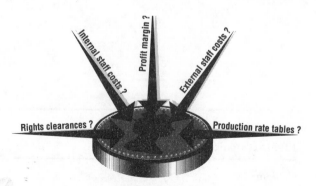

Cost considerations vary.

Finally, some companies work to a defined profit margin which needs to be added to the staff and production costs. Other companies have built this into the daily rates that you apply, so you should understand how your company is working to make sure that you have accounted for all the factors.

When you have your total time and cost go back and look at the time and budget that have been stipulated by the clients. Then you can make editorial decisions of what to cut or add depending on the match. You should now also look to see how much of the cost is real external spend and how much is in overheads like salaries and hardware amortization. The amount of money you actually have to spend to carry out the work should influence whether you ask for some of the money in advance.

Variations on the treatment

These will come to light as you apply the process described above. If you need to cut any major features to suit the budget, you could suggest that these would offer value to the user and the reasons for this. You would already have the extra time and budget implications worked out so you could build these into the proposal.

Outline diagram of the structure

This is best placed at the beginning of the description of the treatment, but the best place to devise it is at this point to see if it is worth offering the variation diagrams as well. It is difficult for clients to understand the navigation routes through the content so a diagram of the main categories and their interrelationships will help.

Description of the human resources

List and describe in general terms the roles that will be part of the project. You will probably have a core team and extras to supplement it at key stages. Most clients are surprised at the numbers involved and it shows the complexity of the project in terms they understand. You do not need to put the time that the people will spend on the project at this point even though you have had to do a rough estimate for the overall cost implications. Using multi-skilled personnel for more than one task is something you should be aware of but, for the time being, it should not be reflected in the proposal. The point of the proposal is to sell the ideas and suggested treatment to the clients. You will be able to manoeuvre time and cost better later if you have not made strong commitments here. You will need this leeway because of the instability of the development process.

Work breakdown and schedule

Even if you have used a computer package to help with your scheduling and costing, it is wise to leave the description here to a minimum for the reasons already stated. It will be enough at this stage to state the start and end dates for each of the options with general timing for research (outline and detailed documents dates) and key development stages, often called milestones. For more complex projects you might break the work down into work packages, each of which has a budget and timing and one or more deliverables. It is easy to forget to include phases for testing the application and these can take a significant amount of time. You should take the lead here in specifying how much can be absorbed into the development time and what sorts of testing are recommended. It is important to establish this at this point and negotiate with the clients so that a realistic level of performance is achieved for the time allowed. How to devise a testing strategy, and how to explain the options and implications of decisions to the clients, is covered in Chapter 18, Testing.

Cost/payment

The total cost should be given with indications of payment policy for the company. Most companies ask for staged payments to improve cash flow and cover themselves for unforeseen circumstances where the project might be stopped or delayed. The stages are often linked to key deliverables or milestones of production. Companies will define these in different ways but many link staged payments to: the phase or phases leading to the detailed agreement of content; first working example of the code and navigation, sometimes called an alpha disc; near final disc, often called the beta disc; and delivery of the final disc master.

Limitations of the proposal

Because the proposal is based on a limited understanding of the overall content, there need to be indications of this to allow for changes from the developers as their understanding deepens.

If you have based any of your decisions on material that will be supplied by the clients you will need a proviso that this is subject to the materials being of the right type and quality. Otherwise you'll need to revise your estimates of how much material will need to be produced.

Technology production is changing rapidly all the time so costs vary quickly. It is wise to put a time limit on the offer subject to costs being reworked. You need to point out that the start dates are dependent on the clients' agreement to proceed in time and that any delay for the start would add time to the finish date. It is surprising how often clients return to you with agreement to proceed after the start date but expect you to complete in the same time without cutting any of the production.

Conclusion

Proposals often need to be turned around quickly. They are difficult documents to draft and there need to be clear guidelines to help the drafting according to company practice. It is the responsibility of management to ensure that these guidelines exist so that whoever writes a proposal for the company covers the scope in the way that serves the company best. The bias within the company towards any specific origin, such as video production, will affect the components in the proposal.

The principles that underlie a proposal are the same, however. The clients will be looking for clear statements of what the company can offer for the time and price. Their attitude will be affected by their own bias towards media and the needs of the project. They can be influenced by good ideas which show value. Defining the added value of one form of media or treatment over another relies on professional expertise and experience.

It is rare for the proposal to be accepted outright and the clients will negotiate on the range, type and composition of the content as well as debate costs. You face a problem if you give a more detailed breakdown of costs at this stage because you have been working from a hypothetical mix for the team. You may have presumed that you could have an internal graphics resource at one cost but until the project becomes a reality, the allocation of resources is notional. It might transpire that all internal resources are booked out on other projects for the period and that a completely new freelance team needs to be formed.

THEORY INTO PRACTICE 4

You have been asked to draft a proposal because there is a deadline and your colleague is sick. She attended the briefing meeting with the client(s) and all you have to work from is the completed scoping questionnaire. You have one working day to complete and fax it to the client(s) while coping with your ongoing projects. This sort of time-scale is not unusual. Remember this next time you look at a program and criticize the treatment.

You have a choice of two completed scoping questionnaires – the museum (Questionnaire 1) or a client-driven edutainment title (Questionnaire 2). Using the information given, derive a proposal for one of them.

Client-centred Project Scoping Questionnaire 1

Project name/no: SMCE / 67

Contact details
Client/Organization name: Brentfields Museum
Address: The Parade
            Brentfields

Tel: 234 444   Fax: 234 445   Email: jane@brentfields.org.uk

Project contacts:
Name(s)   Jane Morris   Positions   Exhibition Organizer
           Libby Turner   History Curator

Direct line:

Previous multimedia experience
    None   x   A little   Fair   Good   Experienced

Experience description

Products: Producer:

Project type

Commercial	x	Corporate		International	
Presentation		Point of sale			
Point of information	x	Training			
Advertising		Education			
Publishing (specify type)		Research			
Edutainment					
Entertainment		Other		(specify)	
Reference					

Content (General statement)

What's the project about? Why multimedia?

As part of their centenary celebrations, the museum is putting on a special exhibition.

There will be five sections covering 20 years each. Each section will feature the five most important acquisitions during the period and have mini exhibitions of work of two/three key local people who won international fame during those times. The history of the museum will run as the main theme throughout the sections.

The multimedia application is needed as a centre point for the exhibition area which will be shaped like a star. The clients want it to complement and extend the other exhibits.

Content suggestions

There's a family portrait of the museum founder and records about the family which they feel could offer good background material. They have a full record of special exhibitions held over the whole period with a copy of the accompanying catalogues which Jane thought might be useful.

Audience/users

Commercial			Corporate	
General Public	x	In-house (all)		
Specific Market		Exec		
Sectors (specify)		Managers		
NOTE: More schools and		Sales Force		
retired people form the		Other		(specify)
audience. Also, tourists,				
surprising number foreigners.				

Estimated number of users (approx.)

1–100		5000–10 000	x
100–500		Other		(specify)
500–1000			
1000–5000			

Estimated number of systems `1` **Location:** At the museum in the centre of the exhibition.

Benefits/achievements wanted

Not applicable ▢ (Reason)

The organization wants the POI:
1. To inform people about the history of the museum
2. To be the centre point of their Centenary Exhibition
3. To add to the visitors' experience in some way
4. To demonstrate the museum's contribution to the locality
5. To instil local pride in the local visitors
6. To encourage people to come to the Centenary Exhibition.

The users need the POI to be:
1. Easy to use very quickly
2. Attractive
3. Motivating
4. Brief and to the point but stimulating
5. Memorable
6. Suitable content for all ages.

Content (existing assets)

Written	x		Contact:	John Barnes, Records
Video Footage		Spec:	Contact:	
Graphics/Stills	x	Spec: photos/slides (top quality).	Contact:	John Barnes
Audio		Spec:	Contact:	
Content expert(s)	x		Contact:	Jane Morris, Libby Turner

Time for development

Client expectation   3.5   (months)   start date   1/5/96

end date   15/8/96

Any fixed dates (demos etc.)   x   Exhibition opens   15/8/96

To be specified in proposal

Platform

Existing platform(s)

Specification: none   Nos:

Location:

Client's suggestion

Specification: none   Nos:

Location:

Reasons:

To be specified   x
in proposal

Factors to consider:

Robustness, child-proof, vandal-proof,
to fit in with exhibition style and decor

Media Mix

Expected total length of program(hrs/min)   50 mins

Client's media expectations

None, wants suggestions		
Video	60	%
Audio	15	%
Text	5	%
Graphics	10	%
Animation	10	%

Budget

£40,000 approx.

Budget Holder: Mike Vincent   Position: Finance Director

Tel:

Cost to be proposed and negotiated

Client-centred Project Scoping Questionnaire 2

Project name/no: **It's a Lion's Life** DN / 37

Contact details

Client/Organization name: Don Newman
Address: The Barns
Highleigh

Tel: 0264 234 234   Fax: 0264 234 234   Email:

Project contacts:
Name(s)   as above   Positions   well-known artist
with good
source material

Direct line:

Previous multimedia experience

None x   A little   Fair   Good   Experienced

Experience description

Products: Producer:

Project type

Commercial x   Corporate   International

Presentation		Point of sale	
Point of information		Training	
Advertising		Education	
Publishing (specify type)	x	Research	
Edutainment	x		
Entertainment		Other	(specify)
Reference			

Content (General statement)

What's the project about? Why multimedia?

Don Newman is a well-known artist specializing in lions in the wild. He has 15 years' worth of various materials – prints, video footage and his own works. He has written and illustrated two books on lions but has refused all encouragement to make documentaries. He wishes to remain anonymous to his public. He recognizes that he has access to good material and is interested in extending the visual impact of books through electronic publishing.

Content suggestions

There are plenty of materials to cover any aspect of the life and death of lions in the wild. The client would like heavy control over the content but does not want to be featured. He does not understand the scope of multimedia and would like to discuss a range of treatments so he can get a feel for what interactivity could offer.

Audience/users

Commercial			Corporate		
General Public	x		In-house (all)		
Specific Market			Exec		
Sectors (specify)			Managers		
			Sales Force		
			Other		(specify)

Estimated number of users (approx.)

1–100		5000–10 000	x	
100–500		Other		(specify)
500–1000				
1000–5000				

Estimated number of systems ?   **Location:** Business and home systems

Benefits/achievements wanted

Not applicable   (Reason)

The client wants the title:
1. To convey the complexities of the animals' lives
2. To cover more than a documentary would allow
3. To educate but entertain
4. To have a section devoted to how to draw animals
5. To advertise his collection.

The users need the title to be:
1. Easy to use
2. Exciting
3. Motivating
4. Interesting
5. Memorable
6. Suitable for general public.

Content (existing assets)

Written				Contact:	
Video Footage	x	Spec:	Variable but enough of good quality.	Contact:	Don Newman

Graphics/Stills	x	Spec:	photos / slides (top quality).	Contact:	Don Newman
Audio	x	Spec:	exists with home video footage but doesn't want own voice used; enough natural sounds though	Contact:	
Content expert(s)	x			Contact:	Don Newman

Time for development

Client expectation	6	(months)	start date	1/8/96
			end date	28/2/97

Any fixed dates (demos etc.)

To be specified in proposal

Platform

Existing platform(s)

Specification: PC and Mac CD-ROM   Nos: ?

Location: For home and business market

Client's suggestion

Specification: none   Nos:

Location:

Reasons:

To be specified
in proposal

Factors to consider: Any similar titles

Media mix

Expected total length of program(hrs/min)		50 mins
Client's media expectations	None, wants suggestions	x
	Video	%
	Audio	%
	Text	%
	Graphics	%
	Animation	%

Budget

The client is prepared to give free use of the visuals and his time for a 60/40 split on the royalties from the title. We would have to finance the development. This needs to go to director level for discussion. Estimate £70,000.

Budget Holder: _____   Position: _____

Tel: _____

Cost to be proposed and negotiated   [x]

Summary

- From the information given, present an understanding of the approach, platform, schedule and cost.
- Work from clients' objectives for themselves and the users.
- Take into account any content suggestions from clients and match these to the objectives.
- Find the gaps left in the objectives and devise content and treatment to fill them *in the time allowed*.
- Check the media mix can be achieved by the platform.
- Cost the proposed treatment and refer back to the clients' budget.
- Tailor the treatment to align the budget. Don't forget to include a testing strategy with options for clients to make decisions on.
- Define the resources that are needed.
- Explain any limitations of the proposal.

Recommended reading

As this chapter was based on experience, there is no recommended reading.

CHAPTER 5

CONTRACT ISSUES 1

Project manager's responsibilities

■ To rework the proposal document's specifications, schedule and costs according to discussions until contractual agreement is reached
■ To elicit as much detail as possible to perform detailed costing on resources and clearances
■ To educate clients in ways of working together

What needs to be covered?

A contract is an agreement between parties that defines the benefit and responsibilities for those concerned. Multimedia contracts will involve several documents and several parties. You will need agreements not only with the clients but with your staff and with any companies you work with during the project. In this book we will cover contractual aspects in several chapters because we are following the stages of the project devel-

opment and the issues have more relevance at certain times during development. The chapters that will deal with specific contractual issues are this one, Contract Issues 2 (Chapter 10) and Rights, Copyright and Other Intellectual Properties (Chapter 17). In this chapter we will refine the proposal into a contractual document and suggest agreements on how you and the clients should work together.

Background to multimedia contracts

The various industries involved with multimedia have their own ways of reaching contractual agreements. Publishing and computing are generally the most formalized. The arrangements in training vary according to company practice, and video production often still works on informal arrangements.

Multimedia is a combination of development stages from the different media production processes and so it is difficult to apply one form of agreement that will satisfy all the stages. Your clients may well have background experience in commissioning some of the media components and will have expectations from the previous work practices they have encountered.

Multimedia production shares most similarities with computing as a development process. A good deal of the development work is hidden in the code which drives the application and integrates the assets. If clients have been used to commissioning computer software then they will be better placed to understand the forms of agreement necessary in multimedia.

Multimedia graphics and video production have several development stages, some of which are hidden. Clients who are used to commissioning text, graphics and video come to multimedia expecting that the work processes are the same. They do not expect the hidden extra stages that occur prior to integration with the computer code. They tend to consider that each of the processes is separate rather than interrelated so that changes can be carried out in a contained way without affecting the other parts. Because of this, clients tend to think that the processes are straightforward, shouldn't take as long as they do and cost too much. They become suspicious because they do not understand the processes and the complexity.

Multimedia is still at the beginning of its life cycle and there are reservations about it. It is difficult for a client to trust something that is expensive and unknown. Consequently, many clients feel they need to exert more control over multimedia projects than other projects. They want to understand the processes that lie behind its development; they want to feel that they are getting their money's worth. As a result they query more, they hesitate to make decisions and they want justification for actions. If they come from an audio-visual background they are also likely to take a detailed interest in the audio-visual content.

Because of this climate of uncertainty and apprehensiveness, it is important to agree how to work together to help smooth the production path. Once you have set up a working relationship with clients or they understand multimedia production because they employ it themselves, this assumes less importance. Throughout the book we take inexperienced clients as the base because they have the most needs to consider and are the most likely to benefit from a set process. However, it is, of course, a mistake to underestimate the knowledge and experience of clients. Your way of working needs to be balanced against their experience.

Refining the proposal into a contract document

As soon as it becomes clear that the new clients have not rejected your proposal out of hand and want further discussions, you need to listen carefully to their redefined needs, then recost and refine your budget. The sooner you recognize any major differences between the initial proposal and the final work specification and costs, the better. If you are still at a negotiation stage, you can influence the budget. Once the amount and type of work has been agreed, you lose this facility, or at least make it much harder on yourself to justify more time and money.

In the rush to produce a proposal you are guided by the media components that are required and the amount of production that these will take. You may have applied a house formula for production costs for, say, 20 minutes of audio with graphics based on using an in-house team, or relied on your experience to quote a production figure. You might have defined the number of staff that would be needed and estimated the staff costs based on a split of some internal and external resources. You would have guessed at a figure that might be needed to clear rights from film or picture libraries and estimated voice-over costs. Many of the cost components would of necessity be vague at this stage. You wouldn't know exactly how many pictures of what type were needed from where, for example, and this can affect the cost significantly.

However, as soon as the specifications and time-scale become tighter, you need to break down the costs so that you are sure that you can achieve the project according to time and budget. This means establishing how long and at what rate the staff will be paid and the maximum that can be paid for each component to stay within budget. It also means refining the estimate of what rights might need to be cleared, how many stills to be cleared at what maximum rate and so on.

You were asked to outline the major cost components in Chapter 4 to serve as a quick assessment of costs. Here, these will be expanded.

We left the proposal document at the point where it was handed to the clients for the first time. In the first draft of the proposal, you may have offered the clients a range of options and costs. If the clients wish to proceed, negotiations will then take place between you to refine the specifications of deliverables. You have to record all the changes from the meetings and rework the costs and schedule accordingly until agreement is reached. The final proposal document will form a major part of the contractual agreements between you and the clients because it will specify the work tasks, schedule and cost. The sign-offs are also contracts. They are agreements that demonstrate certain parts of the work have been completed satisfactorily.

During the proposal refinement, you need to carry out a detailed budget breakdown based on resources and acquisitions and clearances. The clients should need only the high-level summary that was contained in the original proposal with milestones and sign-offs indicated in the schedule. But, your estimation techniques should become firmer to allow you to feed better figures into the summary.

The charts that we used in the first proposal document cover the right areas to prompt you to arrive at estimated figures, but Table 5.1 should indicate the amount of detail you should be refining in discussions with the clients, as well as act as guidelines to make sure you do not overlook anything. Your project may not need all of these resources so you can cross them out. Alternatively, you may have special resource needs to add in.

There will be a wide range of rates that fluctuate according to the internal charge-out rates for company staff who work on the project and freelancers who are brought in to supplement them. You can't affect the internal rates but the external ones can vary a good deal. As you gear up to start the project you should try to get a feel for which resources will operate as in-house ones and which you'll need to recruit. Take a near top rate for any freelancers to give yourself some leeway when you are recruiting, because your recruitment decisions will be affected by the budget

Table 5.1 Multimedia project resource costs.

Resources	Initials	Internal/External	Rate per day	Days/weeks needed	Cost
Management/administration					
1. Project manager					
2. Project assistant					
3. General production assistant					
4. Secretarial support					
				Sub Total	
Video production					
1. Director					
2. Producer					
3. Production assistant					
4. Camera					
5. Lights					
6. Sound					
7. Grips					
8. Make-up					
9. Continuity					
10. Logging					
11. Script writer(s)					
12. Video graphics					
13. Offline editor					
14. Online editor					
15. Film/Picture research					
				Sub Total	
Audio production					
1. Production manager					
2. Script writer(s)					
3. Editor					
4. Voice-over artist(s)					
5. Musicians					
				Sub Total	

you've allocated to specific tasks, the skills of the people interviewed and their rates. However, if cost was an issue with your clients from the first round of the proposal, you may need to use a lower middle rate and cut the quality of the freelancers employed.

An explanation of how you arrive at your team mix and the roles of the various people mentioned in the listings is given in Chapter 11, Selecting the Team.

It is important that all the new details in the specification are recorded in the refined proposal document so that the new agreements are clear. It is easy to confuse which points have been raised, discussed but rejected

Table 5.1 *Continued*

Resources	Initials	Internal/External	Rate per day	Days/weeks needed	Cost
Stills/Graphics production					
1. Production manager					
2. Graphics production					
3. Picture researcher					
4. Animator					
5. Photographer					
6. Lighting					
7. 3-D modeller					
8. Computer graphics production					
9. Scanner/digitiser					
10. Art director					
11. Illustrator/artist					
12. Typographer					
				Sub Total	
Database development					
1. Data collection/management					
2. Integration/development					
3. Indexer					
				Sub Total	
Design/documentation					
1. Interactive designer					
2. Instructional designer					
3. Interface designer					
4. Script writer(s)					
5. Subject matter experts					
				Sub Total	
Computing and Integration					
1. Programmer/Software engineer(s)					
2. Technical manager					
3. Network manager					
				Sub Total	
				Total	

and which points have been accepted at this stage. Good records need to be kept of the meetings during this time particularly.

The refined specification will help determine better costs and scheduling than in the original document. Your objective is to get the clients to sign the document understanding exactly what they will receive for the time and money. Both you and your team will benefit from a sound specification with clear deliverables.

Agreeing how to work together

If we examine the logic behind agreements, and contracts are agreements with responsibilities on both sides, then agreements are made on understanding and understanding comes from knowledge. We should be asking ourselves how we can give the clients knowledge about the working processes of multimedia development and their responsibilities in this. Reaching an equitable agreement is easier if both sides understand what is involved and what each one is expected to contribute.

The education of the client will continue throughout the project but it helps to indicate what is going to happen at the beginning of the project. Once the project proposal has been accepted, the successful completion relies on both parties. At certain points the development company has to pass control to the client and cannot proceed without agreement and the subsequent handing back of control.

The real problems lie in the definition of a client's role. Clients hold the balance of power because they are paying for the service. The customer is always right from a retail perspective. But in a collaborative process where you depend on the client to provide some of the materials and decisions according to a schedule, you should not be held responsible for deficiencies which originate with the client and the impact these have on the development process. It is perfectly acceptable for the responsibilities of both sides to be agreed.

Clients' responsibilities need to be defined and you need their agreement that they will accept the consequences of time, cost and quality changes if they do not fulfil their side of the bargain. The converse is true, of course: the company and project manager also have to accept responsibility and liability for not fulfilling their own responsibilities.

There is one other aspect to take account of in a client relationship. Even if the clients have agreed to the defined dates and processes, the project may be revised in terms of the priority level it receives from them because of other factors. Your contacts within the client company will be subject to their own pressures from their own organization and internal matters will often be given higher priority than external projects. You need to understand the pressures they have because they will affect the project.

Every multimedia project is unique because the products are tailored to circumstances. Some may be similar to others but they all have some characteristics that denote the tailored approach. In principle though they all follow certain stages and rely on certain points of agreement or acceptance.

The way of working may not be defined in a company but it will help your role if you explain the way that you want to work with your client. A definition that is company based carries more weight and it means that there are prior examples that you can use to show the client. It is in your interest to encourage the management to define the stages of documentation and the ways of working. As long as these remain defined at the level of guidelines, they will be flexible enough to allow the project manager to decide exactly which combination may be right for a particular project.

Some companies include aspects of these agreements between client and company in formal contracts but they rarely explain in enough detail what the terms and conditions mean in actual practice. If there are formal contract terms you will need to check them to see if there is enough to help you in agreeing the precise way of working. More formal agreements are necessary to establish ownership and rights, for example, and these will be discussed further in Chapter 17.

You will find the following useful to give the client once there is agreement to proceed with the project:

(1) A short non-technical description of multimedia, its media components, the stages involved in producing and refining each component. A glossary of the more technical terms used within the description is also useful.
(2) A short description of the stages that the projects go through, indicating where sign-off is needed. The company's approach to changes needs to be stated clearly. The stages may vary in name according to the company but could include Proposal, Outline Design, Detailed Design, Testing, and so on. It is wise to break down the sign-off into component parts or you may find disagreements arise about what a sign-off actually meant.
(3) A general description of your responsibilities and the client's responsibilities to ensure a smooth project.
(4) Sample copies of sign-off forms.

Change management

In the previous chapters we have seen examples of the impact that changes in the project can have. There are different causes of change but one of the most common is an alteration to the work specification. The work specification is stated in the proposal and once this is signed, it is a contract. If clients ask for changes, they are asking for alterations to the contract. They need to recognize this. Agreement on ways of working together needs to address how any changes to the agreement should be handled.

The computer industry has had to develop some form of control to contain the impact of changes once production has begun. This is called Change Control or Change Management.

It is not commonly in use in multimedia companies but all of them will recognize the recurring problems of changes and the consequences of the company having to absorb overruns on budget.

Some argue that the basis for agreement between client and company should be based on trust. These people would see change control as a mechanism that would interfere with the client relationship. Trust comes from understanding and respect and as multimedia is not understood by the general public, there is little trust in the professionals. Mainstream

computing still suffers from mistrust but this has shifted towards better acceptance as the mystique has disappeared and its potential becomes more widely accepted.

Software engineering has found that any changes in a project need to be carefully controlled and monitored because the consequences of changes can be disastrous. Several things can happen. If the change is not communicated to all of the team, people working on different parts will end up working in different directions. Then the pieces will not fit together, parts of the program that worked stop working correctly and a lot of time is spent unravelling the problem. Version control is also used in software engineering so that everyone can check which version of the program they are using by looking at a version number and date. Version control helps avoid wasted effort but it is changes which drive the need for new versions so change control precedes version control.

It is not always obvious straightaway that a change will have spin-off consequences even if the whole team is informed. A change to some graphics may cause programming problems, extra audio or video may make the program too big for the disk or platform to run efficiently, and adding an extra section may cause stripping down of the code and rebuilding because a programmer plans coding based on an understanding of the total way the program needs to work.

Communicating the change may seem trivial but the team is usually an extended one where some processes are performed off-site. Contacting up to 15 people to communicate a change and then ensuring that they remember to carry it out is not trivial. Even identifying the change can be problematic unless each tiny component has a unique identification code of some sort.

Apart from informing everyone, any documentation will need to be revised and extra copies given out. This takes time in itself. Documentation for a multimedia project can run into several hundred pages, often with illustrative graphics. If individual sheets are sent out, it is easy for them to disappear in a paper chase particularly if several changes are made per week. It is also common for changes to be made to previous changes as an original idea is refined. It should be obvious how easily chaos can occur.

Clients need to understand the possible consequences of changes and accept a procedure for implementing change. Software engineering recommends using a Change Request Form which would have the following features:

Project name
Date
Change initiated by
Change description
Requirements affected (with identifying numbers)
Other program effects
Other system effects
Planned start and completion
Resources affected (personnel and schedules)
Approvals (this could include the systems manager, development manager, configuration manager, quality manager, program manager)

This makes it clear that any change needs to be considered by all involved for possible impact and the time for implementing the change agreed. A similar process is needed in multimedia development in some way.

At the moment, the way multimedia is working, this level of what will be seen as bureaucracy would be totally unacceptable. The equivalent approvals needed might include: Client, Development Company Director/Account Manager/Finance Director, Technical Director, Project Manager, Programmer, Graphics Artist, Video Director, Video Graphics Artist and so on.

Development time is always at a premium in projects and administration suffers. Because the project manager's role is often split between developing part of the project according to a specialism as well as the overall management, any lengthy administration procedures would add to an already overburdened workload. But without some form of change control, the project can quickly degenerate.

The form as described does not work for a client-driven project because if clients initiate a change, they are not in a position to describe the change or its possible impact in ways that can be understood by the team. The project manager has to work with the client to derive a description, then check out the consequences. In this way the communication time increases in a client-driven project.

The form also does not work for every multimedia project component. It has been drafted for changes to the code and structure of a program. Multimedia changes might affect these but there are also changes requested in graphics, audio scripts, video scripts, video graphics and text scripts.

If a careful object-oriented approach to the software design has been undertaken then many changes to the content will not greatly impinge on the software. The difficulties that changes cause are also related to the time in the project that they are made and whether the components have been integrated with others. If clients are made aware of the last opportunities to make changes for each of the components, the project can run more smoothly and truly trivial changes should be accepted willingly. It is right for clients to adjust components until they are satisfied with them or until the agreed time frame for adjustment has lapsed. Secondly, if clients agree that after sign-off of each stage any changes will incur time and cost penalties, the developers have some form of control.

A compromise solution is needed. This is why it has been suggested that client education needs to address changes. If clients can understand the complications that can arise, they will be more disposed to stipulate carefully at the beginning and within the adjustment leeway. If they understand that after sign-off changes will be costly and time-consuming, they will be more careful in suggesting changes.

Stages of a project

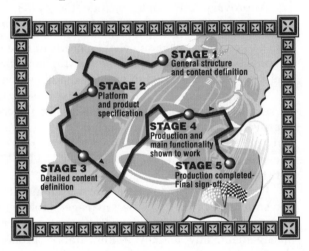

A project generally follows these stages of development:

(1) Agreement to the overall structure and major content areas (the proposal or sometimes the Outline Design should stipulate these). Sign-off Stage 1 and 2.

(2) Agreement of platform and product specification. These can be in Sign-off 1 or 2.

(3) Agreement to the detail of each component – audio, graphics, video, text, navigation methods/menus. These can have individual sign-off stages if the scripts are produced separately.

(4) Agreement that the application operates as stipulated for Phase 1. This is the equivalent of the alpha test sign-off.

(5)   Agreement that the product has fulfilled all specifications and is concluded. Final sign-off.

If sign-off dates are set within the schedule then last change dates can be set ahead of these to allow the last set of changes to be carried out and checked. The overall timing of the project will affect how much time is allowed in total for each stage.

Clients need to know how the project will develop and what they will be expected to do at each stage so that they can plan their time and effort.

Responsibilities

If a list of responsibilities is agreed, this will give commitment to the project as well as educate the clients in how it will progress. The list needs to be tailored to the type of project and company practice. Agreement to the

The project manager's responsibilities

- To work with clients to produce a mutually acceptable proposal which outlines the project content, timing and budget

- To produce a detailed work schedule consistent with agreed start and finish dates which will map out phases of production

- To monitor and record time spent on the project

- To keep clients informed:
  - on general progress, e.g. a written summary every month
  - on any slippage as it occurs and actions to be taken to remedy it
  - on any suggested changes to the specification arising from technical or design factors as soon as these occur
  - on any other factors that affect the project as soon as they occur

- To ensure each component part of the project is produced to the right technical specification

- To ensure the structure and approach to the program is agreed and signed off by the named contact in the client organization

- To ensure the content/script is agreed and signed off by the named contact in the client organization

- To agree the number of turn-around days for the client organization for any decisions/revisions on any of the parts of the project

- To provide deadlines for the client for:
  - the last round of changes on parts of the script (the number of times a client can make changes will depend on the overall time limit of the project and can vary accordingly)
  - the latest time that changes can be made to any graphics
  - the latest time changes can be made to any video
  - the latest time that any changes can be made to any text on screen

- To get final sign-off for the completion of the project

The clients' responsibilities

- To prepare a clear brief for the developers

- To work together on the detail of the specification

- To inform the project manager of any factors that will impinge on the project as soon as they occur

- To appoint one sign-off person in the organization who will be able to devote adequate time across the whole project and whose agreement will be binding

- To agree any subject matter with experts from the company who will need to be involved and ensure they offer adequate time in accordance with the schedule

- To keep within the turn-around time agreed or accept revised time, cost and quality penalties

- To agree that any changes made after deadline dates or sign-off will incur time, cost and quality penalties

- To agree that any slippage caused by delay of any type by the organization will incur time, cost and quality penalties

- To help the developer gain access to any people or materials in the organization who will aid the project

responsibilities is best achieved formally with signing and dating rather than verbally.

The lists show the responsibilities for a project manager and a corporate client, respectively. Although the project manager's list will remain relatively constant for client-driven projects, the client's responsibilities will need to be tailored to the specific project. Remember the edutainment example in Chapter 4. The client there would need a different set of responsibilities drafted, for example.

Does education work?

It works slowly and a project operates better if clients have some understanding than if they have none. However, there are several issues that will arise irrespective of setting up these measures of control.

Clients will be anxious about sign-off points because they recognize they are points of no return. (A sample sign-off form is provided for reference.) They may delay signing because they say they are unsatisfied but the longer the delay the more the end date will need to slip. The partnership aspect of working on a project needs to be made clear. The final product can only be finished on schedule if the components are produced according to schedule. Both of you may need to compromise on some aspects to achieve this so that the components may not be the absolute best that could be achieved but they are the best in the time available. If you

Sample sign-off form

Project name: Brentfields
Project No: 34

Client Name: Brentfields Museum

Components for sign-off:

Outline Design including:

Structure map with main content sections defined
Overall treatment of each section
Length for each section
Schedule
Sign-off authority

Signed on behalf of the company:

Name:
(printed)
Signature:

Date:

Signed on behalf of the client:

Name:

Signature:

Date:

continue to strive for the best with refinement after refinement, the project is in danger of never being finished. To put this dilemma in perspective, the film director François Truffaut once said that he started every project wanting to make the best film ever made but that as the work progressed he ended up thinking himself lucky just to be able to finish it at all.

Clients will be subjected to pressures for change from other factors. If their organization changes their approach or a key member of staff, the content and structure of the original specification may become outdated. This is not a problem if extra time and costs can be established. But with corporate projects particularly, the release date is often linked to high-profile events which cannot be changed. Your clients have to produce something that is in tune with the tenor of the organization at that time. They get trapped politically and you are ensnared in the consequences.

Another problem that still occurs with clients is the thorny problem of them agreeing to one thing on paper but imagining the end result will be visually different. The discrepancy between actual visuals versus a text description of visuals and the difference between static and moving items always causes problems. This is the reason that prototyping parts of the project may be valuable. But this takes time so this can only be scheduled if there is adequate time in the project.

Clients will become suspicious when you make changes but stop them making changes without adjusting the time and cost. This is difficult to justify but the only way to explain it is to refer to your proviso in the proposal and outline designs where you reserve the right to adjust according to the detail which emerges. You need to remind the client that you have made provision for your changes in the estimate of time and cost based on the experience of the range and type of adjustments that occur as the content firms up from a development point of view. You have taken the risk in agreeing to produce a partially defined product to a fixed rate. You may be very wrong in the estimate and have to absorb far more than experience dictated. However, if clients ask for changes to the specification, then you have the right to revise the estimate. Of course you can always ask for more money if you have to make changes because of errors on your part, but you are unlikely to endear yourself to the client by doing so.

If a project has a short life span then some of the phases may well need to collapse or not occur. The tendency is to work according to verbal agreements during the project. Unfortunately, the tighter the project turnaround, the stronger the need for tight specification with no changes and the client needs to be aware of this. It should be up to the management of the company to explain the risks to a client of undertaking a complex task with a short time-scale and how it will affect quality and working practice. This rarely happens because the thirst for business outweighs sense. It appears that multimedia development has not learnt from the software engineering experience:

> ... *false scheduling to match the patron's desired date is much more common in our discipline than elsewhere in engineering.* The Mythical Man-month *(F.P.Brooks, Jr)*

THEORY INTO PRACTICE 5

Try writing a brief, non-technical account of multimedia for prospective clients. You will be trying to convey the complexity and interdependencies of each of the media strands without confusing the reader. You will need to mention the stages of development of each component. Video production could include the following, for example: decisions on video quality and final digital type, research, script, storyboard, shoot, offline edit, online edit, digital conversion, integration.

Your purpose is to give the reader an appreciation of the number and type of stages that a multimedia application can have so that they can understand why it appears to take so long to produce.

Try out your account on a few members of the public who know nothing about multimedia and evaluate if you have succeeded in improving their understanding in the ways you need.

Summary

- Clients often suggest changes to the proposal document which means the specifications, schedule and costs need to be reworked.
- The final agreed document forms part of the contractual agreement between you and the clients as it states the work to be performed, the schedule and the costs.
- It is important to firm up the details so that you can refine the costs – particularly on the resources and rights clearances – if there are any.
- At this time it becomes more important to know which team members will be in-house and which sub-contractors, to cost more effectively.
- The lack of understanding about multimedia development leads to difficulties between the company and the client.
- Educating the client eases the difficulties. Successful development depends on a partnership where each side contributes.
- Building in control mechanisms based on change management and sign-off points helps achieve steady progress.
- Defining the responsibilities of work practice helps to achieve a smoother way of working together.

Recommended reading

Brooks F.P. Jr (1982). *The Mythical Man-Month. Essays on Software Engineering.* Reading, MA: Addison-Wesley

Humphrey W.S. (1990). *Managing the Software Process.* Reading, MA: Addison-Wesley

CHAPTER 6

AGREEING THE CONTENT

Project manager's responsibilities

- To ensure content integrity suitable for purpose and audience
- To establish time for market/content research
- To influence the clients' selection of content
- To guide the clients on commenting on scripts
- To agree turn-around time and number of revision cycles
- To get sign-off on content scripts

The importance of content

It is a sad fact that there are many interactive applications that leave professionals and public wondering why they were developed. In Chapter 2 we saw that design quality is defined in terms of content and treatment so if the program causes a reaction of this type, the faults lie in either the content, the treatment or a combination of both.

If there are comments such as:

'It's a bit lightweight. Not worth the investment of my time really.'
'Great! It's got stunning graphics. Can't say I remember a single thing, though.'
'It took me two minutes of questions and answers to be given one sentence of advice which was obvious. I just felt conned.'
'Very fragmented – all the pieces were fine in themselves but, well, they're just pieces.'
'Couldn't find what I wanted.'

these would point to problems with the content.

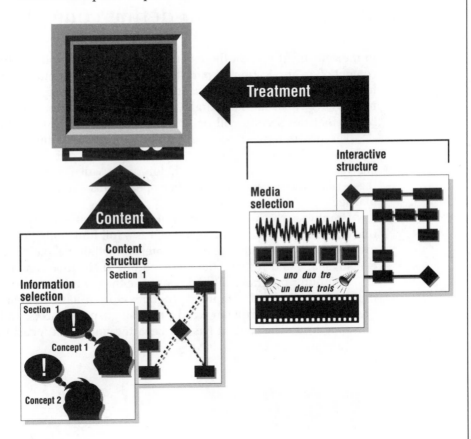

It is difficult to isolate content from its treatment and we should take the definition further to help this process. **Content** means the messages or information contained in the application and how these are arranged. **Treatment** means the media, the techniques associated with the media and the user interface that is chosen for the application. This is usually known as the look and feel. In some applications the treatment dominates because there is little or no content – games programs and some entertainment applications if they are activity or action based. This chapter does not apply to these style applications.

Despite its central role in most multimedia projects, the content is often neglected. More importance is given to the visual treatment than the messages – and since multimedia is about communication where exactly are we going wrong?

The quality of the content depends on a number of factors: the selection, breadth, depth, appropriateness for the audience, pace of delivery, and the sequence in which it is presented. The media techniques can only serve to help the content achieve its purpose better; it cannot make up for poor selection or lack of content integrity.

Whose role is it to define content?

In multimedia at present there is no specialist role devoted to defining the content of an application. In part this is because a lot of multimedia is made for corporate clients and the content often comes along with the brief. It may well be that as the industry matures such a role will emerge. It is hoped that this section will point to the value that could be gained.

The media industries, except graphics and computing, have evolved their own roles for defining content. The author, script writer and training analyst have fulfilled the function for print, video and training. Within these roles there have been further specialisms – comedy script writing, management training, for example.

Graphics, whether video or print based, has always had a supportive role except in very specialist areas such as a full film animation. As a result, graphics artists usually creatively interpret other people's scripts. They extend, shape and reshape the ideas, adding their dimension of visuals.

Computer programs often do not have the equivalent of script because the most widely used computer programs do not have content. The users provide their own scripts in word processing, spreadsheets, and presentation programs. The content has not been the important focus; the support structure and functionality have.

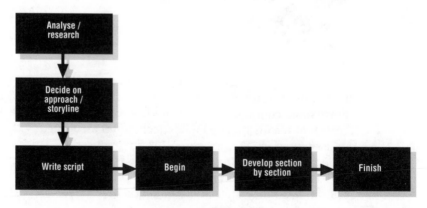

Scripting for linear media.

If computer programs have contained content – educational packages, many entertainment programs, for example – then it has usually been determined by someone in the team who has taken on the role. However, as programs have become more complex and are designed for both experts and the general public, the 'help' content has expanded dramatically. It uses a variety of media to convey how to use the program. Technical writers have taken on the online multimedia design as well as designing the paper manuals. Their skills have not been used in mainstream multimedia applications yet, but this may change. Computer-based training (CBT) has come the closest to developing a recognizable role for definition of content and functionality in the role of the interactive designer.

The interactive designer works with the commissioner or nominated subject matter experts to define the scope of the content. He or she recommends an overall interactive structure for the main sections, then works through each section defining the detailed content with its accompanying detailed interactivity.

Perhaps the best way to describe the additional skills that are needed is to compare scripting for a single medium and multiple media as the equivalent of working in one dimension to 3-D.

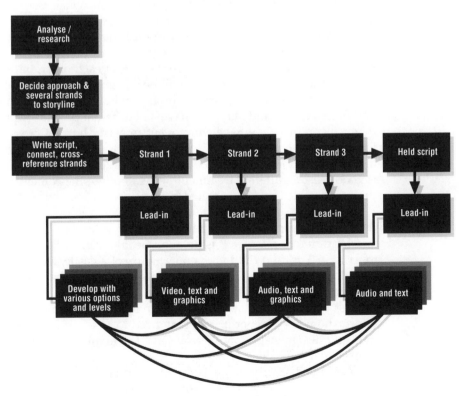

Scripting for multimedia.

This is not meant to belittle the skills of working in one medium which has its own complexities of selection, treatment and techniques but rather to show the scope of the additional knowledge and skills needed. It is more like designing a relational database of knowledge on a subject suitable for different levels of ability and a range of audience profiles.

It is the appreciation of interactivity and how it affects content that is important and is lacking in the traditional content definer's role. Competence in scripting in non-interactive media is a good base to start but it needs extra knowledge and skills to become a good interactive, all-media script writer. At present there is no formal way of achieving this. Multimedia scripting has relied on *ad hoc* solutions either from a person who has gradually acquired the skills through experience or from a team contribution from specialists of a single medium.

Scripting for multimedia

The diagram demonstrates that scripting for multimedia needs a complete understanding of the component parts of the content and where there may be occasion for the user to move sideways or diagonally through the content as well as up and down. It is also important to remember that an interactive viewer has control over the order in which the information is presented – there is no definite beginning, middle or end. Alternatively, the program might need to track what the user has done and tailor access to the rest of the information accordingly. The content is intertwined with media type and techniques because they affect each other, but the possible impact of media and techniques will be covered in a separate chapter.

The main sections of content in an application might involve the use of different media and may well have had different people script them. This might mean that they have component integrity but not cross-component integrity. Another problem might be that each section has different weighting – one could be two minutes long, another 20 minutes long. Unless there is good reason, different treatment of the depth of the content risks leaving the user puzzled and dissatisfied.

The purpose of the communication affects the breadth and depth of the content. People absorb different types of information in different ways and for different reasons. It is no good people using a Point of Information tourist kiosk to find out the opening hours of a castle, for example, if they have to watch and listen to all the information on the castle before that information is given. This is acceptable for a television travel programme but not an interactive system. Interactivity is meant to enhance access to information, not hamper it. You may need to second-guess the user during the early design stages and, if you have the luxury, test your assumptions in user trials.

Multimedia scripting is complicated and demands a complex set of skills but very little has been done to analyse the process. Hopefully this will be rectified quickly.

What affects content selection?

Influences on content: Business and retail

From previous chapters we have seen that there are many factors that can affect the length of a program and its media components. Most of these have been driven by business principles of scoping a solution according to time and cost. These undoubtedly constrain the amount of content and the way it might be presented. But, the content still needs to have integrity and cohesion whatever the length or treatment.

In Chapter 4, The Proposal, the wishes of the clients and their perception of the needs of the user were used to help make content decisions. Multimedia development is thought of as a service industry and is subject to the retail pressures of giving customer satisfaction and the retail premise that the customer is always right. Retail clients are, however, middle-men acting on behalf of the consumer who is ultimately the customer for the product. The clients should know more about the consumer's profile than the developer so their perception can be useful. If the application is being developed for a retailer, their organization should have access to market research on their customers. Decisions on the content mix should reflect market trends and intelligence. Anyone making decisions on content for a retail product should try to tap into this research.

There's an obvious problem of the restriction of time between meeting with clients and completing a proposal. You should try to convince clients of the need to gather market intelligence to help with the decisions on the quality of the content and treatment which need to be settled in the proposal. If they don't grant this then you can only do what you can do in the time. Unfortunately clients will often think that the lack of knowledge at this point is due to your inadequacies rather than theirs. It should be their responsibility to state clearly what they want and they should know what they are trying to achieve with the particular market and why.

Clients also have a responsibility for the level of quality in the program and if they choose to curtail quality of content selection because of time, that is their prerogative and risk, but they need to recognize that this is what is happening. There are other occasions where the clients dictate the content completely. They may insist on a body of content that is inappropriate for an interactive medium. They may insist that a large amount of information is covered when the user may be likely to spend relatively little time on the application. Content inadequacies are not always due to developers.

A few telephone interviews with relevant people from within and outside the organization may help indicate trends in the customers' behaviour that can trigger thoughts about relevant content areas. Finding out what is irrelevant is as useful because you can cut it out of the range. In the Brentfields Museum example, Chapter 4, the extra notes about the users' profile – age ranges, status, nationality – were gleaned from a two-minute conversation with the cloakroom attendant as the developer collected her coat and umbrella on the way out of the client meeting. The answer to the question, 'What are the people like who come here then?' gave a short profile of potential users that should influence the content selection.

Influences on content: Publishing

This is an exciting area that is emerging primarily because for the first time there are enough people who own a platform to constitute a market, namely CD-ROM. There would seem to be no restrictions on the type of content and yet a commercial title will only sell if it appeals to a sector of the market for some reason.

The main difficulty lies in the lack of understanding of the market and what it wants. The second problem is to define what a multimedia CD can offer over printed matter to differentiate it.

The types of questions that are being asked are:

Do you reproduce a book but add a few extras?
Do you provide interactive support material for books that have sold well?
Do you develop a new interactive book template?
How much interactivity should be used?
What type of interactivity?
Is some content better than others to make interactive?

There are significant differences between corporate and consumer markets, principally those of branding and personality. Consumers will be very sensitive to the personality who fronts a project simply because of the names they see on the packaging in the shop. Whereas a corporate client will be interested in your track record as a developer, a consumer will be less so; the instances of branding in the record business, for example, are relatively rare. However, in that arena, when branding is powerful it is very powerful, like Tamla Motown.

Influences on content: Training applications

The concern with cohesion and detail in training stems from the need to test the strength of the overall message and each of its component concepts. It is likely that the users will be tested or have their performance evaluated after doing the program and you can only test what has been taught. Care is taken in presentation of ideas to maximize comprehension and make tests fairer.

It becomes important to know the user's entry level of knowledge in the subject so that the interactive designer can make decisions of what to leave out as assumed prior knowledge. A thorough understanding of the audience is essential to keep the content relevant.

The structure of the content in this case is driven by learning theories. The content needs to be assessed in terms of complexity and the concepts introduced in a sequence that aids retention. Reinforcement is important, as is the chance for the user to apply the knowledge in some way to make sure the knowledge is retained in the longer term, not just stored temporarily in short-term memory.

The distinction of knowledge and skills is useful. Knowledge can be taught by sequential building of facts and concepts from easy to difficult, general to specific. Skills are acquired by the application of combined strands of knowledge to particular circumstances – knowledge in action, so to speak. Some techniques are better than others for demonstrating and explaining the different types and these will be covered in Chapter 8, Selecting the Media and Techniques.

Lately, the emphasis on knowledge and skills has transferred to 'competencies'. This movement has taken place to help people achieve qualifications in the workplace. People naturally employ knowledge and skills to do their jobs. The definitions of the competence levels that are needed to do various jobs have been analysed so that an employee can use examples of work and interpersonal skills to offer to an assessor to achieve a qualification.

It is a reversal of the ideas of traditional qualifications where people are isolated to learn theoretical principles that are tested and then applied later. It is a recognition that application is the true test of worth and that many are already applying themselves in ways that demonstrate mastery of certain skills without traditional qualifications. The structure of the content of these qualifications depends much more on giving enough information so that the learner can perform self-assessment of skill level and present themselves for independent assessment when they are ready.

The construction of educationally sound tests and assessments is complicated. The determination of the content and structure of tests has a wealth of professional experience in its own right. Because the content and assessment of a topic should be worked out simultaneously in a training program, it is important to have a training or educational professional involved when developing a training or educational program. A distance learning professional, instructional designer or interactive designer may well have a better appreciation of the interactive treatment of content and tests than a classroom professional in this case.

Limitations

Traditional learning theories do not link content to media use except to recognize that people learn in different ways so that using various alternatives will help. The areas that have tried to investigate which media is better than another for presenting information are Distance Education and Instructional Design. Instructional Design has enjoyed more popularity in the USA than in Europe where it has a tendency to be labelled Educational Technology. These areas attempt to understand the way media stimulate reaction and have value for interactive developers. The ideas behind Instructional Design and media will be covered in Chapter 8.

Although training and educational applications have principles to apply to guide content selection and structure, these principles do not transfer directly for other types of applications. When the burden of proof for transfer of information is taken away there is more freedom. The principles of:

repetition,
the use of remedial modules,
ongoing checks for comprehension, and
setting up situations for the user to apply the knowledge

do not have to be applied.

It should be evident that the content for training and education packages has recognized principles to apply to ensure content integrity for the purpose. Establishing content for other applications is not so clear cut and there is the added difficulty that the strengths of interactivity are not understood in a consumer sense yet.

Yet unless content is taken more seriously, one part of the quality equation will continue to be neglected.

THEORY INTO PRACTICE 6

Apply the content integrity test shown opposite to three multimedia applications of different types.

How to get content agreed

There are stages of refinement in the production of content, and sign-off should follow these. The first stage is to agree the major sections or topics that will be addressed and to indicate the volume of content for each section. This high-level agreement should set the scope and balance of the application. This usually happens at the proposal or outline agreement stages of the project as explained in Chapter 5, Contract Issues 1.

Some developers do not agree with this definition so early in the project. They say the content evolves as the detail becomes clearer. This is true but unless clients agree to fund an analysis stage separately, which is common in training applications, there is a double dilemma – the developers have to quote a price for the project without creating some form of

Content integrity

Application name

Type of application

Definition of audience

Purpose of application
- To inform
- To entertain
- To train
- To educate
- To sell

	Inappropriate			Appropriate	
	1	2	3	4	5
1. General coverage of subject matter					
2. Breadth					
3. Depth					
4. Suitability of content choice of major sections					
5. Suitability for audience					
6. Suitability for purpose					
7. Weighting for each section					
8. Access to information within sections					
9. Access to information across sections					

Training and Education applications only
By the end of the application:

		Yes	No	N/A
(a)	Were you taught the necessary knowledge/skills?			
(b)	Did you reach the required skill level?			
(c)	Was there feedback to remedy poor performance?			
(d)	Was the content offered in a variety of ways?			
(e)	Was there extra information for remedial purposes?			
(f)	Was there extra information for advanced learners?			
(g)	Were there opportunities to apply the knowledge/skills?			
(h)	Was the material motivating?			

All applications

	Yes	No
Would you recommend this application in terms of content integrity?		

Why?

	Yes	No
Would you recommend this application overall – media, treatment, and so on?		

Why?

guidance for the price, and then the client is at liberty to change or add to the content specification.

The high-level agreement of topic names and volume does not mean that the content cannot be reshaped within the components or that a topic cannot be scrapped and replaced with another, provided the changes are agreed and take place at a point in the project where the changes can be contained.

The developer is in the strongest position here because many of the suggestions for changes from the development team are small but significant improvements – refinements rather than structural rework. Any experienced members of the team will share a common understanding of the shape of development and what can be suggested at which point to improve but not disrupt. Clients are not in this position and do not recognize which changes have structural implications and which do not, or why changes take on different significance depending on the point in the project development.

Stage two for content agreement occurs as each major section is drafted. Here there is another dilemma. The more clients see the more they want to change or at least influence the development. There is also a strange but common reaction to make changes for the sake of change – perhaps to show that they have actually read the script!

The whole question of how a multimedia project is scripted needs a book in itself because developers need one type of professional script to work from while clients fare better with a simplified script. Otherwise, you find they comment unnecessarily on parts of the script such as programming directions.

Another common problem happens when clients comment on the paper versions of the scripts. If they do not have the experience of reading and writing for different purposes, they tend to rewrite scripts in an inappropriate style. They might change short, informal audio scripts, for example, into formal speeches or text appropriate for business reports because they're used to that variety of English. Also, they are reading the script in a written form without projecting the script into its proper setting and so they react to it as written English. If such changes were made, they would act as a good example of the style of English becoming inappropriate for its purpose. Its weighting would be affected as well if the type of information was intended to motivate, not to inform.

You face worse problems if clients do not approve the scripts and they react after the recording or video shoot has taken place, so control has to be established at script stage. Basically you have a couple of options. You take the risk and minimize it by allowing only your one sign-off authority to make any comments or changes to the script. Do not allow your sign-off to hand it out to others as this starts a paper-chase reaction with people disagreeing with colleagues' suggestions as well as the original! This takes weeks to sort out for each piece of script, and rewrite after rewrite, because once people have been involved, they want to stay involved. This is more characteristic of large corporate projects than others. This is why it is important to get as high a sign-off as possible from the client organization because others will tend not to disagree with the authority figure.

In a business application the sign-off may well insist that someone with more expertise in the area should agree the script. This is fine as long as you get it in writing that this delegate has absolute authority in this case and that the main sign-off will not countermand any of the delegate's decisions. This might sound harsh but once you have been involved in a script paper-chase you'll try anything to avoid it again. It is one of the major causes of slippage in projects and one that is unstoppable once in motion.

Another option is to keep clients away from scripts but do mock voice-over tapes without professional artists for audio and video. This helps to set the style and setting better for the clients. It adds an interim stage but allows changes without too much time and expense.

Lastly, you can educate again. If there is a standard way of scripting for projects in-house, you could arrange for a previous application demonstration with accompanying pieces of script. Then you could talk clients through the process of matching the paper to screens. This can prepare them for meeting their own paper script and attune them to what the different pieces mean, who they are aimed at in the team and what their role is.

You need to ensure that clients understand how many revisions they are allowed per script. Otherwise you can find that instead of the changes becoming fewer as revisions go on, they become more. This happens when clients give more time to their script reading as the point of no return approaches. They actually need to understand that their time investment should diminish as the scripts progress so that they should check that their requests have been complied with, not begin to read the whole script again. The project manager can influence clients by explaining how many revisions are allowed – dependent on the time available – and that the first reading should be the most thorough to set the conditions for changes that diminish through the revision cycle.

General principles for establishing content

- Irrespective of the type of application, the purpose drives the selection of content either in terms of education, information or entertainment.
- The age range can influence content selection.
- For general applications, market trends can influence content selection.
- For corporate applications, the company's culture can affect content selection. Sometimes the developer, despite trying, cannot influence this in order to achieve the best result.
- The application's purpose will indicate the length of time the user is likely to spend on the system and this determines the depth and breadth the content needs to have.

- The natural attention span of the audience will be affected by access to and location of the platform. The length of the sections of the application and therefore the depth and breadth of the content should take access and attention span into consideration. This is particularly important in point-of-information and kiosk applications.
- Content that dates quickly should be avoided or put in a format that is easily updatable unless the client accepts the consequences.

Summary

- Content = the messages or information in the application.
  Treatment = the media selected, media techniques employed and the interface.
- The quality of content = the selection, breadth, depth, appropriateness, pace and sequence of presentation.
- There is confusion over whose role it is to define content, content quality and integrity.
- Scripting for multimedia needs complex skills.
- The purpose of the application and the business sector influence content selection. The clients may provide or influence the content.
- Get sign-off agreement to the content stage by stage.
- Control the sign-off process carefully – it is a high risk area for project management.

Recommended reading

Duffy T.M. and Jonassen D.H. (1992). *Constructivism and the Technology of Instruction: A Conversation*. Hillsdales, NJ: Lawrence Erlbaum Associates Inc.

Ellis J. (1992). *Visible Fictions. Cinema: Television: Video*. London: Routledge & Kegan Paul

Gagné R.M., Briggs L.J. and Wagner W.W. (1992). *Principles of Instructional Design*, 4th edn. Orlando, FL: Harcourt Brace Jovanovich

Naidu S. (1994). Applying learning and instructional strategies in open and distance learning. *Distance Education*, **15** (1), 23–41

CHAPTER 7

CHOOSING THE PLATFORM

Project manager's responsibilities

- To discuss the chosen delivery and development platform with the client and advise on the best choice for the particular application
- To similarly advise on delivery medium
- To understand the implications of platform choice

Introduction

Sometimes clients will come to you with a project and they will know exactly what platform they want the application to run on. This may be because they use a certain machine in their business, or because the target market for the application has mostly machines of a particular type. Sometimes they will be a little more vague and often they will ask for your advice. This chapter will not offer any advice for your particular project but it will help you ask the right questions about the requirements and to work out how to decide on the positive and negative factors influencing the choice.

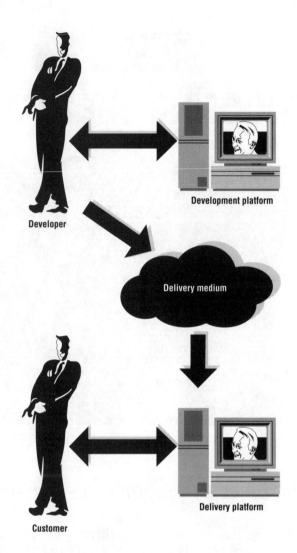

There are three options that will be discussed regarding platforms. The first is the most obvious, and is the delivery computer platform. Then the delivery medium (which is no longer limited to compact discs) and finally the development platform.

What is a platform anyway? The computer platform

A platform is not just the microprocessor, or operating system. For a mathe-matical calculation program it may be sufficient to name the operating system but for multimedia there are issues of screen resolutions and bit depth, sound parameters, the speed of the CD-ROM drive, the way that video is handled, the amount of RAM and the size of the hard disk . . . at least. There may be issues of whether the system is capable of multitasking (doing more than one thing at once) and whether you should take account of that. And there is the shift from application-based programming to document-based programming and the implications of this on the design.

In an ideal world every computer program would run on every computer platform. However, there are serious differences between even the way the basic microprocessors work let alone differences between operating systems. Fortunately there are also similarities.

The 'standard' computer platform for many years has been the PC. Although personal computer is a generic term, the initials PC came to refer to so-called IBM compatibles and clones, based on the Intel microprocessor family (8086, 80286, 386, 486, Pentium . . .). This processor family, in conjunction with a disk operating system produced by Microsoft called DOS (for Disk Operating System), defines the basic platform. The kind of screen available has been the subject of separate 'standardization' starting with screens designed for use with American television sets. Ironically, a screen resolution of 640 by 480 pixels (this is the active size of an NTSC television picture, of which more is said in Chapter 14) has been one of the most standard things about computing systems.

PCs are made by a large number of companies and it is this range of competing manufacturers that has led to the PC becoming so inexpensive and widespread. Only UNIX is as successful, but while DOS is difficult, UNIX is downright awkward and remains successfully in a niche in education, science and technology rather than on the business desktop. The increase of interest in online systems will benefit UNIX because many of the machines that run servers on wide area networks run UNIX.

With the introduction of Microsoft's Windows, the PC found itself a more friendly face and Windows itself became the defining factor for the platform, which was vital as the underlying microprocessors became more powerful and part of the Multimedia (MPC) standard.

Competition for Windows came from the Apple Macintosh, which had adopted a friendly windows (with a small w) approach from its inception. Only programmers drove a Mac from a command line; the users moved a pointer about and pressed virtual buttons on the screen. In some other niche areas there were companies like Commodore (with the Amiga) and Acorn (whose Archimedes machine is firmly lodged in British education but boasted the most bangs for the buck of any desktop machine of its day and was the world's first RISC workstation).

Besides general purpose computers there were games machines (from the likes of Sega, Nintendo, Sony) and home entertainment machines like 3-DO and CD-i. As a multimedia developer your choice of platforms was these and more.

Criteria of choice

It would be really nice to be able to say that, as a multimedia developer, you have the freedom to choose the platform best suited to deliver your multimedia vision. In fact the market is more likely to drive your choice, and often that points to whichever machine is prevalent in your target sector. Businesses have business machines, often not suited to entertainment techniques even if those techniques are appropriate.

You will have to research your sector and find a lowest common denominator for the machinery your customers have. This relates to factors such as:

- Manufacturer and machine type
- Type and speed of processor (and therefore performance)
- Amount of memory (RAM)
- Size of hard disk (speed is less important but should not be forgotten)
- Operating system (don't forget which version)
- CD-ROM drive (speed and, in future, capacity)
- Access to online systems (local networks, Internet, World Wide Web, and so on)
- Resolution of the screen
- Number of colours on the screen
- Ability to handle moving video
- Sound handling (8 or 16 bit, mono or stereo, what compression?)

In some cases you may need to find out how often your users actually make use of their machine. This could be especially true in a business or training situation where machines may be shared between people. It would be awkward for your users to spend half a day using your training package if someone else needed to use it every two hours to read the electronic mail.

Cross-platform chameleons

An alternative to choosing a single platform is to produce the application for a number of platforms. This can be done by using an authoring system that produces versions of the application for several platforms. Macromedia Director is such a package which will produce files that will run on Windows and on Apple from the same 'source'. At a lower level, there are libraries for graphical user interfaces which can be used with C or C++ to run on different platforms with separate compilation.

It is possible for one computer platform to emulate another. A fast processor can run a program which appears, to the application, to be another platform entirely. The more powerful the platform, the more easily it can do this. There are Mac emulators for the Sun and Windows emulators for the Mac where one machine pretends to be the other. It can even be possible (if rather strange) to run a program under emulation where the emulator is itself running under emulation.

A further refinement of this technique is the virtual machine. Here the application code runs in a specified environment. That environment is provided by a program, the virtual machine, that itself runs on the host machine. To run the application on a new platform you only need a new virtual machine. The ancestor of C, BCPL, ran in this way and used a compiled intermediate code (called CINT Code) which then ran on the virtual machine.

This technique is best suited to low interactivity applications because interpreted software runs more slowly than software compiled to run directly on the target machine. There is also the problem of abilities and drawbacks of particular machines. A virtual machine has to have an audio-visual capability (since it is, to all intents and purposes, a platform in itself) and this will be the same as or less than the capabilities of its host.

If there is an incompatibility between the different platforms that can run software then the software might have to run differently. A lesser platform may run the software in a less than optimum way. The way that the application (and possibly the virtual machine if there is one) copes with this is by degrading the performance of the application. Pictures may have fewer colours, movies may run more sluggishly. If this is done well, and possibly even invisibly to the user, it is called graceful degradation.

Graceful degradation.

A classic example of graceful degradation is illustrated in HTML (Hypertext Mark-up Language), the document format that runs the World Wide Web on the Internet. The browsers that display HTML documents have differing abilities and it is recommended that any graphics used in documents are supplemented by words which will be displayed on browsers that cannot display pictures. In this way the document display gracefully degrades from graphics down to text only. If you are designing multimedia applications that will run on networks you might have to account for extreme cases like this. Refer to the CD for an example of HTML document design for different browser capabilities.

What is a platform anyway? The delivery medium

Besides deciding on what computer platform the end user will actually view and use your production, there is the question of how you will actually distribute the end result. To a certain extent this will depend on the size of the application, and might even have been specified up front. It is not unknown for small multimedia presentations to be delivered on floppy disks, with a little help from compression.

Here are some of the options.

Floppy disk

Using a floppy has the advantage of using a standard medium, as you can assume your potential market has a floppy disk drive. However, the downsides are the capacity (1.4 megabytes being the most common), the slow access times and the relative difficulty of replicating in large numbers. Compressing the material on the disk means that it has to be decompressed onto the user's hard disk to run, but this also overcomes the slow speed of the floppy. It is, however, very easy to copy floppies to order if the quantities are small enough.

Compact disc

This medium has become so universal that it seems unlikely that it may ever lose its supremacy as a carrier. Currently it is splitting into more and more different incarnations (Video CD, XA, multi-session, CD-Plus, Photo-CD and the rest). Back in 1984, when CD-ROM first appeared, it was touted as the data carrier to exceed all our requirements; but that was before digital video. There is a higher density format for CDs on the way which will make use of a smaller physical structure to the data on the disc and more layers of data. Replication in quantities is very cheap (almost down to pennies) and the discs are, rumours of deterioration notwithstanding, very robust.

CDs adhere to a group of standards called the coloured books. The original one is the Red Book which defines the physical disc and the original CD for digital audio. The Yellow Book defines CD-ROM and has an extension for CD-ROM XA (Extended Architecture) which provides a bridge across to CD-i (defined in the Green Book). The Orange Book defines magneto-optical discs like the Mini-Disk, and the format for writeable CDs. This writeable format also recognized that such a disc could be written in several sessions rather than all at once – hence the multi-session disc. The White Book specifies the Video-CD using MPEG digital video with the option of simple interactivity. A recent adition to the spectrum is the Blue Book which defines a multimedia extension to audio CDs known as CD+ or Extended CD. Refer to the CD for information on how these coloured books relate to each other.

A related standard is ISO 9660, which specifies file structures. It is based on DOS but has extensions to other filing systems. Importantly, an ISO 9660 CD-ROM can be read on a large number of computer platforms. This means that the platforms can access the data on the CD: they cannot necessarily do anything with that data unless they have the appropriate application.

Delivering on CD-ROM is likely to be one of the major, if not the major, method for interactive multimedia for some time. It will limit your creativity by forcing you to fit everything onto the disc and it will spur your ingenuity by forcing you to try to get around this limit. Compared to a hard disk, CD-ROM is slow, but getting faster. Quadruple-speed CD-ROM drives are now common. Many developers are now able to make their own CD-ROMs on the desktop using CD burners (or CD-R or WORMs) which follow part of the Orange Book standard.

Online

The philosophy behind providing multimedia applications online is somewhat different to that for offline ones. There are four main issues: speed of access, updating, security/payment and the 'unlimited' size of the data space that can be provided online. You can restrict access, charge your users for access and even keep track of who has accessed your information and when. Some of these techniques have spread themselves to CD-ROM with software and fonts being sold by giving away encrypted versions and charging for decryption.

The speed with which your potential users can access your application is unpredictable. If you find yourself frustrated by the access times of a compact disc then the access speed of the Internet will frustrate you further. Unfortunately, speeding up the local link between the user and the network will not necessarily resolve the problem because other links in the system will in themselves be unpredictable, with speeds depending on the bandwidth of the link itself (colloquially 'how fat is the pipe') and how much other traffic there is on it.

The notion of streaming from a networked source has practical problems. Streaming is the method whereby a steady stream of data is expected from the data source and it is processed and displayed as it arrives (on the fly). The classic example of this is digital audio from a compact disc. The 16-bit digital audio data arrives at the decoder chips and is converted into analog audio immediately. There is no storage of the data. If for some reason the stream of data is disturbed then you hear either clicks, where a single sample is misplaced, or pauses and hiccupping.

A way around this problem is buffering and/or caching. For buffering, the data from the source is read into memory at the rate it arrives and is read out of memory at the rate it is needed. In this way small discontinuities can be removed. With a cache the data is read completely into the cache memory and, once it has all arrived, the application accesses it. The disadvantage of a cache is that the application has to wait for all the data to arrive, although the data, once it is in the cache, can be accessed many times. The program can be designed to allow the data to be both streamed and cached, of course, but that is only practical if the data stream is fast enough.

In general, the use of a network implies that people other than your intended user can access the data. If this is a concern then security systems have to be built in, ranging from password protection and access from selected terminals only, to full encryption. In a networked environment it is possible to log the amount of data that a user accesses, whether stock market prices or clips of video. If necessary, the user can be charged accordingly and any royalties required by the data owner can be paid from that money.

A final benefit of the network is the huge data space that can potentially be presented to the user. The 650 megabytes of a Yellow Book CD-ROM is no longer a limiting factor.

Video on Demand (VOD) will provide another market for interactive services and so it will provide a potential market for multimedia developers. The way in which this develops as a platform will depend on which of the two proposed models for VOD is used and where. You can say that in one model the VOD server pushes the application for display in the home on a television linked to the service by a set-top box. In the other model the set-top box itself pulls the application from the server.

The 'push' model works like this: the set-top box functions as an audio-visual version of the dumb terminal and basically passes user commands down the line to the server, takes the data the server sends and displays it. This means that the application itself, usually something to run the movie, is actually being run in the server and not in the set-top box. This can be a crucial situation for the developer because the servers are often going to be very powerful processors running real-time operating systems totally unlike those you would usually find in multimedia. This is unless the servers can operate virtual machines to emulate other platforms. Since the set-top boxes are only operating as dumb terminals, including MPEG decoders, there is relatively free reign for potential manufacturers since only the display and communications need to be standardized, not the application environment because that is in the server.

The 'pull' model has the server operating as a data source, whether for downloaded data or streamed data, and the downloaded application runs in the set-top box, which therefore has to be more than a dumb terminal. This raises a different problem for both the developer of applications and for the service provider. Since the set-top boxes are likely to be from more than one manufacturer, compatability between the boxes and the applications is in question. In practice this can be overcome by only offering applications that the server knows the set-top box can support or that the set-top box itself knows it can support.

Platforms for development

So far, this chapter has dealt with the delivery of your application to the end user: your customer. You will also be making choices about the platform or platforms you use to design and build your application.

It is certainly true that your design platforms have to include your delivery platform so that you can, at the very least, test out the performance and carry out debugging. This can mean that you have to have access to every possible configuration of platform that your customers will have. This is no trivial task.

Even with the Apple Macintosh, a famously self-compatible platform, there is a need to test for users with a range of variations such as these:

- Different models of Macintosh
- Different amounts of RAM
- Different screens and numbers of screens
- Different sizes of hard disks
- Common extensions to the basic system
- Different versions of the system software
- Different CD-ROM drives
- Different network configurations.

With that list, and assuming five possible options for each category, the number of possible configurations is $5 \times 5 \times 5 \times 5 \times 5 \times 5 \times 5 \times 5$, which is 390 625. This is not really practical and you will test for the most likely problem areas such as system software versions and RAM.

You do not have to develop your application on the delivery platform. For a cross-platform application this is especially true since the usual practice would be to develop the application on one of the group of delivery platforms and test it on them all. Even low-level code can be produced on a different computer using a cross-compiler.

More likely is that you will use one consistant platform for your asset creation and manipulation for every application. Even though the IBM PC 'standard' has been the most common delivery platform for multimedia, many multimedia developers use Apple Macintoshes for their asset work and moved the assets across to their delivery platform during integration. The reason for this approach was that the best tools tend to appear first on the Macintosh and that, for the graphically minded, the Mac was already a platform of choice.

It must not be underestimated that moving assets between platforms needs to be done with some care and attention to quality and parameters. Even though both the Mac and PC had 22 KHz sound, they used slightly different sampling rates near to 22. This and other asset formats will need to be checked and tested on both platforms. If you are producing an application for more than one platform, especially if you store your assets in a single common format, this will be even more important.

In fact it does not matter whether you are a Mac fan or a PC fan or whatever. The point is that you can retain your platform of choice for asset creation and manipulation even if your client or market wants a particular application delivered on something else. The only limiting factor is that the asset creation platform must have a display that matches or exceeds that of the delivery platform. It is clearly no use whatsoever to try to do colour graphics on a black and white machine, or to produce sound for a system with CD quality 16-bit sound on an 8-bit system.

Similarly, you should create and manipulate your assets in the highest convenient standard and convert down, if necessary, at the last moment. This will not only give you the option of porting the assets to other delivery platforms if required, but will actually help you keep the quality as high as possible.

THEORY INTO PRACTICE 7

Experience is the best teacher on moving applications from one delivery platform to another. You can learn a lot by talking to people you know who have direct experience of this and discussing the detailed problems they may have encountered.

Look at a multimedia application (such as Electronic Arts 3-D Atlas, which was separately developed for Mac, PC and 3-DO) that is available on more than one platform and compare the versions. There are other examples, and you will be able to judge from the boxes on the store shelves which are cross-platform.

Summary

- The choice of delivery platform will usually be decided by either your client or your target market.
- You do not have to do all your development on the delivery platform, especially when it comes to working with your assets.
- It is possible to develop an application that will work on more than one platform, but moving from one platform to another can lead to changes in performance and you should be aware of what is likely to happen.

Recommended reading

Vaughan T. (1994). *Multimedia: Making it Work*. Berkeley, CA: Osborne McGraw-Hill

CHAPTER 8

SELECTING THE MEDIA AND TECHNIQUES: THE TREATMENT

Project manager's responsibilities

- To define the project constraints that affect the use of media and techniques
- To understand the strengths and weaknesses of each medium
- To involve experts from each medium for the detailed treatments, if possible
- To keep the focus on interactive use of media and the needs of the user
- To keep abreast of research because this area has few guidelines to date

Constraints

Platform

It may seem to be counter-intuitive and negative to start from the constraints that affect the development team but in reality this is usually what happens. If clients specify a platform you need to find out as much as you can about it quickly. It will affect your decisions about what is possible, what is likely and what is impractical because of the platform's capabilities and limitations. This is true especially for the range and technical quality of the media components that it is able to support.

If the platform is already in place – perhaps in hundreds of installations – then you may find that you have no leeway and will have to work with the hardware provided. This could be equipment that is several years old. As technology advances quickly, this can mean that the team has to work to a much lower specification than they would like.

With this situation, if there is a possibility that the clients would upgrade their systems to allow better use, the arguments need to made early for them to find the extra budget. They need to understand the factors that have driven the decisions for your solutions so that they recognize the constraints their systems might be imposing and the benefits that a better system would bring.

If you demonstrate examples of previous work to clients who already have a platform, you should exercise care. If there are features and quality levels that are not possible for them to have on their equipment, this needs to be made very clear indeed. It is difficult for anyone, let alone the clients, to see some stimulating demonstrations that imprint themselves on the memory while listening to passing remarks about why some of these features will not be possible. They will often hark back to these features later and comment on the difference in quality that they are getting. They will have forgotten that it is their machines that caused the restrictions and they will have forgotten that you pointed this out to them.

Another problem occurs if clients see or read about the latest developments in technology and expect to be able to have them halfway into the project. Clear, straight talking backed up with written records is the only way to cope with the change in expectations as clients become more versed in multimedia and its possibilities. This change is healthy for the next project because specifications will be clearer, cleaner and faster.

It is more useful if you can show clients examples of the range and type of features that their platform can handle. Alternatively, by working from previous examples of work they have had developed, you can show them the difference in quality levels that might be possible with upgrades. This will be your only chance to influence clients to improve their systems if improvement is possible.

Budget

The biggest constraint on the selection of media and techniques is the budget. Many clients do not have systems already in place so the outlay for both the platform and the application is expensive. Many projects of this nature are pilot projects and because of this clients want them done cheaply even though their purpose is important. Pilots are used to impress the organization to move towards using multimedia. The purpose and budget do not match well so you have to work hard to compensate.

Table 8.1 Media components.

Component	Type	Cost	Production time	Analog forms	Digital forms	Notes
Video	Drama	High	Long	1 inch	Broadcast Digital (CCIR 601)	Rights and clearances can be costly and time consuming.
	Interviews	Low to medium	Short/medium	Betacam-SP	MPEG, Video for Windows,	
	Studio shoot	Low to medium	Short/medium	VHS	QuickTime formats	
	Location shoot	High	Long	Hi8		
Audio	Drama	Medium	Long	Audio cassette	DAT	Good voice-over artists and actors for drama can be expensive.
	Voice-overs	Low	Short/Fast	Quarter-inch	Compact disc	
	Interviews	Low	Short/Fast			
	Music	Low to medium	Can be off the shelf			
Video graphics (graphics as found in video facilities)	3-D animation (high quality)	High	Medium/Fast	1 inch	Broadcast digital videotape, computer streamer tapes	Costly and difficult to transfer to computer but improving.
	Animation (high quality)	High	Medium/Fast	Betacam-SP		Grabbing from video is usually easily done in the same facility.
	Sophisticated tricks	High	Fast	VHS		
	Static graphics (high quality)	High	Fast	Hi8		

Table 8.1 *Continued*

Component	Type	Cost	Production time	Analog forms	Digital forms	Notes
Computer graphics (graphics as found on the desktop)	3-D Animation (high quality)	High	Long	N/A	Hard disk	Production time relative to video graphics production but the number of graphics needed often means the computer wins because of cost.
	3-D Animation (medium quality)	Medium	Long			
	3-D Animation (low level)	Medium	Long			
	Static graphics (high quality)	Low to medium	Medium			
	Static graphics (medium quality)	Low to medium	Fast			
	Static graphics (low quality)	Low	Fast			
Text		Low	Fast	Paper	Disk	Text can be expensive in particular cases where you have to develop or use special fonts.

Resources

Within each kind of medium there are a range of possibilities that affect the cost. Because of this you need to decide the best for the purpose, platform, price and user. The costs are not straightforward since they depend on other factors. Examples of these can be: access to the right equipment at the development site, the need to hire facilities, whether the right expertise is in-house or if there is a need to hire it. Your resources can constrain you to work in certain ways.

Table 8.1 gives guidance on some of the media components, their major categories and the relative development times and costs. This presents them in general terms and the time and costs need to be considered in a work context to refine the generalizations.

Once you understand the constraints you are working with, the challenge is to produce the best within them. Constraints do not stifle creativity: they shape the way it can contribute. Each combination of media, message, techniques and interface can have unique features that are suitable for the content and the users.

Matching the media to the message

If the developer had complete freedom, there are definite occasions when one medium will convey some concepts better than others and there would be a natural selection – video for coverage of action-based events, for example. The power of a medium does not just lie in the way it offers us messages – audio, visual, text or combinations of these. It is also dependent on the techniques that have evolved in each medium – sequencing, ways of editing, morphing, time lapse photography and so on. This is difficult to analyse because it is very subjective and difficult to identify which techniques or which combination of them has caused a reaction. The power of the media and messages and techniques is only released when the person receiving the messages interprets them, so we need to consider the skill level of the recipient as well as the impact of the techniques themselves. Basically, the ease with which viewers 'read' the grammar and syntax of television and film changes and becomes more sophisticated as the medium develops. The interpretation is not a conscious activity. The techniques have symbolic significance and influence the viewer's interpretation in this way.

The impact of each media component depends on a combination of the quality of the content, the media itself and the techniques employed by the media specialists. For example, a great deal of research has been done with printed text. Specialist techniques would include decisions on layout, use of space, length of sentence, readability, style and tone among others. These fine details all contribute to the quality of the product and increased reception of the messages by the reader. Some of these can be useful for screen-based text but the size of the screen and the electronic nature of the environment mean that parameters that work on the page have to be adjusted.

There are several problems with making recommendations for use of media components. The first is that new forms or new quality levels of display occur – overlapping windows and MPEG video are examples – and these evolve quickly. The second is that research into different forms of media and their relative merits for imparting similar information has been inconclusive. As there is conflicting information on the 'right' use of single media, the use of multiple media or combinations of them remains subjective, based on experience.

In view of this we will present the individual media and discuss their strengths and techniques. We will indicate wherever possible where the context and platform may influence use and how multimedia may cause extra considerations.

Video – background factors

As video becomes easier to use and control in digital form, its use in general multimedia applications will increase. Developers will find it as liberating as the advent of audio, but its use needs to be considered wisely within the constraints that still operate. Not all systems allow full screen video and the size permitted affects the type of content that should be communicated. Even the term full screen can be misleading since the video often only fills the screen because it has been expanded to do so. MPEG-1 as used in Video CD is a case in point since the real resolution of MPEG-1 is only a quarter of the area of a standard screen. When a Video-CD is displayed, the pixels of the digital image are blown up to four times their original area.

It is easy to demonstrate the size versus content issue when you consider the inappropriate use of video for a well-known theatre drama that was transferred to CD-ROM and shown in an inch-square box! At the time of development that might have been the technological constraint for video on the system.

However, size can also be influenced by the necessity to juggle all the components to fit into the disk space. Because video almost certainly takes up the greatest space in an application, it constrains how much will be left for other component parts. If the application grows too big, video will have to be sacrificed in terms of duration or size to accommodate this. Video also uses the most processing power to run and accounting for the space is not enough. Often, even though there is space, the use of video can lead to slow access and slower interactivity while it is being played. You need to know early on how much and which components are going to be used in order to calculate if the mix can fit into the space, or if the speed of access will be affected.

It is as well to remember that users are familiar with good quality visuals because of television. Their expectations are high and they will be critical of poor quality, as will your clients. Any undue waiting during the use of the system also causes universal annoyance so this needs to be avoided or made explicit to the client from the beginning. If you remember the example of 'Just a small change' in Chapter 2, it is easy to get carried away once the project is under way and agree to what appears to be a small change. It would be tempting to include extra minutes of video because the material that is shot is so good, but the repercussions need to be thought through from every angle – space, speed of interaction, sacrifice of other material.

Drama needs to be displayed in a size that is large enough for detail to be visible. This would seem to be a self-evident guideline but sometimes the drive to try out what is possible with technology seems to blunt common sense. A talking head, shown in close-up, is likely to be satisfactory in a small window, but the same could not be said of a group of actors in a dramatic scene, or several people in a discussion. Anything that relies on wide shots of detailed scenes will suffer in such circumstances. The video needs to be big enough to suit the circumstances for the user.

Video of this type in a kiosk, for example, should be at least half-screen since the user tends to stand further back from the screen than if sitting at a system. Kiosks also tend to be used for communal viewing because people share the interaction with whoever they are with.

Video used on CD-i must be as large as possible because the user uses a remote control and sits at least six feet from the screen; just as they do when watching television. CD-ROM users tend to operate on a one-to-one basis with the application and sit very close to the screen, so there is a case for the video to be smaller. However, this should not affect the size to the extent that the video cannot be viewed adequately. An option is to allow the user to choose whether to view the video in a window, with other screen components around it, or to see it blown up to fill the screen.

From these few examples it should be evident that the strengths of a medium are affected by the total context in which it is used. The guidelines for the use of media that will be cited here need to be adapted to the context of platform, needs of the user and interrelation with the other components. Many of the general guidelines that exist do not indicate that these factors affect the decisions for use. A lot of the educational research guidelines do not recognize that their own context and purpose affect the validity of the findings for other types of media use. For example, a completely incongruous use of sound effects juxtaposed with weird graphics that make no sense would break all the rules for design, but it could also be very powerful in an entertainment application for that very reason. This type of use would fall foul of guidelines for both general and instructional use of media, however.

Video

Video is already a combined medium because it generally uses sound to accompany the pictures in some form. It is the nearest current medium to reality since our lives are full of moving images and sounds. Watching and listening are the natural way we process our understanding of the world and we are comfortable with this realistic medium.

Film and television have developed some interesting techniques which relate to the treatment of information and its sequence of presentation according to time. Our own perception of time in the form of days, months and years is always linear and, to start with, the so-called grammar of film making followed this convention. But over time, as audiences grew accustomed to watching movies, film makers began to change the grammar to enhance the story-telling abilities of the medium. Time becomes non-linear and therefore closer to being interactive. The use of flashbacks or parallel action, for example, allows a non-linear progression through information so that the viewer gradually builds up a complete picture. Action replays allow a concentrated focus on particular events. These non-linear techniques provide a basis for helping people relate to other non-linear techniques that come under their control as computer inter-activity is added to sound and motion.

Video can be used for a whole spectrum of purposes – explanation, humour, demonstration, exposition, fiction. In general it is used for appealing rapidly to the senses and transferring impressionistic information very quickly. Viewers cannot absorb and retain all the information that passes, so they filter it according to their preferences and prior understanding. This happens internally as the video passes across viewers' consciousness, but computer control will allow a greater manual selection of preference within a topic. Viewers will be able to pre-select pieces to view. This is a proactive filter of information although they will continue to filter the detail of the information even as it is delivered.

This control that the computer element allows when added to sound and motion means that information can be marked unobtrusively into smaller units of meaning than usual so that each piece can be searched and selected. This might mean in practice that the equivalent of a 20-minute video programme might be classified into themes or sections and viewers might select to see two or three minutes of the material most relevant to them rather than watch the whole programme.

Of course this level of control will be more useful for some information than others. Drama needs to develop and the story needs to resolve over a period of time, for example, so tiny pieces might be disconcerting, even frustrating. But put in a learning context where specific use of gesture or look is being studied by actors and actresses, such fragmentation can still be very useful.

The type of application will govern the amount of control and the size of the pieces of information. Kiosks, for example, will need to offer people fast, interesting information. Advertisers are used to getting their messages across quickly but powerfully, so developers could learn a lot from their techniques. Advertisers are the masters of short sequences of video and they innovate continually to motivate people.

The combination of sound and vision can appeal to people's logic, imagination and feelings. But sound and static visuals can do the same, so what is the difference? The difference lies in how much viewers bring to the interpretation of the content and how much they have to do to construct meaning. The combination of sound and moving images is easier to process because viewers' senses are fed with stimuli that are realistic and are absorbed effortlessly and almost unconsciously. Static images and sound require viewers to contribute more to their interpretation.

In the extreme case, when only text is used, readers have to consciously apply decoding techniques to extract meaning from the letters. The skills of reading take several years to learn because the information is removed from reality into a complete system of symbols. There are various levels of symbolism used throughout the mix of media but there is a gradual move from the realistic to the symbolic as you move from video to text. When the mixture uses more symbolic than realistic elements, the viewer needs to decipher more and this takes more effort.

Viewing and listening are not passive processes and this is often forgotten. The combination of vision and sound is more powerful with the majority because they stimulate reaction more easily. They appeal to a larger range of possible reactions. Stimulation and motivation are closely linked so it is easier to motivate the viewer to respond to an appropriate mix of sound and vision.

Appropriate use is the key factor and the more media that are combined the harder it is to keep all the factors appropriate. For example, an historical video needs to ensure historical accuracy to be convincing. This includes location, location detail, dress, accents, type of language used, type of music used, and so on. Exactly the same criteria need to be applied to interactive video sequences. Details such as the tone and look of the presenter need to be be appropriate for the purpose or the audience. Carefully and correctly chosen, they can be the making of the application. Any music used can motivate, be ignored or demotivate the audience.

Most people are used to controlling videos in a limited interactive manner on their VCRs. The controls allow a combination of forward, back, search, play, stop and perhaps slow motion. Viewers cannot jump around the video following links or backtracking to the point they started from. They are used to a semi-interactive environment within the one medium. This will have implications for the interface design where the control or navigational features for applications are used.

A few finer points of visual grammar

When film was invented it was believed that the camera had to remain static and that the action was framed as if it were on a stage and the film frame was the proscenium arch. In time directors and cameramen developed the techniques of framing, moving the camera and editing and, as they did so, the audiences learned with them. Today an audience is sophisticated enough to know that if the film shows a car drawing up at a building, the camera looks up to zoom in on a window, we cut to inside a room and two people walk through the door, those people were in the car and the room is the one we looked up at. The film is edited to remove time and so speed up the action.

At a simpler level the very way in which a shot is framed can convey information. If, during an interview, the camera gradually moves close in to the speaker, then the impression is of a sharing in a secret or of some momentously important point that is being made. Often this visual metaphor will override anything that is actually being said.

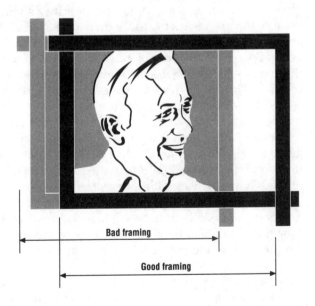

Bad framing

Good framing

The way a face is framed in a picture is important. This is true for stills as well as movies. The face should have space to look into, otherwise the effect will be unnatural. The strongest points in an image are a third of the way across or up and down the image. You can increase the impact of an object by framing it to make use of this rule of thirds.

Of course, there are more straightforward ways of drawing a viewer's attention to something, such as zooming in on it or panning to follow it, and viewers now know these conventions. You might, if you are feeling devious, actually distract the viewer by using the visual grammar to draw attention to something completely inconsequential so as to hide the real action which can be revealed later. This technique was used to great effect by Alfred Hitchcock in his films and if done well, as he did it, can completely unnerve the viewer. There was the way the viewer is made to identify with first the girl and then the private eye in *Psycho*, only to have them killed. In *The Birds*, there appears to be something significant about the two lovebirds that the hero and heroine are carrying, but in fact they are another of Hitchcock's McGuffins, as he called them.

Video and applications for education and training

It may seem odd to single out training and the use of video but there are many factors that make the imparting of information for learning purposes different from its use for other reasons.

As explained in Chapter 6, Agreeing the Content, if the user is going to be tested on the knowledge and skills covered in the application then the information needs to employ certain structures and techniques to aid this. One of the strengths of video in other contexts – the ability to cover a great deal in a short time – is not necessarily a strength in a training context because the user needs to absorb more of the detail. This explains why there appear to be inconsistencies between educational research findings and general practice in the use of video. When the viewers have no control over the media – as in television – they cannot look at the material again for revision. They have the one chance to listen and absorb.

Video players and computer-based interactive materials offer the means to control the video and so provide viewers with the opportunity to revise the information if necessary. Computer control can offer more than just replay opportunities. It can be used to pinpoint the concepts the user finds difficult and re-route to remedial material where the concepts are offered in a new way with different explanations.

Role plays and simulations are recognized as good techniques for demonstrating skills in action. Video is very good for showing interpersonal skills, whether handling meetings or dealing with difficult customers. An interactive role play could allow the user to take one side of the role play while the video character asks or answers questions accordingly via prompts through the computer. Here is an example of the combination of video with computer control and text with audio serving the educational purpose possibly better than a linear video. The other obvious advantage is the use of the computer for testing the transfer of knowledge during and at the end of the application.

A computer mixture of media-based information can also provide a superb reference set of materials where the learner is asked to research or discover information. There are several defined approaches to how people learn. People have preferential learning styles – the way they prefer to absorb, process and classify information so that it makes best sense to them. Educationalists can choose to present information based on progressing from easy parts to more difficult ones. Alternatively, it can be left to learners to impose a structure on the information through discovering links themselves. This is called discovery learning. The only problem is that discovery learning takes longer and there is no guarantee that what is discovered covers the whole range that would be appropriate. Luckily, multimedia can be set up to cover both approaches with the same data depending on the requirements.

Audio

Audio is a very versatile medium which will usually be an integral part of any video but can be used alone or to accompany graphics, text, or both simultaneously. It uses relatively little space so can be used quite freely. The space it consumes depends on the quality level that is used but the levels are easy to choose because there are guidelines matching the types of audio information to the quality level. These are explained fully in Chapter 13.

Before audio was common in digital form, text and graphics had to be used for all information. This made explanations onerous. Screen after screen had to be used for the main content and all the help explanations. Access to relevant pieces of the information became problematic because there was so much of it. Applications tended to be tedious and linear.

Audio liberated developers from lengthy text explanations. The main problem is overuse because it is cheap and efficient. Its efficiency fails when too much information is given too quickly for the user to absorb and there is no opportunity to repeat it. Its effectiveness is increased when it supports text and graphics appropriately so that the information, like video, addresses both sight and sound senses for better reception by the user. The use of audio feedback for help in applications has increased mainly because it can be played at the point in the program the user needs. This means that users do not lose their place in the program and the audio supports the visuals that are on screen with extra explanation. It can be repeated easily. The alternative used to be endless scrolling text boxes which took the user away from the main program and could cause disorientation.

Audio includes speech, music and sounds. Both radio and television have developed techniques to use with sound which makes it a sophisticated medium but as it is so easy to listen, the sophistication is not appreciated. The sympathetic blend of music and speech with variations in pitch, volume and style can add greatly to static pictures and text. These can be effective alone, of course. But it is precisely because listening is effortless that the subtleties of its qualities have been almost completely ignored in applications, to their detriment.

It is no accident that both radio and television choose to introduce many programmes with a signature tune. It identifies the programme (a form of branding), it settles the listener and viewer to be receptive to what is coming next, or alternatively brings them in from the next room. It emphasizes the end of the programme. During the programme it can form part of the continuity strategy to blend segments together when there may be little overt connection. In a non-broadcast context such as video or multi-media some music at the front also helps the viewer to adjust the sound volume and even check that the sound is getting through.

Sound can be evocative. It can appeal to emotions and in this way influence the reactions of the listener. It can set an atmosphere. These are good points for applications that need to persuade, like presentations, demonstrations and Point of Sale. Equally, it can jar and demotivate when used wrongly.

Most applications fall in a neutral middle ground in their use of sound. They have missed opportunities – but the opportunities are difficult to spot. Few recognize the full potential of a well-planned and well-executed sound track. The extra effort means extra money and time for something that is intangible. It is hard to prove its real worth until you compare one that has professional touches and another that does not. Listen to the examples and explanations on the CD to improve your appreciation of sound quality.

Sound has its own techniques to appeal to the listener. A fade-up implies that the listener is evesdropping on something already under way and and a fade-out signifies that we are moving on and leaving them to it. Sound effects can be humorous, intriguing or realistic. Ironically sound effects are not always what they seem. You can try this experiment. Take a piece of paper and crunch it up into a ball. Open it out and gently manipulate it. The sound is not unlike the crackle of a fire. Quarter-inch audio tape could sound like walking through grass, and we all know about horses and coconut shells.

Interactive sound does have differences for developers to consider. Sound used on computer systems to attract passers-by irritates other people who might have to stay in the vicinity. Kiosks and demonstration programs can be prone to this misuse. A phrase becomes annoying if it is repeated often as the user navigates around the system. Developers need to consider how sound can have a good initial impact but then becomes irritating. They might need to consider giving control to the user so they can switch it off when they want. Alternatively developers can build in control themselves where repetitive audio turns itself off after a couple of times of use by the same person.

Another problem with kiosks, and any other installation in a busy area, comes from high levels of background noise. Any sound needs to be carefully manipulated to make sure that it is still audible over any extraneous noise without sounding distressingly loud.

Computer and video graphics

Computer graphics systems, whether they are on desktop machines or dedicated sophisticated television or video graphics machines, are capable of very impressive results. Desktop computer graphics are very versatile and can range from simple line drawings to 3-D animations. More than any of the other components, they can be manipulated to suit the budget allowance. However, many of the specialist skills within graphics are still needed. Original material might need to be created, like cartoons for example, before it is processed and integrated into an application. The manipulation of source materials and their successful integration are the two computer graphic processes that figure most in multimedia. Their quality can be affected by the platform and software.

The strength of graphics is to provide a visual stimulus that can trigger reaction in the user. It can be the prime source of the reaction or offer support for other media components so that their impact is improved. Because systems have become more sophisticated and have more memory, it is easier to use many high quality graphics. This has changed the look and feel of applications considerably away from a text, menu-driven approach to a visual selection in the form of icons.

Even though graphics can be realistic – as realistic as photographs – their advantage over video stills lies in their ability to be representational in a symbolic sense. This can add a dimension, a unique program style and feel to an application. The style is often set by the first main selection screen or menu. It usually is the key feature, the hallmark of a program and one which is used the most and seen the most by the users. Refer to the CD for an example main menu and a description of its style.

Sophisticated graphics allow superimposition of one picture on a representation of itself and animation could add to the understanding of transformation. For example, this technique can be very effective when there are layers of visual material like the bones, muscle, tissues and skin of a person or animal that need to be shown or even the relationship between the outside of a machine and its internal parts. This type of technique is found useful in developing analytical and discrimination skills so can be extremely useful for educational purposes.

The exact use of each graphic will be driven by the content, the existing assets and the skill of the artist.

The expense of dedicated video graphics has meant that they have been used very little in interactive programs, except for developers with a broadcast video connection. However, this kind of equipment has special hardware which allows for very fast working and video graphics can offer high quality animation faster than most computer generated animations. So when speed is crucial and there is enough budget, video graphic sequences could provide an answer. Also, if an application has video as part of it, the use of video offcuts from the main sequences to construct video graphic images can offer a continuity of style and quality through the application. A lot of these decisions can only be made once the size of the application and content treatment have been established because video graphics sequences, like video, eat up space. A lot of small sequences can be too costly and space intensive for an application once they are totalled.

The use of graphics in education and training applications

As with the use of video, there is research that applies particularly to the use of graphics for instructional purposes. The choice of a particular type and style of graphic still lies in the joint decisions of designer/producer or whoever takes this role and the graphics artist but they can both be served in making a selection by some of the insights from this research.

Instructional graphics have been categorized into representational, analogical and logical:

■ Representational graphics share a physical resemblance with the object or concept that is portrayed. An example of this might be a picture of a particular style of architecture that demonstrated the points that were being addressed. A photograph, such as the edit suite in Chapter 14, would also be representational.
■ Analogical graphics display something that has similarities with the issue under discussion but in an abstract way that uses analogy to help convey meaning. An example would be a time-lapsed video graphic that used a leaf decaying as an analogy to the decline of a dynasty, corporation or whatever, as shown here.
■ Logical graphics are symbolic representations in the form of flow charts, graphs and charts. The flow charts describing linear and multi-media script writing in Chapter 6 are examples of logical graphics.

It was found that although learning theory recommends the use of graphics to support and extend text to aid comprehension, this was being

Analogical representation of decay.

ignored in computer-based courses. Representational graphics were used the most with analogical used the least. This may be related to the history of education and training where text has played the dominant role. The visual side of communication needs to be recognized in those teams involved with developing interactive education and training so that the effort put into defining well-structured content achieves better success with balanced use of media. This might be achieved by making sure a graphics specialist works closely with the person whose role it is to define the content.

The instructional use of animations has also been researched and these findings can be applied across different types of applications. It was found that users can be easily distracted by other factors so that the relevance of the animation is only partially understood. This is particularly true when the users are inexperienced in the subject matter.

The guidelines recommend that animations are kept simple enough to be understood but sufficiently complex to convey the important information. Users can fail to notice aspects if too much happens at once. Because of this, the use of cueing strategies like narration and the use of colour become important. They help direct attention to salient parts of the animation at the right time. It is recommended that users should be given control of parts of the animation like the speed, triggering factors and so on as this involves and focuses them. Animations were found good for representing motion, trajectory, spatial organization and otherwise invisible events, but overuse can be distracting.

Text

The value of text tends to be overlooked by multimedia specialists but is an integral part of any application and needs to be thought through as carefully as the other media components. Whereas a few years ago text was a dominant feature on screens, the amount and function of text has changed as the other media components have come to the fore. This shift is linked with the fast-moving technological environment. Many of the problems that made it difficult to integrate all the media components in a digital domain have now been solved. Previously, text had to bear most of the communication load, aided with some graphics. Even the graphics were limited since they took up a seemingly enormous amount of space. Now, although space can still be an issue, it is easier because the storage capacities of disks have increased dramatically.

The function of text information in multimedia has become supportive rather than dominant. It is used most for: help explanations, reinforcement or summary information, summaries of decisions made by the user, titles, names of hot-spots, quick-scan information like opening times and admission charges in a tourist application.

When it was a dominant media component, it was important to pay a good deal of attention to screen layout, readability and legibility. Now it is even more important because poor typography is immediately evident beside the quality of the other media components. For an application to have integrity, components need to blend into one another without a noticeable drop in quality. This may not be easy. If text has been added onto the video at the video edit, other text added over computer graphics and some screens are text screens alone, the difference between them can be very great.

This is because the final integration process can affect each component in slightly different ways and can have a knock-on effect. Text is one element that suffers in video encoding, for example, because of its sharp edges. Of course, if text has been added into each component, control over font use, characteristics and size need to be consistent across all and has to be established early. It may be better to generate all the text with the computer to keep more strict control but these decisions have to be made by the core team members.

Making text easy to read is more complex than many imagine. Readers are adept at deciphering text but their job can be simplified or complicated by the techniques employed in its layout. The users of the application will have certain objectives once they see text because they will make the decision of whether to read it thoroughly or not. They will employ their own reading strategies of skimming and scanning the information to appraise it. It surprises a lot of people to find that many readers of Western languages do not start to read at the top left of the screen. They may not scan the text from left to right until the bottom right piece of text. Instead, they might skim the headings to get the gist of the material; they might scan the material looking for a key word that could indicate that the information they require is in the vicinity. These types of strategies are used more often when the text is giving information as opposed to text narrating or explaining. In sound there is a phenomenon called the cocktail party effect, where listeners will clearly hear a word across a noisy room just because the word has a special meaning for them, like their name. A viewer picking out a word from text is a similar phenomenon. Of course, the word may be misread or hyphenation may result in anomalous groups of letters being at the start of lines.

The layout can help the reader by having clear headings or markers of some type. Line length is also important as the comfort of eye span across words is linked to the length of a line. Because screens are generally small, it is tempting to cram as much text as possible into the space. However, this will not necessarily help readability. Because of the limited space, it seems logical to have a small font size and as many words to the line as can fit but this will only increase the difficulty of reading. The size of the font will also affect the legibility of the text. You need to consider the distance of the viewer from the screen when making decisions of how large and how much text will be viable.

The use of space helps reading because the reader needs natural prompts to understand how much concentration and attention to give to the information. If there are few or no paragraphs, the reader quickly reaches overload. Headings stand out if there is space around them but if you need to sacrifice space, other cues can help. The use of bolding, colour and size can help establish the importance of some parts of the text over others.

See the CD-ROM for examples of readability and legibility.

The use of colour alone to distinguish some text from others should be handled carefully because a sizeable minority of the general public suffers from colour blindness – particularly red and green tones. It is also wise to remember that not all cultures share the same reading pattern of left to right, top to bottom. If the text is going to be translated there is more to consider than whether the translations will fit into the same space. The block of text may be better placed in a completely different part of the screen according to the reading conventions of the country.

Text is still a powerful way to communicate. It allows readers a lot more control than the other media components because they control their pace of reading. They decide how and when to assimilate the information. They can re-read and pause, if necessary, to think things through. It is a versatile medium which has changed with the times.

The use of computers has changed the way that text is organized and this in turn affects how people relate to it. They need new reading strategies to suit the new types of organization. Developers need to understand that just because reading printed matter can be taken for granted, reading on computer screens cannot. The use of layers of text instead of pages as used in hypertext and Windows, for example, represents a different form of structure for text. The stacking of related and unrelated information needs readers to develop new reading strategies. They are expected to keep track of detailed lines of investigation across time and space instead of reading sequential text that has been pre-ordered in logical patterns that they recognize.

The research on hyperdocuments and the confusion that they can cause in readers is fascinating. Readers can easily get carried away when they select link after link across cross-referenced text until they lose sight of their original line of investigation. Worse than this, they find they are lost in the depths of a seemingly never-ending document.

THEORY INTO PRACTICE 8

Getting lost with associative logic is easily demonstrated if you play a game of associations for a minute verbally with a friend. One person starts with a word and the other has to reply immediately with the first word that comes to mind. At times this can operate like a trapdoor, where the association works in one direction but becomes virtually impossible to trace backwards. It is difficult to retain the thread of connections for long unless they are recorded.

Look at the following example and try to guess the flow of logic of the blank spaces. The answer is provided underneath the diagram.

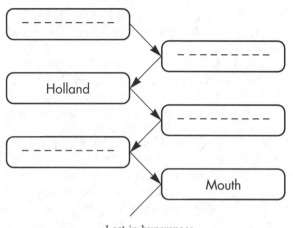

Lost in hyperspace.

Answer: Light, Bulb, Holland, Cheese, Food, Mouth

If you think that was difficult, remember that in hypermedia there would be multiple choices at each point.

Overlapping windows that have many selection possibilities can present a daunting image for newcomers. They forget what they have opened, forget where a particular function is hidden, and may never be able to find something because they do not know what it is called.

These initial problems will multiply as text documents themselves become multimedia documents. In multimedia documents a piece of sound information will be cross-referenced to a bit of video which will be cross-referenced to other sound, text and video components. Multimedia archiving and office automation are accelerating so this scenario is no fantasy. There is much to learn from the analysis of reactions of users to the new forms of structuring information on computers. Some of the problems have simple solutions. For example, to stop people getting lost in hyperdocuments, maps tracing the routes people have taken are recorded and these can show the origin and development of their searches.

Overview maps of multimedia applications are becoming common and when users complete a section, the map indicates that this has been done. The concept of a bookmark is also being used more frequently. This records how much of an application users have completed and what remains to be seen so that when they return to the application they can continue where they left off.

The difficulty for the developer is to decide how computer literate the audience will be and how much guidance will be needed as part of the application in the form of help explanations or aids such as route maps. These are aspects of the computer interface and will be dealt with in the next chapter.

Where does this leave us?

Media selection will remain complicated because of the constraints, whether these are mechanical or influenced by humans. It is a complex subject that needs much more attention but because multimedia is embryonic there are no set answers yet. We can only try to understand where and why a certain combination succeeds and where and why other combinations fail. There needs to be broader research that crosses the traditional media demarcation zones so that interdisciplinary insights can emerge.

THEORY INTO PRACTICE 9

Windscreen wiper instructions.

Look at the set of diagrams which illustrate how to attach a new windscreen wiper. It is a single use of media – namely graphics – used to convey instructions. Imagine that you need to change your windscreen wiper and both the wiper and wiper hinge have changed in design. In this case, removing your old one won't help you much and you need to rely on the diagrams more. Think your way carefully through the diagrams imagining you are carrying them out.

After completing this, go to the CD, Chapter 8 Support Material, Windscreen Wiper Example 1. What difference does the sound commentary make to your understanding?

Finally, look at the CD example 2. What difference does the movement make? Is animation more effective than video would be in this case?

Summary

- Understand your constraints and work within them.
- Research offers few conclusive principles to help match media and message in specific multimedia contexts.
- **Video:**
  - The display size of any video needs to be appropriate for the content, needs of the viewer and platform.
  - Video uses more space than other media and may affect the interaction speed.
  - Video use for education and training has extra considerations from research.
- **Audio:**
  - Audio is a versatile medium which is cheap.
  - Saves overuse of text.
  - It appeals to emotions.
  - Its range and scope are unappreciated in most multimedia to date.
  - Care is needed for sounds that become irritating when repeated in an interactive environment.
- **Computer graphics:**
  - These are versatile and have a wide range of quality.
  - They can offer realistic and symbolic representations.
  - Educational research findings have value for all applications.
  - They handle transformations between layers of visuals well, for example skin and bones.
  - Video graphics can be faster to produce but more expensive than computer graphics.
  - Video graphics can give continuity of style in applications where video features.
- **Text:**
  - Although used less now, care should be taken to keep its quality in line with other media components.
  - Its role has changed to a supportive one rather than a main component.
  - Integrating text and maintaining its quality can be difficult.
  - Layout, size and legibility are still important.
  - The new ways of organizing text in interactive environments can pose problems for readers. Ensure help and aids are provided.

Recommended reading

Bordwell D. and Thompson K. (1993). *Film Art: An Introduction*. New York: McGraw-Hill

Clarke A. (1992). How are graphics used in computer-based learning? *British Journal of Educational Technology*, **23** (3), 228–33

Clarke A. (1994). Human Factors Guidelines for Multimedia. *European Commission RACE ISSUE Project 1065*, HUSAT Research Institute, Loughborough University of Technology, UK

Ellis J. (1992). *Visible Fictions. Cinema: Television: Video*. London: Routledge & Kegan Paul

Foley J.D., van Dam A., Feiner S.K. and Hughes J.F. (1990). *Computer Graphics, Principles and Practice*. Reading, MA: Addison-Wesley

Gagné R.M., Briggs L.J. and Wagner W.W. (1992). Selecting and Using Media. In *Principles of Instructional Design* (Gagné R.M., ed.), 4th edn, pp. 205–23. Orlando, FL: Harcourt Brace Jovanovich

Jonassen D.H., ed. (1982). *The Technology of Text*, 2nd edn. Englewood Cliffs, NJ: Educational Technology Publications

Koumi J. (1994). Media comparison and deployment: a practitioner's view. *British Journal of Educational Technology*, **25** (1), 41–57

Leher R. (1993). Patterns of Hypermedia Design. In *Computers as Cognitive Tools* (Lajoie S.P. and Derry S.S., eds), pp. 197–228. Mahwah, NJ: Lawrence Erlbaum Associates Inc.

Lowe R. (1993). *Successful Instructional Diagrams*, London: Kogan Page

Milheim W.D. (1993). How to use animation in computer assisted learning. *British Journal of Educational Technology*, **24** (3), 171–8

Monaco J. (1981). *How to Read a Film. The Art, Technology, Language, History, and Theory of Film and Media*. New York: Oxford University Press

Neilsen J. (1990). *Hypertext and Hypermedia*. New York: Academic Press

Preece J., ed. (1994). *Human–Computer Interaction*. Wokingham, England: Addison-Wesley

Watson R. (1990). *Film and Television in Education*. London: The Falmer Press

CHAPTER 9

INTERFACE DESIGN

Project manager's responsibilities

- To recognize that different types of interfaces are needed for different types of application
- To understand the components of an interface and their significance for users
- To analyse the target audience to find possible problems with the symbolic meanings embedded in the interface
- To test the elements of the interface early with the target audience if at all possible

What is an interface?

Each application has an infrastructure that links the component parts together so that users understand what the application contains, how the information is organized and what they need to do to activate the separate pieces. An analogy that is often used refers to navigation within the application and the routes that the users can explore.

Application navigation.

The interface is this structure. At a detailed level it means the selection screens where choices are given to the user, the style with which the selections are denoted, the transitions from one part of the application to another, how options are linked or cross-referenced and the method of input for any data the user needs to give.

Interface design

If you glance back at Chapter 4, The Proposal, you will see that the foundations for the interface needed to be laid then. The main content sections were suggested and agreed. This gives a shape to the intentions of what the application will contain. The decisions about the content will indicate the best way of organizing the information and will take the audience and platform capabilities into account. Even at the proposal stage the decisions will be shaping the interface in an irreversible way, since the amount of material and the number of sections it will have tends to govern the style of the interface.

When text was the dominant medium, applications were structured through menus. The user made a choice that led to another text menu and so on. The user went down through the levels and returned by selecting Exit or the equivalent. This led the users back through the levels to the top menu. This type of structure is known as a tree structure.

There can be variations on this structure where the user can select other routes to return to the top level instead of the reverse decision mode. It all depends on the links between the content areas and the options the

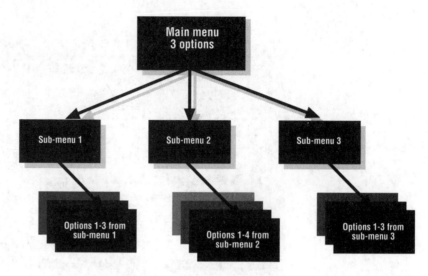

Diagram of tree structure.

users are given to move around the program. The tree structure has survived text menus and can now be identified with icons instead of text on the menus.

As it became easier to have graphics, icon-driven menus started to become common. Icons have certain advantages over text. They can take up less space. They are not language specific. They're more aesthetic and appealing. They can make access through an application easier. However, the research on the use of icons has inconsistencies. Sometimes they're good and sometimes they're bad.

What are icons?

The research on icons can be linked with that on signs and symbols. In multimedia any pictorial representation that a user can select is called an icon. But in the theory of signs, icons are images that are readily recognizable. They are not symbolic; they are realistic to the extent that they are recognizable without explanation. Commonly, icons in multimedia encompass the complete range of images from abstract symbols to realistic representations. The user quite often has to learn what the symbols mean to be able to use the icons effectively. One distinction that is sometimes made in multimedia relates to the use of high quality graphics that are so realistic they are like small photographs on the screen and these are called Picons. If there are the equivalent of icons with moving images that can be selected, these are sometimes referred to as Micons. (Examples of icons, picons and micons can be viewed on the CD.)

In the theory of signs, icons can be classified into iconograms, pictograms, cartograms and diagrams to help define their individual functions. Iconograms are like picons – realistic pictures. Pictograms are equivalent to icons so are related to more symbolic, abstract images. There is no equivalent of the miniature moving image in sign theory as by nature it is a study of static images.

Considerations for designing icons

Interactive media allow the combination and manipulation of information in new ways. Icons form part of the new vocabulary. They show that the user has choices and try to indicate what sort of information could be activated if the icon is selected. However, present interface research could learn from past research. This has shown what happens when new techniques that are symbolic are used when the user does not have the ability to decode the meaning.

There are classic examples of cross-cultural misinterpretation that it would be wise to note as new forms of structuring information emerge on interactive platforms. Health educationalists in developing countries found that commonly understood visual techniques used in Western communication were completely misunderstood. In Peru when demonstrating how to identify and eradicate lice, they used magnification to show the insects in detail. This only served to distract the viewers. They did not link the visual image to any insect they understood and so did not think the information relevant to them. The modern equivalent may relate to the use of new techniques for manipulating information such as the use of icons. The use of a trash can icon to represent getting rid of unwanted files has been noted as culturally unsound for many countries that do not share this method of disposal.

As soon as you begin to design an interface it becomes obvious that some concepts will be difficult to encapsulate into an icon. Even something as simple as Exit is not that simple. There may be several forms of the concept 'to leave' in the program. Users may need to leave a section but stay in the application, they may want to leave the application completely or they may want to leave a screen, check something and return to the same screen.

The functions have similarities and so any icons used to represent these functions might need to have similarities. But as there would be different results when using these icons, they would need some differences as well to indicate the different consequences of use. Firstly, this example shows that an application can need many icons to indicate the functionality. Secondly it shows that it can be difficult to choose symbolic pictures that demonstrate the functionality clearly using symbolic pictures. Designers also need to take into account that there will be a saturation point for the number of icons a screen can support, even though icons take up less space than text.

If there are many icons, users will take longer to learn their meaning. In some cases for multimedia, especially where users are not expected to spend much time on the system – kiosks, for example – it is best to limit the use of icons to the minimum. Users will want quick access to information.

Some concepts are by their nature more abstract than others and are difficult to represent visually. In packages where the concept 'save' has been needed to indicate the transfer of work to memory for storing, various icons have been used to indicate this meaning. Many have tried to follow the principle of relating icon use to everyday objects but this can lead to strange anomalies. The 'save' icon has been represented by a piggy bank and a monetary symbol. There is a link between save and money but the saving money metaphor is out of context in an application for storing information.

Using everyday metaphors helps people remember icons if and when the set of icons relate to an overall metaphor. The overall metaphor of a book or an office has been used successfully with individual icons relating to specific details consistent with the metaphor, for example. But some of the concepts of dealing with information electronically, such as Undo, are new and these pose problems for relating to everyday items in ways that will make sense. A compromise solution seems to be more common now where an icon is used and its text name is either written underneath or appears when a cursor is placed over the icon.

This technique will provide answers for some of the problems but not all. Guidelines for international use advise against the use of text names in this way because they cause problems in translation. Often translations cannot be fitted into the same space.

The decisions about interface design seem to lead you round in circles. The guidelines can seem inconsistent. However, a lot of progress has been made because of the use of icons. Their use has widened the use of computers from specialists to the general public. Overall they do provide better access to the functionality despite their limitations. Instead of having to remember sets of symbols and codes like computer languages, icons provide prompts to help anyone activate the power hidden in applications.

Get to know your target audience

The more you understand your target audience, the better your design will be. At present the hardest audience to design for is the public because, in general, their use of interactive media is so limited. There is little profile of use for different types of applications and until the market increases, this will not improve.

However, if and when your application is tied to a specific target group, you need to spend time building up a profile of them, their multimedia literacy level, how they achieve results in their role without the multimedia application, what they would like from the application, their expectations of what information/results they want from the interactive application.

If we use the set of icons used in this book as an example, their design was influenced by the need for them to be used in black and white text. Gary Weston, the designer, decided to emphasize the black and white medium by using the strength of contrast of the colours and by using

strong clear lines. The size of the image affects the amount of detail used as well as the concern with the possible deterioration of detail in the printing process. This approach was carried through all the illustrations and provides a cohesion in look and feel throughout the book. This consistency is a factor that needs to be achieved in electronic applications as well because it helps users to identify the application and recognize the navigation paths faster, and provides a sense of harmony that contributes to a feeling of satisfaction for the user.

If you look at the transfer of these icons to the CD where they are in colour, you should be able to assess how Gary has maintained the continuity of feel in their design by maintaining a colour hue and strength to give consistency once again. The strong, stylized lines and shapes also maintain their original purpose. However, if the icons had only been needed for the CD or the book had used colour, the whole conceptualization would have had a very different starting point and would have looked different as well.

The stylization in the icons shows the identification with you, the readers, as a specialist audience. Some presuppose in subtle ways that you have a certain level of computer literacy and think in certain ways. The Summary icon not only stylizes bullet points but also changes their usual horizontal position. This presupposes that you are comfortable with the link between summaries being denoted by bullets or the equivalent and that you are familiar enough with them to compensate for the angle shift in perception. The Responsibilities icon links the concept of someone having a finger on the button with the implication of having the knowledge and responsibility to make decisions. This is particularly true with interactive media where the user has control to access or even delete information, for example. The Theory into Practice icon uses an arrow to denote direction and the split format of the icon enhances the concept of change from one stance to another representing the transfer of theory into practice. The arrows also reinforce the idea that this is not a linear action. There is an interplay between theory and practice as people move back and forth between them – referring to the book and trying something out then referring back to the book or CD again.

These icons had to represent more abstract points than the others, but they needed concrete clues within their stylization to help establish their meaning for the reader and to re-establish the meaning every time they are seen.

All the icons are based on the design of buttons as denoted by the frame around them and this gives them their integrity as well as reinforcing the subject matter of interactive media. The diagonal split between the reversed images will trigger some people to think of negative images and therefore photography – this has yet another level of meaning of a medium that is used in multimedia. So, there are various triggers within the design to consciously and subconsciously link the icons to their overall purpose as well as their specific one.

Hopefully, this analysis of the way in which the design of some of the features of an interface assigns meaning to a particular audience will indicate the complexity of maintaining integrity of look, feel and sense in an interface. It is not an easy task but it does provide the key to good application design. You need to build up an empathy with your audience and there are several ways to do this. Some of these are outlined below.

Needs Analysis was introduced in Chapter 3, Scoping a Project. Task Analysis forms part of Needs Analysis. This is particularly important if the application is going to form part of the workplace as a job aid or offer an alternative service to a human one outside normal work hours. Task Analysis means the study of how a set of actions are carried out, what processes/procedures and questions need to be followed to achieve a satisfactory result and what results match which set of circumstances. The analysis is usually carried out early in the project so that all decisions can be based on the findings.

If the type of application does not warrant task analysis then concept testing may help to give a profile of expectations and preferences from the target audience. Concept Testing, also called Focus Groups, means that people are told what the application will do and what it will provide. Their reactions are monitored to see if the design principles have predicted their needs/wishes accurately or if they have common agreement on suggestions that arise during the discussion. These may be used to tailor the design so that the application matches the user profile better than before. Concept testing takes place at a stage when there is a very limited prototype or no working prototype of the application. It is not to be confused with usability testing which takes place later in the project when a good working model is available. The target group in this case actually uses the application instead of reacting to the ideas that will be embodied in it.

Testing interface design

If there is any way to get the budget to build a prototype application that would include usability testing the interface, then get it. Experience can help predict certain problems with a certain audience but you learn more with every application you work on. There are always one or two aspects that just do not work out in the way that was planned, but by the time the team has spotted the deficiencies, there is often no way back. Usability tests provide a wealth of information but they are of little use unless they are carried out methodically and professionally. Unless this happens, conflicting results and recommendations will be made.

The theory and practice of usability testing is too great to go into here but its principles are important and so some of the insights will be mentioned briefly to encourage you to look into this further.

It is too easy to base interface decisions on your experience rather than on the experience of the target audience. This does not mean that insights gained from experience are not valuable. It also does not mean that you have to suppress any creative ideas about interface design. It is an evolving area so there is scope for flexibility and experimentation as long as these are recognized as such and tried out with the intended audience. It may be that they will experience some difficulties with the interface design. But the important aspect is that you notice where and why there are problems and reach some decisions of (A) how to eradicate them or (B) add help to educate the users into using the new aspects successfully.

One of the misconceptions about usability tests is the number of people you need to have valid results. The more recent research has shown that up to 80% of the problems were found with between 4 and 5 participants and that 90% were detected with 10 users.

This however needs to be put in context. It is important that:

■   the selection of the participants has been made according to a predetermined profile of user groups;
■   the environment for the test has carefully prepared;
■   the participants have been inducted into the test environment and know their rights;
■   the tasks to be performed have been created to mirror the aims of the product and the needs of the users;
■   the ways of collecting quantitative and qualitative data have been agreed;
■   the testing team have been thoroughly prepared and tried out in a pilot test;
■   the ways to organize and communicate the data have been agreed.

See Chapter 18, Testing, for more information on these and other forms of testing.

The interactive environment

If the purpose of the interface is to make the interaction smooth then this is the criterion that needs to be applied for quality. The users' levels of competence and understanding need to shape the design of the interface. The project manager takes on the responsibility to act on behalf of the users. The biggest problem is deciding what can be assumed as prior understanding of the interactive techniques. This is harder for the general public than for other groups since the application would have to appeal to the naive and experienced user simultaneously.

Any interactive communicator aims to trigger the user's interpretation of the messages embedded in the application. This ability holds the key to good communication with media. But if techniques are used that are alien to the users, they may miss the point completely. If they do not understand the symbolism of the techniques that are used, they will not reap the full benefit from the application. The new forms of interactive structuring employ techniques that take time for users to understand – just as using magnification was outside the comprehension of the tribe in Peru. Understanding, in this sense, is not an innate ability; it has to be acquired. Media techniques are culturally based and depend upon shared experience. The shared experience can be part of a subcultural group or cross-cultural group. The Internet would be a good example of a cross-cultural group that shares common understanding of particular symbolic codes and techniques.

Just as icons are part of the new vocabulary of multimedia, the layering of information associated with Apple Mac and Windows has become a common technique. Windowing with option bars and icons have proliferated. The techniques associated with the use of a mouse, namely point and click, free the users from typing in their selection. It becomes easier to organize access to information with small drop-down menus. This approach lends itself to structuring access to a mass of information by splitting it into small pieces. But does your audience have the experience to use this structure efficiently? Will you need to train them in it? The example given in the last chapter about the problems users had with hyperdocuments is relevant here.

Many multimedia applications fall in between tree and window structuring and it is common to have picons, arranged on a screen. Picons often reveal the text names of the content section they represent as the mouse pointer passes over them. These are called hot-spots. Other applications have scrolling graphical menus where the screen width and/or height extends as the mouse pointer reaches the edge of the screen.

All of these share the same purpose; they show the scope of the program. The initial selection screen is very important. It sets the expectations and understanding of the user. It gives an indication of the scope of the content and the techniques needed to navigate through it. It establishes if there is help available at all times or if the user needs to discover aspects about the program. It should set the example of:

(1) how users are to select an option – find the hot-spot and select, click on an icon which expands into a menu, and so on;

(2) how they will know if they have made the selection. For example, you may use a sound to show something has been successfully selected, or the button/hot-spot/picon may change shape, size, colour or stay in a depressed position.

Once users have started the program you need to establish how they can move around in it. Do they have an option to select to return to the main selection screen? Do they have a map to show them the overview of where they are? Are they allowed to go up, down, sideways, forwards and backwards and if so how do they know this? Do they have to complete certain sections before others? How will they know this?

Once certain ways of working have been established, these need to be consistent. The interface and its working needs as much integrity as the other factors we've looked at. If users become confused, lost or irritated by the operational side of the program, their concentration on the content will suffer. They will become demotivated. They will tend to leave the program before they have found what they wanted or before they've explored all the possibilities.

Interface antics.

Designing an interface that helps people reach all the application information effortlessly is far from easy. It usually provides the longest discussions between the graphics artists, programmers and producers. The high-level structure will affect how the programmers set up their code. They need to be clear how it is meant to work to ensure that they construct an adequate frame for the application. They will have opinions on what functionality the platform can support and because they have studied interface design as part of their courses, they often feel that it is their role to design it. The graphics artists feel exactly the same. The interface graphics are one of the prime ways they can exert their creativity and style.

The project manager will have the best understanding of the scope of the content and the clients. These have an effect on the interface design. There may be corporate conventions that irk the programmers and graphics artists but they will have to prevail. There may be special considerations for the intended audience – poor second-language speakers, for example.

Your research on the intended audience and their multimedia literacy level is crucial. It will help determine the best methods of interaction, their prior experience, if they will be receptive to innovation, and how many levels of help they might need.

Sometimes, as with games and activity-based entertainment programs, the consideration is not to make the interaction too easy as this is not the purpose of the interface. With these the purpose is to excite, surprise, demand attention, and to use fast reactions to interpret a changing environment. These types of applications need different considerations for their interface and many of the guidelines covered in this chapter will not apply.

The use of sound

Sound means any type of audio use. This can include speech, warning bleeps, alarm bells and so on.

When sound became easier to digitize and store on CDs, it became apparent that overuse was unwise. People become irritated by repeated sounds. Some sounds that are initially attractive or entertaining pall quickly. You need to guard against inappropriate use of sounds at the planning stage which is difficult since it is easy to react with your mind rather than your ears at this time.

It helps if you take time to look at the use of sound independently of the other factors and see how likely it is for the sounds to be repeated inadvertently. The prime example is the use of audio to state the function of a picon. The sound occurs even when the users are trying to move to a picon in a different part of the screen. The information is useful at the beginning but annoys users after that. As indicated in the chapter on media selection (Chapter 8), you need to consider giving control of volume and silence to the users. Control of these could help make the application more versatile for partially sighted and hard-of-hearing people. These users might form a strong sub-group of the audience profile and if that were the case, their needs would drive the total interface design, not just the use of sound.

The use of colour

Because the use of high quality colour is easier and more common in applications, and the resolution of screens has increased, the concern with the general use of colour has diminished. Prior to this, the use of background colours, the colour of text against a coloured background, colour linked with layout and the awareness of colour-blindness in a percentage of the audience were all factors that were researched. The major problems were poor selection of colours in relation to each other causing difficulties in readability and legibility.

Now it is normal to use graphics artists to design the visuals in applications but this was not always the case. They bring their knowledge and skills to bear on the problems of style, design, consistency of visual approach, layout, legibility and readability. Their training in making the best combinations of colour is invaluable. There can be several uses for colour – attention cue, aesthetic, styling and branding. As with the use of sound, colour can please initially then become annoying for users. If colour is used badly then all the factors that applied for earlier applications remain true.

One of the problems that still prevails is the changes that occur in colours depending on their origins, the platform, the software and the encoding processes. So even with good planning, colour shifts can occur. It is a good idea for the project manager to get the graphics artist to check out the effect of the varying processes and to tap into contacts who have used the combinations before to see if there are any adverse but unrecorded reactions. With some applications, colour consistency is vital – medical applications are notoriously difficult for colour integrity and can need special processes to ensure accuracy.

Finally, another problem associated with colour remains. There are cross-cultural associations in the use of colour. This is part of the aesthetic appeal of colours but it may become more important as applications need to reach international audiences. The retail sector has noted the variations in response to combinations of colour. They sometimes adjust the packaging of products for various countries. Some cultures respond better to bright, strong, primary colours and other cultures prefer pastels. For applications that need to sell, this could be more of a factor than other types of applications. Common examples of Western colour psychology are:

Red   =   stop, danger, heat, appliance is on
Blue   =   cold, water, sky
Green =   go, environmentally friendly

There is little research in this area at present.

Packaging and related materials

It is easy to forget that applications need to be packaged and that this forms part of the interface; in fact, it can help set expectations before the users actually begin the interactive part. The attention given to book covers, record labels and music CD cases show the importance of the initial impression. The consistency of design in the applications needs to carry over into the packaging and labelling to give a professional stamp to the materials.

Although unusual a couple of years ago, additional printed materials and even videos can sometimes be part of a total package that includes some interactive multimedia material. All extras need the same attention to their design as the multimedia component. If it is the dominant part of the package, then elements of its design should be carried through to the other materials. This might include colour combinations, layout, montages of graphics from the application, and so on.

The planning and budgeting of any such extras need to be linked to the multimedia production phases to ensure they are all ready simultaneously for release.

THEORY INTO PRACTICE 10

Use the Interface Assessment Form, which follows the Summary, to assess your next interface after discussions and initial decisions have been made in the team but before the client has been given the decisions. Use your appraisal to go back to the team if necessary for rethinking any issues.

Use it also to appraise any applications you look at to help focus on their true strengths and weaknesses.

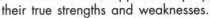

Summary

- The interface is the infrastructure of the application.
- The use of icons and the method of organization – tree, windows, hypertext – are symbolic so the users' correct interpretation of their meaning is the key to good design.
- These need special care, explanation and possibly training, when the target audience has little exposure to such symbolic structures.
- Usually, the aim of the interface is to provide smooth, easy access to any part of the program the user wishes. But games or activity entertainment titles can have different aims.
- The use of sound and colours in the interface also need attention to ensure best use.
- Materials which form part of the total package are part of the interface 'look' and need to be treated accordingly.

Interface design appraisal

Tick as appropriate

Application profile	**General interface assessment**

1. User profile

	Inappropriate			Appropriate	

a. Naive ☐ Specialist ☐ Mixed range ☐   Match to users 1 2 3 4 5
General public ☐ Other ☐ ☐

b. Application use   Match to use 1 2 3 4 5
National ☐ International ☐

2. Proposed style of use

	Disagree			Agree

Sustained/regular use by people ☐   Functionality matches use 1 2 3 4 5

Brief/occasional use ☐   Simple functionality matches use 1 2 3 4 5

Mixed usage ☐   Range of levels match mixed use 1 2 3 4 5

3. Application purpose   Style suits purpose

To inform ☐   To sell ☐   1 2 3 4 5

To entertain ☐   For reference ☐

To train ☐   To educate ☐

Other ☐

4. Overall marks for: General impression

	Poor								Excellent	

a. Ease of use   1 2 3 4 5 6 7 8 9 10
b. Design style   1 2 3 4 5 6 7 8 9 10
c. Consistency of selection methods   1 2 3 4 5 6 7 8 9 10
d. Consistency of functionality   1 2 3 4 5 6 7 8 9 10

e. Consistency of icon design   1 2 3 4 5 6 7 8 9 10
f. Clarity of icon meaning alone   1 2 3 4 5 6 7 8 9 10
g. Clarity of icon meaning with text   1 2 3 4 5 6 7 8 9 10

5.   Inappropriate   Appropriate

a. Use of colour in interface   1 2 3 4 5 n/a
b. Use of sound in interface   1 2 3 4 5 n/a
c. Use of moving image/animation in interface 1 2 3 4 5 n/a

6. Help

a. Suitability for user profile   1 2 3 4 5
b. Amount of detail   1 2 3 4 5
c. Tone   1 2 3 4 5
d. Effectiveness   1 2 3 4 5

Recommended reading

Clarke. A. (1994). Human Factors Guidelines for Multimedia. *European Commission RACE ISSUE Project 1065*, HUSAT Research Institute, Loughborough Institute of Technology, UK

Del Galdo E. (1990). Internationalisation and translation: Some guidelines for the design of human computer interfaces. In *Advances in Human Factors/Ergonomics 13*, *Designing User Interfaces for International Use* (Nielson J., ed.), pp. 1–11. Amsterdam: Elsevier

Deregowski J.B. (1980). *Illusions, Patterns and Pictures. A Cross-cultural Perspective.* London: Academic Press

Dumas J.S. and Redish J.C. (1994). *A Practical Guide to Usability Testing.* Norwood, NJ: Ablex Publishing Corporation

Jonassen D.H., ed. (1982). *The Technology of Text.* Englewood Cliffs, NJ: Educational Technology Publications

Kennedy J.M. (1982). Metaphor in pictures. *Perception*, **11**, 589–605

Maissel J. (1990). Development of a Methodology for Icon Evaluation. *National Physical Laboratory Report DITC 159/90*, Teddington, UK

Marcus. A. (1992). *Graphic Design for Electronic Documents and User Interfaces.* New York: ACM Press; Reading MA: Addison-Wesley

No. 77 UNESCO Press Reports & Papers on Mass Communication. (1976). Cross-cultural broadcasting: psychological effects.

Salomon G. (1979). Media and symbol systems as related to cognition and learning. *Journal of Educational Psychology*, **71**, 131–48

Shneiderman B. (1992). *Designing the User Interface: Strategies for Effective Human–Computer Interaction*, 2nd edn. Reading, MA: Addison-Wesley

CHAPTER 10

CONTRACT ISSUES 2

Project manager's responsibilities

■ To understand legal issues that can affect multimedia contracts
■ To carry out the company's policy for binding clients and subcontractors to its terms and conditions

Introduction

In Contract Issues 1 (Chapter 5) we concentrated on establishing ways of working between you and the clients. Without these agreements, your work could be affected by hold-ups out of your control which would impact on your deadlines. These risks we recommended you controlled by defining the work flow responsibilities between you and the clients. Change management principles were also explained and it was suggested that they were included in the agreement for the way of working.

In this chapter, we will return to the process of developing more detailed costing that should form part of your background estimates for the final proposal document. After all, you are in business to make a profit so you have to predict the costs as accurately as possible to stand a chance of coming out on top. Secondly, we will note the more formal legal details which may need to be addressed.

Costing rights and clearances

This is a complex area. The background to the types and the processes involved in rights is covered in the Rights, Copyright and Other Intellectual Properties chapter (Chapter 17). If you are not experienced with these, you might benefit from reading that chapter first. Here we're concerned with approximating the numbers involved and their costs to help stipulate a workable budget. Rights and clearances are a good example of knowledge that applies across many stages of development. The project manager needs the knowledge here to define the budget. Whoever takes on the role of rights clearer needs a good grasp of the varieties to be able to negotiate the best deal from owners of materials across media during development.

Still pictures

Scanning and rights.

Any reuse of an existing photograph, picture or slide, or even extracted details from any of these for which neither you or the client has copyright will incur costs to clear permission for use. The amount charged varies according to the location of the visual – museum, picture library, for example – who owns it, the purpose for your use, where your program will be seen, and how long your program will be in use. This list does not cover all the variables, so you can begin to get a feel for how problematic this is. Unlike Europe, the USA has a tradition of freedom of information that leads to a large number of free sources of assets. NASA is the best known example. There are also many sources of clip art for which no royalties are payable. It would help if your company found out about free and royalty-free sources as you never know when they will come in handy.

Music

This is the most complex part of rights and clearances. Conditions change according to the artists, the length of the music, the publisher, whether an original work, library music or a recording. The costs change accordingly.

Voice-overs

These are usually cleared through the voice-over's agent. Rates vary according to the artist, the length of time spent recording, the type of use, the length of the clearance, and the number of countries.

Video footage

This is rather like stills clearance and depends on the owner. Costs may depend on the length of the footage, and if the videos come from different sources and have to be edited together you may have to convert them to a common format which will affect quality and cost. Video footage, if it is being licensed from a television programme, can sometimes contain material with many secondary rights implications including stills, music, artists and scripts. This can contribute to the clearance costs significantly and it is vital that the rights situation is known comprehensively.

Table 10.1 gives an indication of some of the variables that can occur and some examples have been given to demonstrate the variation in costing across the range of media. There isn't a standard rate per photo from museums, for example, so you may be negotiating individual rates from different museums depending on where the originals are kept. Rates vary from country to country.

You should make your clients aware of the problems of costing clearances and stress the estimated cost. You will really only know the true figure once the job is completed. So, it may be wise to negotiate an estimate for this part which you will affirm and renegotiate during the project as you become clearer about the numbers involved.

The nature of the task should now be clearer. The complexity should show that a person who will research, negotiate rights, keep accurate records and keep track of the assets to send back, is not performing a trivial task especially when different types of assets are involved. It may be as well to mention that you get penalty payments from some libraries if you do not send the original photo or slide back by a stipulated date. These unknown costs that can occur should be covered by having some of the budget defined for contingency. Also you should remember that courier

Table 10.1 Rights and clearance costing.

Category	Clearance type	Numbers/length	Market covered	Time cleared	Other factors	Ball-park rate	Total
Stills	Photos from museums	approx. 60	Commercial/ World	3 years		£75–100 B&W £100–150 colour	
Video footage	Library	10 minutes	Commercial/ World	3 years	Technical costs can be high	£250–1000 per minute + rights	
Music	Commissioned Title music	3 musicians 3 minute piece	Commercial/ World	Indefinitely	Buy-out on rights. One single payment	£1000 upwards	
	Library (background in 2 sections)	approx. 15 mins	Commercial/ World	3 years	MPCS negotiation	£100 per 30 seconds	
Voice-overs	Professional artists	2 artists 1 approx. 35 mins 1 approx. 15 mins	Commercial/ World	3 years	2 payments, one for recording, one for rights	£150 per hour +100% for rights	

companies like FedEx and DHL may be used to carry the assets and the cost of shipping is not insignificant. Consider whether your researcher has to travel to look at images.

The legal issues

There are a surprising number of multimedia projects that are undertaken on little more than a handshake and often on simple letters of agreement. Also, of course, legal aspects would indicate access to lawyers, preferably specializing in multimedia, and they are expensive professionals. It is true that in the majority of cases, the projects progress with some hiccups but these are resolved amicably. In cases where things go wrong they tend to go horribly wrong and people end up saying 'if only we'd . . .'. On the other hand if the project is very successful, that can also lead to queries of who can exploit it and how, and who should be getting what from the sales!

The major problem lies in the uncertainty of how to treat multimedia in a legal sense because it is still emerging as a delivery medium. In mature delivery media like broadcasting, music and film, the issues of primary rights in materials and the use of the materials for secondary purposes have been sorted out. So, for example, a contract to write and record a talk for BBC radio will include several clauses explaining in detail what the residual payments are, as percentages of the original fee, for such things as repeats, translations, printing in publications and sales to foreign broadcasters. See Chapter 17 for more details.

We will look at several key areas and highlight why some formal agreements might help, but each company has to take responsibility for its own terms and conditions.

Rights and clearances of assets: Liabilities

The methods to use when clearing rights are addressed in Chapter 17. Here we will be concerned with establishing and agreeing which rights and clearances need to be addressed. Your clients may give you permission to reproduce, edit and reuse many of the visual assets they have. But, they may not own the copyright to be able to give you permission. They may believe they own the images but ownership of visual images is not straightforward. Visuals prepared for a company brochure may have been given solely for that purpose and no other. So reuse would constitute a breach of conditions from a former contract. Originators of work have particular rights that protect them from other people editing their original work. It is a difficult area which changes according to country. The clients may own copyright for the original purpose of the materials but not have the electronic rights that are required for multimedia.

So it is in your interests to get written agreement, called an indemnity, that the clients own the electronic copyright in all the assets they provide to you as a safeguard in case of any future dispute over the rights.

Other assets you may have to find and clear for the purpose of the project – music, for example. You will be asked for the purpose, audience type and countries where you want permission to use the application. These are known as markets and territories you want covered. This is not as simple as it sounds. Many applications begin with one purpose but evolve into others. A consumer product may be produced for a national audience but is found to have international appeal. If the rights were originally only cleared nationally, they would have to be renegotiated. An in-house training application may be released on the consumer market after a period of time in the company. The market would have changed and the necessary rights and clearances may need revision. It is cheaper to negotiate once than have to renegotiate later. For any who are incredulous still about the burden of renegotiation, consider this example.

It has been recognized that reuse of some of the best film footage from television programmes in interactive programs would seem sensible, but many that have proposed this have fallen by the wayside once the cost of re-clearing electronic rights with all those who took part was worked out.

The duration of rights is also established at the time of negotiation so you need a good idea of the life span of the product to determine how many years to ask for or you may consider 'buy-outs'. These mean paying a once-only payment where you get agreement to use the material indefinitely.

You need a clear directive from the clients on their short- and long-term plans for the application. You should state what markets and territories you will cover when clearing rights and how long the clearances will be valid. If you put this in writing and have their agreement to this formally, there can be no confusion as to who should have done what when if circumstances change.

If you intend to remake the application in another language then you must have cleared for such use. In some cases a rights owner will count a direct translation as part of the original agreement, but in others they will not. It will be easier to cover multiple languages if your agreement provides royalties because more languages attracts more sales. For a buy-out this argument does not work. A similar situation occurs when an update of the application is required, to change information that has become outdated. The extreme situation in this chain is the derivative, which is another project based on the first.

Other liabilities to note

You will be using other companies' code in the form of libraries, tools and authoring packages under licence to develop your project as well as producing your own code as and when necessary. You cannot guarantee that bugs from these will not affect the performance of the end-product. This is not as uncommon as it sounds since multimedia is an experimental environment and code gets used in circumstances that were not originally envisaged and may therefore fall over. You do not want to be held responsible for problems originating with other people's software so you should include clauses to cover for this. The same is true of hardware that can have unforeseen and unstated idiosyncrasies.

Payment structure

You can see that your company will have put in quite a significant investment in terms of time to reach the agreed proposal stage. All this has been unpaid. On a large project, you might be working for a year or more to completion. Even smaller projects can mean considerable outlay of money during the production stages. The company needs to define a payment structure so that payments are staggered according to specific points in the project.

Sign-offs are well defined and represent agreement points so these might be linked to staged payments. Others follow the computing model and define milestones that represent phases of the project. Payment could be linked to achievement of these. Or, payment stages could be linked to calendar months and achievement of schedule to dates. Yet others ask for a certain amount up front, staged payments through the project and final payment of the remainder at completion. Whatever option is chosen, some form of phased payment would help your cash flow.

Your clients, on the other hand, will be interested in containing the costs. This is why they begin by trying to get an estimate from you and then haggle about the fine details of the deliverables to get the best deal for the money. Effectively, you are signing a fixed-term contract when you agree to the final proposal. It states what you will produce in the time for the money. Your only safeguard in a fixed contract is agreed, comprehensive specifications with as detailed costing as possible done up front. So you have to be confident in your costings.

The alternative to fixed-price contracts, which are notoriously difficult to achieve in any ill-specified projects, is a time and material contract. This means that you indicate what you expect the cost might be but that you will keep strict records and bill according to the actual amount it takes. You should be able to see that clearances are so difficult to predict accurately that this approach makes sense. Unfortunately, as time and materials is more open-ended, clients are not receptive to this model although it may be fairer on the developer.

There is another model, which is a shared development where the client clears the rights in the content but the developer undertakes all other work to a budget. This is a likely model where the client is a publisher or asset holder.

Ownership of code and other assets generated

Part of the way developers survive is to build up a stock of code or libraries which help them in the production of other projects. This does not mean that they will produce an application that looks and behaves exactly the same as the original product where the code was generated. Most often the code is adapted to fit the new requirements but forms some of the building blocks. If your clients are not computer companies, or developers themselves; they will probably not have any use for the source code that underlies their application. It is best to try retaining copyright in the code but issue a free licence to the clients for its use.

The company needs to establish where it stands on this issue so that it will not infringe any rights in reuse of the code later. There is an added problem that the code used may well be a combination of third-party code as well as its own. This makes it problematic to identify exactly which new code might belong to the clients and which you would not have the right to sign away anyway as it belongs to the third party.

Many clients are reasonable once they realize the lack of value to themselves in having the copyright in the code. You might have to agree to provide access to source codes under extreme circumstances, such as your company ceasing to do business.

If clients have been used to commissioning video productions then this will seem a new concept for them. They would never expect a video production facility to retain rights in what they do. It will help if you explain that this is not usually the case with software. It is common practice for application software never to be sold but only licensed, with restrictive conditions on usage, copying or decompiling.

Establish your right to demonstrate and promote the product

It is important for winning new business that, as a developer, you are able to demonstrate your capabilities to new clients. Some clients will bind you to confidentiality agreements and you need to recognize the effect this might have for demonstrating the program after completion. Some clients will not grant permission for competitors to see the product but may be happy for non-competitors to see it. There are several ways to approach this to establish limited demonstrations with the company's permission but this will be onerous on you.

If the clients themselves will be demonstrating some aspects publicly, there should be no reason for them stopping you doing the same. Often confidentiality agreements have a proviso or time limit where once the information is in the public domain, then the clause no longer applies. However, it is one more aspect that needs a clear statement or your company may find that it cannot use the application as part of a repertoire to show at exhibitions or to prospective clients.

Similarly, you should consider what happens if you wish to publicize an application by advertising it or getting editorial coverage in a magazine or on television. Can you show any of the application under these conditions?

Moral rights

As developer, your company can ask for its moral right of paternity. This will allow your company and its members who worked on the project to have a credit; otherwise, no one will recognize your involvement once the product is released. See Chapter 17 for more details on moral rights. There are other considerations you might wish to consider.

Severance

Problems can arise from many quarters that may make it important for your company to extricate itself from any agreement, mainly to protect it from further damage. If your clients' company is taken over and you hear that they will be closed down as part of an inevitable downsizing operation, then you may wish to pull out earlier rather than later. Make sure that you still get paid for work done if the project is stopped. Or, if the key person in the client organization leaves and the new person makes it impossible to continue along with the project as previously specified, you may wish to terminate the contract.

A severance clause works both ways so that clients can extricate themselves as well, if they have cause.

Force majeure

This means that a major unforeseen disaster like an earthquake or terrorist bomb stops your company fulfilling the contract. Although unlikely, major catastrophes do happen and then you want your liability to complete the contract to be contained. This avoids your company being sued for non-completion when it was no fault of your own that you were unable to do so. It costs very little to include in an agreement, but a lot if you don't and you need it.

Which law?

If there is any need for legal action to be taken – non-payment, for example – then it is to your company's advantage to state which country's law your agreement complies with and which country's law any proceedings will comply with, since the law on certain points varies around the world. Also, your costs will be easier if the hearings are in your own country. So, again, it is easy to stipulate which country's law is to be used up front but possibly very costly if you do not.

These are a few of the main considerations but it is in your interest to establish your terms and conditions and ways of working so that you can capitalize from your time and effort. It should not be the role of the project manager to draft the legal clauses in the agreement, just to know enough to make sure that the main risks are covered. Each company will have its own way of drafting, issuing and checking agreements, some through the legal section, others with a contracts manager, others, after guidance from lawyers, will do so on their own behalf.

It is the company's responsibility to have enough support for the project manager to ensure that agreements conform to their requirements.

Freelancer and contractor contracts

When you need to recruit extra people for the team, you also make agreements with them. These will have separate issues that need to be covered or you may find that your graphics artist's company owns the copyright in the visuals that are developed, not your company. Employees are different from contractors as long it has been established that all work that is created in the course of their work belongs to the company, and this would be stated in their contract of employment. Any of the team, whether in-house or external, have the same moral rights as the company does in relation to the work and the client. So the company may need to establish an overall policy for themselves and employees, depending on how moral rights are treated in their country – if at all. Note that in some countries moral rights cannot be signed away.

The company may be comfortable with employing a contractor who then subcontracts the work, but on the other hand it may not. Clauses indicating who is responsible for the work and if and how subcontracting can be done are necessary to cover the type and quality of the work. If you have agreed any confidentiality clauses with the client, these usually put the onus on the developer to bind any staff to the agreements, so you might need to be very clear who is working on the project to comply with your confidentiality undertaking.

Again it should not be the project manager's role to draft the contract agreements, only to agree the work tasks, the length of the contract, the rate of pay and possibly payment terms. It is the company's responsibility to provide the standard contract where the project manager completes the relevant parts.

Conclusion

The project manager needs to understand the background to many issues about rights, clearances and legal obligations to reach a well-defined contractual agreement with the client. The proposal document becomes part of the agreement where the detailed specification of the work to be done, the time and costs are contained. The more detailed the understanding of what rights and how many will need to be cleared, the better. It can have a big impact on the costs, so it is in the project manager's interest to define this, particularly before work begins. Finally, there are legal issues which are more the responsibility of the company to determine for each project, but knowledge of them is in the project manager's interest to ensure that the project fulfils both the clients' and the company's interests.

THEORY INTO PRACTICE 11

Improve your ability to predict costs on projects.

There are hidden problems that arise with most projects where you need to have allocated a percentage of your budget for contingency purposes. Your company may have a percentage it recommends that you add on to the cost figure. You need to build up your knowledge about hidden factors to help you predict that your project is likely to run into them. Ask as many colleagues as you can about any overruns on time – remember time means paying more for your resources so is an extra cost – and extra hidden costs that they have encountered on projects. Check the percentage of the total budget these factors cost. Build up a profile of factors related to type of project to define the risk factors and the percentage contingency to cover risks. You may find that some are not risks, that they were costs or tasks that were overlooked. In this case you can detail these into the true costing rather than contingency.

Summary

■ Clearances can be complex depending on the nature of the assets and the owners. It will be impossible to cost accurately because there are so many variables. You either need to get the clients to agree to an estimated price which will be firmed as the project proceeds, or work from the top rates that you know to cover yourself.

■ There are legal issues which you should understand although it is the company's responsibility to determine its terms and conditions.

■ Apart from clearing rights in assets you acquire from sources other than the clients, you need to avoid liability if your clients give you assets but do not own the electronic copyright.

■ You need to establish ownership in any new assets created by the project – code, pictures, and so on – and where you stand in development of any derivatives from the project.

■ Other aspects for attention include your right to demo the application, moral rights, severance clauses, *force majeure*, and which country's law will apply in any proceedings.

■ You are not only involved with contractual agreements with the clients. Some of these issues carry over into the contracts needed for subcontractors.

Recommended reading

See the reading list for Chapter 17, Rights, Copyright and Other Intellectual Properties.

CHAPTER 11

SELECTING THE TEAM

Project manager's responsibilities

- To match the skills needed to the project requirements
- To check the in-house resource availability – align the requirements
- To determine the roles and responsibilities of the core and extended team
- To interview and select all key team members
- To establish a list of criteria for each role
- To ensure the company policies on contract terms and conditions are carried out
- To ensure the correct rights and clearances are made
- To provide clear and detailed briefs to those employed

Introduction

Although the selection of staff was touched on in Chapter 3, Scoping a Project, the consideration there was to demonstrate how to assess the cost of the project rather than the skills, but these two happen in unison. The aim of this chapter is to give a more detailed account of the staffing decisions and demonstrate the complexity of the process. You need an appreciation of skill sets across several disciplines to be able to match your project needs to personnel requirements, while balancing the cost of the resources against the needs.

Identifying the skills needed

The mix of skills needed for any project depends on its content, use of media components, size, platform and amount of administration. As project manager, it is your responsibility to ensure resources are available at the right time to keep the project on track. This means that you plan who you need at which points of the project and then ensure that:

■ these resources are on hand,
■ they are properly inducted into the project,
■ they have been contracted under the right terms and conditions,
■ they have the right skills for the job,
■ they have the right tools for the job,
■ they have a good working environment.

Because of the nature of multimedia, there is often a core team who work together for the majority of the project and then an extended team who are brought in for particular tasks – a video editor, for example. The core team may well be full-time staff members from the company. But because projects can be long and complicated and therefore lock people into a time frame, quite often it is necessary to contract-in one or two people to form part of the core team.

It will depend on the company you work for if you are expected to carry out the interviewing process or if there is a specific personnel role in the company to take care of the search and selection process. In both cases it will pay you to define the skills and experience level you need to make sure you staff the project correctly.

Once you have a feel for the scope of the project and the expectations of the clients, you should be in a position to identify the staff needed. Your decisions at this point affect the budget decisions and the costs. You need to assess the position for a core team first by matching the core skills you need with the availability of the nearest match to these in-house.

Once the clients have agreed to the proposal, you have to move fast to assemble the team. Situations change quickly. Even though a few of the core team appeared to be available at the time the project was scoped, they might have been placed on another project if the go-ahead for that came first. This can leave you with the difficult task of recruiting very quickly to ensure that the project begins on time. Any delay can be vital to achieving the deadlines so this is another dangerous time for the project manager – the time between a proposal and confirmation – because some of the circumstances may have changed.

Many companies try to build in some flexibility to their organization by having a list of independent contractors that can be brought in for specific projects. A project manager needs to work up a good set of contacts across all the multimedia sectors to help the recruitment process. There are agencies that specialize in multimedia recruitment and some companies use these to help construct teams. Remember that if you will be using an agency to help, you need to budget for their fees as well as the staff costs.

Whatever way your company works to solve its staffing needs, someone has to do the interviewing and make the final decision. It is wise to become involved in this process to build up your own skill set. It is not an easy task and is very time consuming but unless it is carried out effectively, you could be landed with a poor team for a difficult project.

Your core team will probably comprise the following:

- one or more programmers,
- one or more graphics artists,
- yourself as a producer/project manager.

Your extended team might include:

- Video personnel
  - a video director/producer
  - an assistant producer
  - a production assistant
  - a video editor
  - a video graphics artist
  - actors/actresses

■ Sound personnel
  – voice-over artists
  – sound editor

■ General support
  – a personal assistant
  – secretarial support

■ Specialist support
  – technical support
  – script writers
  – a training specialist
  – an instructional designer/interactive designer
  – subject matter experts.

Because some multimedia specialists have built up experience across a range of skill sets, one person might be able to take on a couple of roles. But when exactly do you need any of these roles and how do you assess if you need them? The profile of each skill set and the type of project that warrants their use will be defined to help decision making about resources.

Considerations for interviews: general

It is as well to remember that interviews are a two-way process – you are assessing the candidates but they are also assessing you and the organization. It is better if a couple of people can attend the interview so that impressions can be consolidated through discussion and comparison. Those interviewing should have:

■ established what to say about the company and the project to introduce the candidate to the set of circumstances, the requirements and the set up;
■ established a set list of questions to ask all candidates;
■ established the skill criteria needed and thought of ways to assess if the skill set is present at the levels required;
■ defined the role needed with the level of responsibility;
■ gained an impression of the candidate from pre-reading a CV;
■ formulated extra questions specific to the information contained in the CV to ascertain:
  – the accuracy of the information
  – the reasons for any apparent discrepancies or breaks in employment
  – the strengths and weaknesses of the candidate;
■ put a time-scale on the number of minutes to be given to each section of the interview and have appointed a person to be time-keeper;
■ allowed a few minutes between candidates to discuss reactions and findings and make notes.

The interviews should start on time and progress according to plan. If the plan overruns, any waiting candidates should be kept informed of progress. Some people have the same reaction to interviews as they do to examinations and it is not an ideal way to form solid impressions. Some larger companies use group interviews for full-time jobs where the candidates are set tasks to assess their abilities in a range of factors such as leadership, teamwork, and so on.

However, this is not a practice that prevails in multimedia at present mainly because the majority of workers are employed on an *ad hoc* basis. It is a good idea to allow members of the core team to meet candidates for other core team roles because they will need to work together. This can be done after the formal interview while the next candidate is being interviewed. The project manager should then collect any additional comments from the other core team members prior to making decisions.

Skill set profiles: Core team

Programmers

The skill set of programmers is wide ranging. As project manager, the decisions that affect your programming resource are:

■ the development platform,
■ the software that will be used for development (authoring, scripting or computer language),
■ the delivery platform considerations.

You need to understand what hardware and software you will use in the project to help pinpoint the exact skill set needed in your programmers.

The first major decision will be the development platform your project will use – Mac or PC, for example. The programmers specialize at this level and then have specialisms within these two main groups. There are other development platforms such as Sun and UNIX but these are less common. Often it will depend on the company which development platform is used. Under the Mac and PC categories, there are different sets of authoring tools. These packages allow programmers, and non-specialists who have programming aptitude, to develop straightforward applications. You need to have a good understanding of what the tools allow, or take advice from your technical support, to decide whether the tools can fit all the project requirements.

Authoring tools have become much more sophisticated over the past few years and can cope with far more than they used to but you need to become informed of their limitations and nuances. Some authoring packages have their own scripting languages. These allow the tailoring of the package to specific needs but add a level of complexity to the skill set needed. Scripting languages bridge the gap between authoring tools and computer languages. The difference in the levels is equivalent to prefabricated house segments (authoring languages), prefabricated building blocks (scripting languages) and constructing your own bricks (computer languages).

A further category of programmer is an analyst or systems analyst. This group have experience in defining the requirements for projects. They are the most likely to convert into project managers since they deal with clients and supervise other programmers to deliver the specification as well as having programming ability themselves. They will have been trained in using structured methods to specify and document computer projects. There are differences in the skill sets of managing computer projects and multimedia projects but this group will have a better starting point. The very formal approach to defining requirements by using a functional and technical specification as well as having a user requirements study is seen as over-complex and off-putting for clients in the business sector. The principles are sound but the methods have to be adapted and extended for multimedia.

Cross-platform.

The application platform does not necessarily dictate the development platform, so a PC application may be authored in a Mac tool set, for example. Sometimes, applications need to work across platforms and this is where expertise from both camps is needed to ensure that the development takes account of the cross-platform restraints. You have to be confident that the right decisions have been made about the choice of development hardware and software to fit the delivery platform requirements. If you are non-technical, you need to have complete confidence in the technical support and/or programmers who make the decisions on your behalf.

If the application cannot be developed in an authoring environment, a programming language will be needed. Although there are exceptions, non-specialists have not got enough experience and training to use computer languages so usually a specialist will be needed. Different languages suit different purposes and accomplish certain tasks better than others. This is why your technical support needs to understand the whole scope of the project to make an informed decision as to what combination of hardware and software will be needed.

Programmers can apply past experience to learn new languages/ packages as they work. Some packages share similarities in approach so that the learning curve is relatively fast; others have a totally different approach to their logic so they take longer to learn if the past experience is not compatible. Quite often, the programmers you employ will have to learn as they go along and you need to be aware of how much extra time to build in to allow for their learning. This might sound like poor project management – to employ the wrong skill level – but several circumstances can lead to this. Firstly, you may have to use full-time members of staff with a lower skill level for your project because they are available and therefore it is cheaper for the company to use them than employ contractors. Secondly, some specialisms within programming are harder to find and you may not be able to find contractors with the right skills. Thirdly, when skills are scarce they become expensive so even if you find the right contractors, you may not be able to afford them within the budget. In this case you have to gamble on the extra time for someone to gain the knowledge against the speed of experience. This would tend to mean the lower cost for longer or a higher cost for a shorter period of time.

This is a difficult decision since estimating the time it takes for programming is not an accurate art, particularly in multimedia development.

Considerations for interviews: programmers

Pre-interview

You need to have worked out the skills you want, the skill level you'd be willing to accept and 'grow', the length of time necessary to complete the project and the cost range you could work with within your budget. Ask candidates to bring examples of their work.

At interview

There are good and bad traits within professions that are part of their 'folklore'. Programmers can be creative, versatile, act on initiative, quick thinking, adaptable, precise, accurate, work to time-scales, and reliable. However, the profession suffers from labels from the business world that indicate erratic time keeping – both personal and project specific, poor communication skills, stubbornness, a wish to fulfil themselves rather than the project in hand, a tendency to be wilful, seeming to live in a world of their own. The problem is that some of the best programmers are not easy to manage.

You have to decide whether solidity or finesse is needed more in the particular project if you end up with a choice of candidates who display different traits, and you need to recognize your own strengths and weaknesses in your management style to assess a fit within your team that you can manage successfully.

If you are technical, you could conduct the interview to assess the technical ability of the candidate. You also need to assess the candidate as a project member. You may well be looking for different attributes than in a full-time employee. Project-specific work can make it easier to manage a more diverse range of people than those you need to work alongside continuously. In a project-specific situation, the expectations are different for all involved.

Computer graphics artists

Applications can demand a certain style because of the content and ideally a graphics artist should be selected to bring the best to the content and to the interactive environment. The development platform and the delivery platform will dictate the level and skill set that is needed for the graphics artist in the same way as they did for the programmer. The artists will come either from a PC or Mac background and have experience in the respective graphics packages.

The artist needs to be both creative and technically minded since creative ideas in multimedia graphics have to be achieved through technical means. Many adjustments have to be made because the graphics process is not straightforward. Colours can shift quite often as the graphic moves through its various stages to the final image and for applications where accuracy of colour is needed – selling items that have a range of colour options, for example – this can be a major problem. The sizing and placement of images cause other problems. Text often becomes corrupted at the last stage. It is difficult for the client to realize how much rework is needed because the graphic may have to be taken back through stages to correct such problems. The technicalities and inconsistencies mean that the graphics artist needs patience and logical, analytical thinking as well as creative flair. Your application may require more of one of these attributes than the others.

The programmer and graphics artist have to work closely together. The graphics person constructs the images to a certain stage and then passes them to the programmer to integrate them with all the other pieces – sound files, text, position in the program, the means of access to the image and so on. They work out together exactly how to produce and transfer the images between them. There are often hundreds of images and pieces of images that have to be assembled so the naming convention for the assets and the version control between them is important.

Because people may have worked in various companies with diverse approaches to working and have different ways of expressing concepts, bringing the core team together can be problematic. Some of the skills overlap and the graphics artist might have been used to taking the image process further than the programmer expects, or might be used to liaising with clients directly when the project manager wants to avoid this. There may be a strong split between the technical and creative skills. A technical artist may depend on the source images being produced by conventional means and then they scan, adjust, assemble and integrate ready for the programmer. This will always be true for specialist areas such as cartoon images, for example. But if the artist has a strong technical bias, it will affect the resources and costs of the project if you do not recognize that one graphics resource will not suffice. Often this is the case where there is one main artist and input from others as and when needed.

As with programmers, you may find you have to work with an artist who is available in-house but who doesn't have the full skill set you need. The erratic availability of contractors can also mean that you may have to select a person who displays many but not all of the attributes you need. Then you will face decisions of how to build up the balance of skills according to budget.

The project may form part of a set of projects so several artists with a variety of skills might be needed. If there are several people, they need to be managed and a senior graphics artist could be appointed to take on this role, or an art director might be considered.

An art director is usually employed by larger graphics studios as the creative ideas person who is responsible for managing the overall style of projects. You may have a set of projects that need to show continuity of graphic style – a certain look and feel. Also, if you have several computer graphics and video graphics artists involved in your project, someone needs to coordinate the artistic direction and personalities. Although the role of art director is unusual for multimedia projects at present, the role may develop as the number of projects increases. Now, a senior graphics designer usually takes on the responsibilities of the art director but whether the person should come from a video graphics or computer graphics background will change according to the bias of the company and their production routes.

Pre-interview

Although there is usually one main artist for the project, you will often need several for different functions during the development. You'll need to define exactly how you intend the project to run with any split of work needed between video and graphics artists, for example, so that there are no misconceptions about what type of work each artist will be doing. Some tasks are more laborious than creative, and tensions can occur if an artist thinks he or she will be doing creative new work rather than repetitive conversions from source materials. It will depend on the size of the project whether these tasks are combined for one person to do or whether the tasks are split. Also, one person needs to have responsibility for artistic direction or clashes in opinions, style and approach will show up in the application.

At interview

The definition of roles is easy to state but difficult to achieve because you will be working blind until the fine detail of the project is teased out. So, you can explain to candidates how the graphics appear to split but remind them that the circumstances may change once the project is under way.

It is important to see examples of the candidates' work and understand exactly their role in the production process, whether technical, creative, managerial or all three. Graphics artists will be happy to discuss their preferences and styles and might be able to come up with a feel for some treatments for the project once they understand its scope and their expected role. Because multimedia graphics production is not straightforward it is a good idea to probe where the candidates have experienced problems and how these were solved. This will give you a feel for the depth of experience and knowledge of the idiosyncrasies of the graphics packages.

You may be working on a project that has a 'house style' and this might mean that the artists will need to adapt their style appropriately. Some find this easier than others so you should check their disposition for this.

Because the synergy between the programmers and graphics artists is important, it is good to allow them to meet if possible and get their reactions. If the contractors have worked for the company before, it is also wise to gather informal feedback from those that worked with them.

The extended team: Skill sets

Video personnel

If your application is going to include video footage, you might need to use a video director/producer, an editor and perhaps a video graphics artist too. The directors/producers will have contacts and preferences for using certain facility houses, editors and video graphics people so it may save you some effort if you trust your main video contractor to organize the other video needs. Again, depending on the company bias, you may have access to all the video personnel you need in-house.

The difference between a video director and a producer is not straightforward until you define the roles for a full feature film where the director has the creative role and the producer is more of an administrator. For shorter pieces of work, you need to check what a person will be prepared to do if you interview directors and producers, so that you are aware if they will collapse the roles together, or whether they expect support themselves. A lot will depend on the amount and type of video footage you require.

As video becomes more of a key component in multimedia applications, the traditional roles from video production will figure more in multimedia teams. Production assistants have had a key role in video productions helping the director and producer. The role involves organizing and administration but can extend to supervising edits, directing part of the shoot, clearing rights, organizing facility houses, and editing scripts. A good production assistant is well organized, used to troubleshooting,

Use of video is increasing.

well skilled in audio and video production and has a useful range of
contacts.

Personnel with a video background find the seeming disintegration of
pieces of a script and the lack of control over the user's sequence of using
the material an anathema. Their backgrounds have prepared them for
continuity, flow, strong storylines, methods of story development, build-
up, characterization and unity of a whole. They lead the viewer through
the material. Interactivity destroys this to a certain extent and it takes time
for traditional directors and assistants to come to terms with the changes
that are needed in material development. They have a tendency to be critical about the technical quality and the structure of interactive programs
they have seen because they compare them with video programs.

Although the addition of interactivity and working with programmers
is a new area, video personnel are used to dealing with a mix of materials
and people. It is possibly a little harder for those coming from a programming background to pick up the creative aspects of audio and video
production than it is for video personnel to adjust to interactivity. But it is
easier for them to learn the technicalities of audio and video production
than it is for video personnel to understand computer graphics and
programming technicalities. This might mean that some personnel from a
computing or graphics background will claim to have audio and video

production skills. You need to decide if these people have full creative, administrative and technical skills or if audio and video specialists are needed.

Assistant producers help the producers with the creative direction of the video footage. The producer may delegate some of the responsibility for shots and edits to an assistant but still maintain a strong directional line. This means that some assistants have a wide range of skills and are capable of directing smaller projects. You may decide that an assistant producer could fulfil the role you need depending on their experience. It would be rare in multimedia to need both producer/director and assistant producer.

Production assistants can be invaluable when a project needs video footage, photos or pictures from picture libraries, video, sound and graphics rights cleared and if several strands of the project need to be completed simultaneously because of the time-scales. They have an administrative role supporting the director and producer.

The casting and directing of actors and actresses might form part of your overall responsibility. If your footage needs extensive detail such as external locations or studio sets, you will need a full production team. This is why and where video footage is expensive and might take up a good portion of your budget. The producer would usually coordinate, recruit and manage the video team, and take care of casting, but you may have to sit in with the clients to check that the actors and actresses fulfil their expectations and needs.

So much depends on the scope of the project and the budget that the number of people involved and their roles is difficult to quantify. Multimedia at present tends to expect people to collapse a few roles and responsibilities together because the amount filmed is generally shorter and less complex than for videos and films. Sometimes you might find yourself in the position of selecting and organizing facilities houses and personnel, like video editors, to work on pre-shot footage. Your need for a producer or director diminishes in this case, but you still have to clear the rights and re-edit the material to suit the purpose.

Video editors work to directions so if your application needs existing footage reworked, you need to consider whether you can handle the direction or whether you need help. This could depend on your own background and experience and whether the scripts are straightforward. Or, the editor might be prepared to work with the scripts without direction. The range of possibilities within video production and the variety and level of skills within the personnel mean that identification of which personnel are needed and recruitment is much easier with someone who has been part of the industry.

Your video editors will work in two stages – offline and online editing. The offline is where all the decisions are made around cheap copies of the footage. The editors will work and rework according to direction. They will make suggestions based on their experience. When your director, or whoever is taking responsibility for the footage, is satisfied, you'll move on to the online. No changes can be made to the material after the online without incurring great expense. The online transfers the decisions that were made at offline to the original material. You have to have client agreement and sign-off prior to online to avoid detrimental and acrimonious negotiations.

Sound personnel

If you are using audio over graphics and text, you will need to:

- book a studio with a sound editor,
- select and book your voice-over artists,
- select any music needed,
- have all the scripts ready and signed off,
- specify exactly the format in which you will need the material.

You will be asked how long you'll need the studio and editor so you have to make sure that you know how much work is involved in the scripts and estimate the amount of time needed to edit the material afterwards. You have to work out the timing sequence of all these aspects so that they come together at the studio. Selecting the voice-over artists is no trivial task. You'll more than likely have to go through an agency. Your company may hold banks of voice-over tapes from different agencies that you can browse; you may have a voice in mind and need to find out the agent, or you may have specific requirements for voice qualities and need to match them to people. You can phone agencies and put your specifications to them and they will suggest some alternatives, then send through some demo tapes.

The voice-over industry is well structured and used to responding quickly to enquiries. The agencies have several questions about use of the voice-over which determine the basic rate for the artist and any clearance and rights fees. For non-interactive productions, the negotiations are straightforward and clear. They are based on the type of use, type of audience, period of time and countries for clearance. However, the industry is confused about multimedia and there are no standards set.

This makes it difficult for you to predict costs for audio work and you can run into problems as each agency seems to operate differently with multimedia. One of the standard categories that's been used – number of times for broadcast or use – is impossible to predict for multimedia since the user may or may not access the particular voice-over every time. It has also been unfair to apply a mature market strategy to a small emerging market so that the specification of audience as 'the general public' and the costs associated with that are applied to a multimedia application for the general public when 'the public' is extremely limited.

Some sound editors/studios will usually take on the clearance of the performing rights for the music used which are separate from voice-over rights. But here too, a well-understood and well-used structure with the Mechanical Copyright Protection Society (MCPS) for other forms of use does not apply to multimedia use. At present, each application is negotiated on its own and it is a problematic area so therefore needs good project management to ensure that the artists and your company are served fairly. (See Chapter 17 for more detail on the various categories of clearance for rights.)

If you are employing production assistants, it is invaluable if they have had prior experience with clearing multimedia rights. As it is an area which is constantly shifting and the regulators are trying to address the problems, you need to keep up to date with the changes either through them or by yourself.

Voice-over artists work quickly. They often have sessions before and after yours so if you have miscalculated the amount of material, or there are too many changes, you will be looking at the hire of all concerned again. The artists usually charge a minimum of an hour however little they say.

The sound editors will use a variety of techniques to deal with any retakes that are necessary owing to mispronunciation, wrong intonation or whatever. The way they choose to operate depends on the sophistication of the equipment they are using. Some studios are digital and some are still tape. If there are very specific subject terms, it is wise to have a representative from the clients at the recording to check the pronunciation.

The artists should have the script a couple of days before the recording so that they can prepare, although many are excellent sight readers. The scripts need to have been signed off by the clients prior to the recording. The editor will mark up the script to show where there were retakes but you or your delegate should also keep check and decide which out of any that are disputed should be used. The clients or their representative might prefer to make these decisions but they have to be made then and there.

It is important that the editor knows what the tracks will be used for, and the quality level needs to be stated clearly.

Multimedia applications have underestimated the importance of the use of sound as discussed in Chapter 8. This starts at the script stage when speech and stills are often put together without the atmospheric use of music and sound effects. However, until the clearance and rights problems are sorted, the expense of quality audio might be too much for many projects and it is easier to compromise on its quality than many of the other components.

Audio production is a large administrative, creative and technical part of the project and carries its own risks which the project manager needs to understand and control. A video producer or experienced assistant producer would have the skills to manage and coordinate the audio production as well as the video if necessary but they would have to be made aware of the technical specification for the audio so that the next stage – encoding – can proceed smoothly.

The audio and video move to the next stage in preparation for integration. Because the tools have matured quickly, it is becoming easier to encode them. It is so much easier that both graphics artists and programmers can shoot and record pieces of material, then integrate them without the need for all the personnel, studios and facilities houses. If your application only needs this level of quality, there is no reason to go to the expense of full-blown audio and video production. You still need to clear all rights and ensure that there are no accidental infringements such as advertisements on a wall used as a background in the video, or uncleared use of any music, and so on. There are lots of traps to avoid when this in-house approach is taken and the creative personnel are often not aware of all the administrative angles that need to be covered for legal reasons. If this is the right approach for your project, you have to take full responsibility for ensuring that all the administrative procedures are carried out and recorded correctly.

General support

Personal assistant

If the administration in the project is going to be heavy, you may well need a personal assistant instead of or as well as a production assistant. The skills of organizing are parallel but personal assistants will not get involved with the audio and video production to the same extent. They may book facilities, arrange, and clear rights under your direction if you will be performing these tasks. They should possess secretarial skills so they can assist in documenting the project and collating scripts as well as contributing to the general communication with the clients and team.

If the project is an international one with all the administrative extras that this entails, a personal assistant may be the answer. If the project involves details of the client's products, for a kiosk for example, it can be a large task to ensure the information is accurate and in a form that will facilitate integration.

Clients will be used to changing their details on a daily basis until the products are on sale and it is difficult to keep track of the current situation on prices, colour descriptions, product dimensions, product specifications and so on. Unless the application links online to the client database as part of the project specification, you will most likely need to reproduce the details and get sign-off on a version at the time you need to do final integration. You will have to build up the relevant details and keep updating until the last moment.

This is one of those grey tasks that several people might do or share – an instructional or interactive designer might see it as a task to ensure the quality of data and be prepared to take this on, programmers might be persuaded to have this as part of their role particularly if the technicalities of merging data from the sources can be streamlined, you might see it as part of your liaison and sign-off role, or you may set up a process between companies where your personal assistant will liaise with the appropriate people to maintain the records. A lot will depend on exactly how much data there is, how unstable it is, and how it will be integrated into the application.

The role tends to evolve according to circumstances and aptitude of the people.

Secretarial support

All projects generate a good deal of general administration and some level of secretarial support is always needed. If you have to type and produce all the documents and letters yourself, make all phone calls to book facility houses and contact the various contractors, clients and officials, you need to block out at least half of your time for this and have other forms of backup support for the other functions to compensate. Lack of administrative backup is one of the most common causes of problems in multimedia projects because the amount of time it takes is underestimated and undervalued by management. This is not a major problem if you do not have to perform several of the core tasks yourself on the project, but if you are expected to do part of the programming, perhaps produce a prototype with an authoring tool, cover all the liaising with the clients and maybe write a script or two while recruiting and managing all the other staff, then the day-to-day administration becomes problematic. This is where the value of being multi-skilled can become diminished because it is considered the norm rather than the exception.

If you need to have support, you may be able to identify the busy administrative periods and survive with temporary secretaries. However, inducting people often eats up vital time and so continuity of personnel across a project needs to be carefully weighed against other factors.

Project managers in other business spheres are not expected to perform any of the core tasks themselves. In many ways, the practical skills are seen as non-management functions and therefore not part of the role. Multimedia is still embryonic so the boundaries are not as defined. Also, the skills are not as plentiful because of this, so doubling-up is natural at this stage. This may change as the profession matures.

Specialist support

Technical support

The day-to-day running of the technical side of the project can range from straightforward to very complex depending on the mixture of hardware and software that will be used. In some research and international projects your partners might be producing the hardware and software as part of the project and you may be dependent upon them meeting their deadlines and testing the efficiency of the tools, prior to you using them. Inevitably with new hardware and software the unexpected happens and it is at this stage that good technical backup is essential.

The company may have a technical director, a production manager, a network manager and technical assistants or it may not. It is essential that any work on the project is properly backed up. The administration for the technical side of the project such as registering software licences, general maintenance, chasing parts and creating backups can be onerous.

You cannot assume that graphics artists and programmers will perform any administrative aspects unless these responsibilities are defined as part of their role. Depending where they have worked, this might be considered normal or highly irregular. This is where a good definition of roles, responsibilities and general work practice pays off because then there is no assumption made by anyone. Very often, it is the assumption that someone else is doing something that suddenly provokes a crisis for the project manager.

The amount of technical support should increase according to the number and type of projects that the company has. If, however, your project warrants extra for the whole period or part of the time, this is yet another resource to nominate and budget for.

Script writers

Many script writers could form part of the video personnel team if their experience lies in writing video scripts. If video script writers are employed, they tend to work with the director or producer. But multimedia scripts, as we have seen, can combine any variety of audio, video, interactive instructions, interactive design, and text. You might find one person to write all the scripts for the project or you might have to employ several for the different parts. Your prime concerns are to:

- maintain quality across the scripts so that every media attribute is used to best effect;
- ensure consistency of style;
- check there is correct adherence to the overall interactive design;
- keep the script writers on track;
- make sure the scripts keep to the size and specifications worked out for each section;
- determine that each script is technically achievable in the time and budget.

The precise content can take time to determine and this can sometimes form part of the writer's brief; at other times, the subject experts, interactive designers and/or training analysts will work to decide which issues need to be addressed and then work with writers to achieve the scripts. The whole area of script writing is one of the least defined in multimedia and therefore one of the hardest tasks to control for the project manager. As each piece of script is addressed, there is a tendency for the writers to want to add and expand the original ideas beyond the scope of the budget or beyond the space allocated for the section, and this needs to be contained. Experience of working with interactive scripts helps writers understand the new constraints that have to be taken into account, but if they have little experience you need to monitor them closely.

Prior to interview, you need to define a brief to direct the writers. The brief needs to cover the content treatment needed, the scope, style considerations, the audience profile, the company profile and the time-scales. The briefing documents should be written and include as much detail as possible so that there is no misunderstanding later. If there is an overall interactive design, sometimes called the high-level design, the writers should be briefed to explain where and how their piece fits into the overall design. A structure diagram proves invaluable when discussing the project with most of the personnel involved and always helps script writers. They will have a different approach if they know that they are not responsible for the whole program and will want to ensure that their piece fits the overall specification as well as the individual section brief.

If the writer is meant to take on a fuller role and produce the interactive design as well as the detailed scripts, your brief will be different and you will be checking for a more complex skill set. The type of application will direct the needs for designers and script writers and the precise skills they should have. The script for a sales kiosk, for example, would need to be very different from a medical education project.

Training specialist

As already discussed, training has its own approach to defining content and scripts, so if the project is a training application, you need to make sure it conforms to the principles of the discipline. The training specialists you recruit would need to have had experience in Training Needs Analysis if you expect them to define the overall scope of the content. Their role may stop there and the script writers could take over, or, if the training specialists have interactive experience, they may be able to take the project through the next stage of high-level design. They may possibly be capable of writing all or some of the scripts themselves. A lot depends on the application and the experience of the training specialist. So-called 'soft skills' such as assertiveness, leadership and counselling are harder to recruit for than other training areas. You should be looking for a fit in experience of the content, a match with experience in training analysis for a similar audience and experience in developing interactive or distance learning materials.

You may find that you need to pair a training specialist with an interactive designer, subject matter experts and script writers at different stages of the content development. If the application is an in-house training program for a large firm, this mix of people would be quite common. If the training specialists were from the client company, and you had to utilize their skills, they might have little or no interactive experience. Then your role would be to recruit enough support staff around the training specialists to help achieve the right mix of skills needed for this part of the project.

Instructional/interactive designer

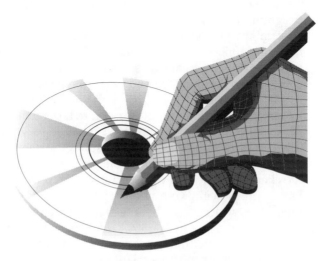

Interactive design.

One of the key skills you are trying to cover is that of interactive design. Because this is bound up with defining the sections of the content, the interface, and the routing or navigation paths through the material, it spans several of the roles – programming, graphics, script writing, producer and interactive design. Your programmer or graphics artist may well be experienced in producing the equivalent of a high-level design but not scripts to support it. They may on the other hand not be very experienced or happy in liaising with clients to extract the salient information and prefer building to a specification that they are given.

An interactive designer takes on some or all of the responsibility of defining content plus specifying the high-level design and probably can write some or all of the scripts. The fine detail of the interactive design has to be negotiated between all the core team members because they all have relevant input to help shape the decisions. In this way, an interactive designer might sometimes be part of the core team.

If one of your core team, including yourself, cannot fulfil the functions of interactive design, you should consider recruiting an instructional/interactive designer. Other roles will be able to script for text, audio and video but the 'help' script, which explains how the program works, may also include text, audio and video. This is often forgotten but is vital. It is unlike the other scripts in style and tone. It can be the key to a successful application. As applications are now more complex, the help script is growing in size and importance. You need to determine whose responsibility it is to take care of this.

Subject matter experts/Personalities

Commercial applications tend to use a public figure because the name helps to sell the product. They may be experts in the field or have strong links to the subject. Sometimes, the experts will take an active part in the program by being in the video or doing some of the voice-over. Sometimes, they might just endorse the application. On other occasions, they might help to define the content and check the scripts. There can be a pairing between training analysts, subject experts and instructional designers or combinations of these, as and when the project needs it.

It is important that you and your clients are confident about the integrity of the content so it is useful to tap into subject expertise. However, the more people that are involved in vetting scripts, the more problematic it becomes to stabilize them. The subject experts have to be given a clear brief of their roles and responsibilities in the project. If the experts are from the client company, they can influence the project strongly. They can cause havoc if they begin to stray out of their area of expertise into criticizing the interactive structure or the interface, for example.

Their advisory and critical role has to have strong boundaries drawn around it to allow the rest of the 'experts', the core team, to do their job effectively. You need to explain to the clients that the experts' advice has to be put into the complete interactive context and that when this happens some compromises may have to be made. This is more of a problem when the experts suggest complete new areas that need to be incorporated into the application too late for you to reconcile with time and cost.

Subject matter experts and personalities are quite easy to locate and recruit but their guaranteed allocation of time to the project is more of a problem. Your clients will often recommend their preferred experts. It is important that you explain how time-critical their input will be and get a signed commitment.

THEORY INTO PRACTICE 12

ALLOCATING ROLES AND RESPONSIBILITIES

The check-list at the end of the chapter covers many of the tasks that need to be performed during the multimedia project cycle.

Apply the list to your present or a past project by inserting the team's initials into the relevant boxes to see how the roles and responsibilities pan out. Put 'not applicable (n/a)' where appropriate. Beware any gaps and ensure they are covered next time.

The listing can be useful during your pre-interview and interview stage. If you are going to use in-house resources, then you can map out their roles and responsibilities, indicate where 'not applicable' applies and get a feel for the personnel you need to recruit and the tasks they will need to perform from the gaps that are left. You can then make a note of the skills that lie behind the tasks to get a skill profile for the people you need. This check-list would not be comprehensive for international projects where more tasks are used, but it could serve as a starting point for you to adapt if necessary. The check-list can also be found on the CD.

Summary

- The project manager needs to identify the mix of skills necessary for the project and then assemble an appropriate core and extended team.
- Recruitment is not an easy exercise. It should be handled professionally with good preparation, briefing and role definitions.
- Knowledge of what multimedia roles exist and the contribution each can make to the project is important to help in decision making.
- Each multimedia role has its own range of skills and considerations. Careful assessment of the skill level needed has to be balanced with the project needs, budget constraints and management style.
- Clear assignment of responsibilities is necessary to ensure all project tasks are covered. It's a good idea to list all the tasks and assign the person responsible for each as a check that all aspects have been covered.

Multimedia project task and skill set check-list.

Client liaison	Initial	Recruitment/selection general	Initial	Video production	Initial
1. Attend meetings		1. Identify resource needs		1. Direction/production manager	
2. Write up meetings		2. Cost resources, align to budget		2. Identify resources needed	
3. Be the main telephone/fax contact		3. Organize deskspace, equipment, etc.		3. Cost resources, align to budget	
4. Respond to queries		4. Organize appropriate CVs		4. Organize recruitment	
5. Organize sign-offs – proposal, contract, content, scripts, database		5. Select interviewees		5. Select interviewees	
6. Handle scheduling		6. Define roles and responsibilities		6. Define roles and responsibilities	
7. Monitor budget		7. Write job descriptions/criteria		7. Interview	
8. Handle disputes		8. Define skill mix needed		8. Recruit or delegate recruitment	
9. Inform of project status		9. Interview		9. Recruit: Script-writers, Camera, Lights, Sound, Grips, Make-up, Continuity, Catering, Communications, Logging, etc.	
10. Negotiate changes in time and cost		10. Select appointees		10. Negotiate contracts	
		11. Negotiate contracts		11. Negotiate with agents	
		12. Negotiate with agencies		12. Organize shoot (locations, props, etc.)	
		13. Induct new recruits to company		13. Clear locations, liaise with police	
		14. Induct new recruits to project		14. Cast artists	
				15. Organize facility houses/edits	
				16. Recruit Video Graphics: 3-D animator, computer compositor, Harry operator, etc.	
				17. Direct edits	
				18. Edit offline	
				19. Edit online	
				20. Approve edits	
				21. Film/picture research	
				22. Clearances and rights (footage, pictures, music, voice-overs, etc.)	
				23. Liaise with programmers/technical quality assurance	
				24. Monitor and approve costs	
				25. Organize video encoding	
				26. Encode video	

Audio production	Initial	Stills/graphics production	Initial	Database development	Initial
1. Direction/production manager		1. Direction/production manager		1. Identification of data fields	
2. Scripts (main and help)		2. Graphics production		2. Collation of data	
3. Organize studio facility		3. Picture researcher		3. Verification of data	
4. Organize recording/edit		4. Rights and clearances		4. Liaison with clients	
5. Organize translations		5. Electronic asset management		5. Integration into project	
6. Direct edit		6. Animation production		6. Indexer	
7. Select voice-overs		7. Photographer		7. Help script	
8. Select/commission music		8. Lighting		8. Spell check and editing	
9. Negotiate rights and clearances		9. 3-D modeller			
10. Liaise with programmers/technical quality assurance, formats		10. Computer graphics			
		11. Paintbox operator			
11. Organize M & E tracks		12. Scanner/digitizer			
12. Organize encoding		13. Art director			
13. Encode		14. Illustrator/artist			
14. Monitor and approve costs		15. Text/page layout			
		16. Typography			

Design and documentation	Initial	Computing and integration	Initial	Administration	Initial
1. Produce final contract agreement		1. Programmer/software engineer		1. Typing	
2. Produce technical specification		2. Technical manager		2. Filing	
3. Product outline/high-level specification		3. Network manager		3. Answering/making phone calls	
		4. Maintenance		4. Collating personnel and project documentation	
4. Produce interactive script – interface functions, help script		5. Backup/archiving			
		6. Software librarian		5. Sending and distributing faxes/messages	
5. Define content sections				6. Organize meetings, book rooms	
6. Define detailed content				7. Organize couriers, cars, post etc.	
7. Liaise with subject experts				8. Photocopying	
				9. Collect timesheets	

Recommended reading

Belbin R.M. (1981). *Management Teams: Why They Succeed or Fail*. Oxford: Butterworth-Heinemann Ltd

Belbin R.M. (1993). *Team Roles at Work*. Oxford: Butterworth-Heinemann Ltd

De Marco T. and Lister T. (1987). *Peopleware: Productive Projects and Teams*. New York: Dorset House Publishing Co.

Honey P. (1988). *Improve Your People Skills*. London: Institute of Personnel Management

Katzenbach J.R. and Smith D.K. (1993). *The Wisdom of Teams: Creating the High-performance Organisation*. Boston, MA: Harvard Business School Press

Phillips N. (1992). *Managing International Teams*. London: Pitman Publishing

Raudsepp E. (1963). *Managing Creative Scientists and Engineers*. New York: The Macmillan Company

Tjosvold D. (1991). *Team Organisation: An Enduring Competitive Advantage*. Chichester: Wiley

CHAPTER 12

TEAM MANAGEMENT PRINCIPLES

Project manager's responsibilities

- To negotiate with higher management on behalf of the team
- To motivate the team and set the direction for them
- To create good communication between the team members
- To employ a variety of management styles appropriate for the occasion
- To identify and remedy any deficiencies in the team make-up in functional, decision-making and interpersonal skills
- To resolve problems occurring in the teams
- To recognize and address environmental factors affecting the team

The project manager and team culture

Most multimedia projects take place in a team culture. A good team culture can be defined as:

- everyone pulling together to achieve well-defined tasks
- respect for each other's skills
- a sharing of success and failures
- mutual support when needed.

The team will be affected by outside conditions such as recognition within the organization, being valued, being treated fairly, receiving support, receiving adequate resources. A team culture will often take its lead from the organization culture but it can develop its own. So the manager has a dual role: to try to provide the conditions which will help motivate the team to work well together, and to create an open, constructive working atmosphere to allow the individuals to achieve their best in a way that also serves the project best.

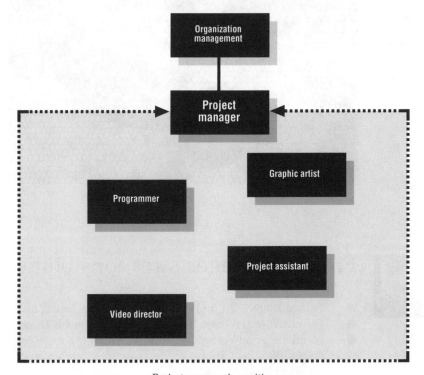

Project manager's position.

To provide good conditions, the manager has to negotiate with higher management for the necessary resources. You may need to justify how they will improve the success criteria of the project. As the team's representative to higher management, the manager takes the lead on their behalf. For many, this representation role appears a contradiction of the idea of leadership. Leadership seems to imply being in front of others, being ahead of them, making the decisions for them, but this is true only in some cases. Team leadership is also about being the representative of the team's needs, views and skills.

To create an open, constructive working atmosphere is not easy. Individuals have their own aspirations, their own personality traits, their own strengths and weaknesses, their own defence mechanisms, their own way of interacting with other people. To unify a disparate group who come from different disciplines, with different skills and different ways of describing multimedia, might seem impossible. However, the team will respond to the tone and form of interaction you set. You can be the catalyst by being open and informative, supportive and straight-talking.

Team leadership is also about giving direction but this should not be confused with being directive. Setting the direction in a multimedia project means performing all the background tasks that have been described in the preceding chapters which help define exactly what each member needs to achieve and how each task relates to the whole project. The administrative tasks, such as defining everyone's role and responsibilities, in itself sets a working direction and this in turn gives unity of purpose. Maintaining the overall vision of the application also helps set a direction. Individuals can become too involved with their own particular pieces to maintain the overview. Constant focusing on the needs of the user also sets a unifying direction for all concerned.

Management styles

Being directive, on the other hand, is linked to management style. There are many ways of defining management styles but we'll concentrate on directive, consultative, collaborative and delegation. Good managers employ a mixture of styles appropriate for the occasion and circumstances. The hard part is recognizing which to use, when.

Management style: Directive.

Directive is appropriate when you have the knowledge and experience to make the necessary decision, you have to accept the responsibility for your decision, and the decision is needed quickly. Under these circumstances, you make the decision and then direct the team members to carry it out. If you communicate this to the team in an open manner, you can be directive without making them feel manipulated. They may challenge the decision from their perspective and experience. You should see this as a chance to broaden them by giving an explanation, rather than as a challenge to your authority – as long as you are confident that you are right.

Management style: Consultative.

You can employ a consultative style when you need to make a decision and you are fairly confident about it but you have some time to check the views of team members. They may influence you or may not. You have the time to think things through and take all aspects into consideration before reaching a decision.

Collaborative decisions occur when you recognize that you do not have the right knowledge, skill and experience to come to a conclusion

Management style: Collaborative.

yourself, so you seek the team's views to pool experience and take a decision based on the majority view. Collaborative decisions may not involve the whole team. You may seek the views of some of the team who have the relevant skills and take the decision based on their expertise.

In multimedia management, where there are so many strands of expertise, often you do not have the same level of knowledge and experience in specific areas as members of the team, so you will need to collaborate with them often.

However, sometimes you will be forced into making decisions in time-critical circumstances where you cannot contact the right team members. Both sides need to recognize the constraints and accept that some decisions may not always be the best. They can be the best for the time and the circumstances, which may be your only consolation. You will maintain an open and honest atmosphere by admitting the decision was forced and that you were aware of the risks but that you were left no choice.

This can happen, for example, at a meeting with clients very late into the project, where they suddenly include an important visitor from their head office who states an opinion contrary to the one your clients have stated in the video. You can see that they are as surprised as you, but they agree with the visitor wholeheartedly. You are placed in a very unfortunate position. You cannot embarrass your main clients in front of their important visitor by explaining that they have already stated their original position on camera and signed off the video which has been encoded and integrated into the relevant section.

But once the visitor departs you have to address the situation. You recognize that there is no way that you can now keep that opinion in the section but also you cannot rework it in the time and money even if the clients agree. There is little else to do but suggest that you'll look at the section and try to edit out the offending part, or cut it out. The clients insist that the new position has to be included. You know that a new video clip is impossible and that the clients will not move from their demand. The stakes are too high for them. You appreciate their circumstances. At the same time, you realize that your knowledge of the specific content is not accurate. The script writers would be the ones to comment on the impact and usually, you'd have telephoned them. But as their work was finished a few weeks earlier, their contracts ended and they are no longer around. With a public launch in a few days, you decide to go for the lowest common denominator – to cut out the old message and then insert the new one with text and graphics, knowing that this is against the design continuity of the application but is achievable.

When you and the team fully analyse the situation back at work, the new slant actually has much more of an impact than imagined because several of the associated ideas are affected as well. The whole section needs rework rather than one contained piece. So much is affected that it becomes better to scrap the video and reform the section into text, some saved audio, and new graphics. Your team are furious with you, your clients are furious – more with themselves and their top management for not communicating changes in policy faster to them, but they take it out on you. However, a decision had to be taken and the consequences accepted as part of your responsibility.

With hindsight, there may have been alternatives if you could have thought things through and talked things through. But with other pressing points on the meeting agenda, you needed many decisions and agreements, not just to fire-fight with that one. Your only consolation might be that other project managers would understand, and if you'd warned the clients not to include time-sensitive information in a video, they had ignored the advice!

Management style: Delegation.

Delegation means that you transfer the powers of decision making on some matters to members of the team. But you must meet certain conditions to be seen to delegate otherwise this can be abdication not delegation. If you delegate, you need to make clear:

■   how far the delegation is allowed;
■   that you delegate with complete authority within the limits set;
■   that you will support all decisions made on your behalf.

If you fail any of these criteria, you have not delegated effectively. There is nothing worse than a manager who confuses delegation with abdication. This can lead to unclear ideas of how far, when, and to what level the other people can make decisions. With no clear boundaries and with a confusing brief, it is easy to make mistakes. If your own manager has abdicated not delegated, you'll quickly find that there will only be support as long as you are right!

For example, you may decide to delegate the video production to a video director who would take care of the casting, the shoot and the edits and hand you a master tape. You could allocate a budget from your budget for the completed tape and then monitor the spend. You might prefer to take over at the encoding stage so that the key points for you to monitor would be the quality of the content, the technical quality and the compatibility of the tape source. This would then be delegation. The video director would know the precise tasks, the authority limits of the budget, where you would want sign-off, where you would take over and the criteria of acceptance of the tape.

This has been a quick overview of some of the styles that have been identified. It is impossible to cover this area in greater depth here but it is important to introduce it as a topic because your performance as a project manager can be affected by your management style. Many multimedia project managers do not recognize the extent that good people management contributes to successful projects.

It would be a good idea to include some more reading on management styles in your own development plan for the next year to get a better appreciation of the insights that can help with managing people.

Teams: Lessons learnt so far

From the last chapter, we understand how to identify the technical or specialist skills needed for a particular project and recruit accordingly to make sure all the tasks are covered. But this is not the complete recipe for success. A project needs enough people in the team with a capacity to bond the individual pieces together. This means that they are willing to attend to detail and compromise their individual professional drive for the sake of the total project performance. The project manager needs to take the lead in this. A good team needs the complete set of technical or functional expertise, problem-solving and decision-making skills, and interpersonal skills.

The problems of managing talented specialists have been recognized in investigations into teamwork. Personality attributes and behaviour characteristics can account for the success or failure of projects. Interaction skills within the project team can make or break it. Belbin offers detailed insights into personality mixes, teamwork, success and failure. Although his experiments were conducted with management teams selected on the basis of extensive psychometric testing, the personality attributes could be applied to any set of individuals who need to work in a team setting.

The use of psychometric testing as part of multimedia recruitment would not fit into the way the industry works at present. It is difficult enough to find the right technical and creative skill mix. But the project manager can benefit from understanding group dynamics and may use the knowledge wisely to help in difficult situations.

Belbin's findings which appear to have relevance for multimedia will be summarized in the following paragraphs.

The premise that very high levels of mental ability in all team members make the best combination proved disappointing. It appeared that critical debate was a characteristic of these teams and that there were difficulties in them reaching coherent decisions. They were difficult to manage. The emphasis within teams of high mental ability was analysis not synthesis, and in teamwork, the analysis needs to be synthesized to move the ideas to tangible development. The teams performed best if there were one or two people of high mental ability and worst if there were none. The profile for teams from high-technology areas was one of high mental ability and so there could be correlations between multimedia teams and these findings.

There is little that the project manager can do as many of the necessary skills for a multimedia team warrant high mental ability. Critical debate is necessary in a creative, high-tech field, and specialists thrive on it. It forms part of their drive and motivation, both of which you need in the project. But if you recognize that the avenues explored lack cohesion, and no one else in the team provides a unifying stance, it becomes your responsibility. There will be a balance between allowing constructive debate and letting it run away with itself.

High-tech teams also portrayed the inability to have a rounded approach to viewing problems. This is a weakness associated with teams that have a concentration of specialists. Specialists were often found to have anxious-introverted personalities and this was also noted as a cultural prevalence in high-tech companies. If the specialists had risen to management levels, they continued to display specialist tendencies. This also showed in the type of projects that they selected. The projects tended to aim high within the specialisms rather than consolidating and refining known techniques.

There is a dilemma here because the literature has also shown that every project needs to be personally challenging for the team to give their best; otherwise they become bored or indifferent. The specialists may only be employing these principles but because they are specialists, they aim higher than others would. Again, you have to find the balance between personal challenge and achieving the project within time and budget. The business principles will help give the rounded perspective needed, or you might opt to invite a business specialist into some of the initial meetings to add balance.

The other option might be to share the criticisms of high-tech teams with your team as part of the critical debate. People can learn. They can begin to recognize when the team displays these tendencies and can move towards accepting the need to balance them. They may come up with some surprising strategies to compensate for them.

This would seem to leave multimedia project managers themselves in a vulnerable position. As indicated in earlier chapters, they often still carry a split role within the project, acting as specialist in one area and general project manager in the others. It is important that your own specialist views, as well as those of the other specialists, are considered within the business context of the application so that the criticism of narrowness in the team vision is avoided.

There are some points in favour of the project manager being a specialist where other specialists are present in the team. They are difficult to manage but they are more predisposed to respect people who are achievers within a related specialism. It will not make the role easier necessarily but it will be easier to voice your opinion with confidence.

Belbin noted that if teams were composed around those who showed creative criteria, there appeared to be weakness of follow through. There was an abundance of ideas but they were not utilized effectively. A team needed a creative source but also needed the backup of people who would create the opportunity for the ideas to move into action. There are, by definition, many creative people as part of the multimedia team and so this might present possible difficulties.

From Belbin's research, the team leaders who were most effective with computer application development teams were selected not for their experience and seniority in the field but for 'chairmanship' qualities. These were defined as the ability to recognize the strengths of the others in the team, explore options that were raised, back the right person at the right time, and obtain good results. This does not, and could not, define how the leaders knew who to back when and therefore influence the final decision. The data seems to support that the leader should not be the cleverest person in the team but should appreciate the strength in others, help them communicate in ways appropriate for the whole group to understand, and keep them focused on the objectives. However, the tasks the team need to perform can also define the type of leader that is needed. If the team has been in a rut, someone who is extrovert can galvanize it into action and drive it forward and therefore might be more appropriate than the 'chairman' character.

Eight role types were defined as necessary for potential management team excellence:

(1) a solid organizer;
(2) a catalyst who would draw the best from other members;
(3) someone with drive and a readiness to challenge;
(4) a creative, imaginative person;
(5) someone with the capacity to shape the ideas into action by using contacts and resources outside the team;
(6) a hard-headed judgemental figure;
(7) a person who responded well to people and situations and who would engender team spirit;
(8) someone with the capacity to follow through.

These roles represent the concept of an 'ideal' team mix where there is balance for the variety of management tasks that could arise. Often, each team member may have to fill a few roles as and when they arise. The dynamic nature of teamwork means that the needs shift and therefore team members adjust their roles to cover the needs.

THEORY INTO PRACTICE 13

If you are working in a team at the moment, put the initials of the team members most likely to fulfil the role types into Table 12.1. The names are shorthand for the roles described above, so refer to that paragraph for confirmation of the role types. They are not the original names used by Belbin and have been adapted to suit a multimedia audience, but the role types conform to the original research.

Remember, one person can switch between several roles over the course of a project if necessary although one role tends to dominate. If there are any gaps left, what are you going to suggest to try to achieve a balance for the team?

Table 12.1 Team role profile.

Role type	Team member's initials
Solid organizer	
Catalyst	
Driver	
Creative	
Explorer	
Judge	
Carer	
Completer	

It was very difficult to find the last type of team member – the one who would finish the task and follow through on the detail. Many managers admitted that they lost enthusiasm for the tasks once the exciting and challenging first phase of definition had passed. This dwindling of interest is unfortunately characteristic of multimedia projects and project managers. The production phase is often beset with numerous adjustments after adjustments for a variety of reasons, and this is wearing for the team.

The end of the project spins out. Everyone wants to reach the final sign-off but it is the hardest to get. There is also a problem of reallocation of energy and resources from the team onto new projects, as these are phased in as the old ones are phased out. The team members are invigorated with the new, exciting challenges. The old project's appeal becomes stale.

This, one of the hardest phases for project managers, is made worse if the lack of finishing power is part of their own weakness. If the team members lack the will to complete tasks, and this is more characteristic of creative and analytical personalities, there is a problem keeping the team on-track to the end. It becomes the project manager's responsibility to get the project finished. The management of the company needs to recognize these problems, which are inherent in this type of teamwork, and back the project manager in the allocation of enough time and resources, as well as give encouragement to the team to finish.

The other role that is a problem to fill in a team is the one of handling conflict or difficult situations. There is a tendency for the team members to opt out of this and leave it up to you even if the cause is related to a particular team member. The move between a hierarchical system where the team leader is accepted as the one who is directive, and the open team structure where whoever has the best fit of skills for the task takes the lead, is a strange feature of team interaction. There will be situations during the course of the project that need strong, hard decisions.

Take for example a graphics artist who likes working at night and so ends up arriving for work late afternoon. This becomes the norm. It is true that in multimedia there is tolerance for erratic hours because the team will work hard and long to reach a milestone. But if the work habit of one member means that the rest of the team find it very difficult to communicate the necessary tasks, then some action has to be taken. The behaviour increases the time taken to complete a phase, and the error rate for the work is likely to increase because of the mis-communication. You will have to decide the course of action. If after explaining the reason for the request, the team member fails to rectify the situation, what are your options?

You will need the backing of the rest of the team to take further action or you risk alienating them, but if they agree with the problems it is causing, and that the member's actions are detrimental to the project, you have the backing to become more formal with the treatment which could lead to a change of staff for the sake of the project. The main problem lies in getting a replacement up to speed versus the disruption caused by the present situation. But the longer the situation remains unresolved, the more unsettling the effect on the team. You will need to take the lead in these situations because you have the nominal authority and the links to higher management. The main problem is the switch between the open, less formal management style you need to adopt to allow the ideas to flow within the team and the traditional role of a strong director.

The only other way that these tough team problems are resolved is by getting the core team to commit to mutual accountability for the project. If your company employs performance monitoring, there could be scope for doing this so that team objectives are set rather than individual ones. This might exert more influence over the team needing to work together and accept mutual responsibility for achieving the total project rather than expecting to fulfil the specialist role only.

If the team is performance driven and the tasks have been determined and agreed between all, then this should help keep the group working towards common goals and feeling mutually responsible for achieving them. Then, the team itself should help coerce errant members, because everyone's work is interdependent.

How the organization can affect team management

Because it is hard enough to recruit the functional skills for the core team, balancing the interpersonal skills so that there is a blend that will cover the eight role types may be like looking for needles in a haystack. The mental ability, creativity, and personality factors needed for multimedia development almost seem to work against teamwork and project management.

But understanding the blend that can provide a good team mix is a tool in itself that should help you analyse some of the problems you'll experience better than before. It may provide some answers to the need for key extra resources that might have to be brought in at various stages as cement, for example.

In Chapter 2 specific examples were given to show how the structure of the organization you work for can affect your role as project manager. It can influence your team management if the in-house team members report to a functional boss as well as yourself. The team members can have split loyalties which may affect their work on the project. They may be pulled to work in different directions by both of you and find it difficult to reconcile their duties to the project and the company at large. The company management needs to recognize this potential conflict and define the respective roles for the functional manager and the project manager so that the team is clear how they should relate to both.

The team will need frequent meetings to communicate how individual parts of the project are progressing and for you to pass on detailed information of the clients' latest reactions. The organization can facilitate these meetings by having meeting rooms which are accessible and well laid out. People can take communication seriously or not, but the environment can help provide the right stimulus for good communication. There is nothing as frustrating as holding a team meeting in the corridor or in part of an open plan space with the constant noise of telephones ringing, copying machines, and interruptions from other people. Clear communication in a pleasant room takes a shorter time and disrupts not only your own team's work less but also other people's work less, than the disorganized, patchy communication that takes place in crowded environments.

The layout of a meeting room can influence contributions from the team so you need to recognize this and organize the room accordingly. A round table or a circle of chairs gives the best non-hierarchical feel to a meeting and encourages everyone to contribute. If you are trying to engender an open, constructive team culture, the circle will help. An oblong table encourages a hierarchical feel particularly if you sit at the head of it in the traditional leader position. If you have no choice in this, at least sit on one side instead of at the top of the table.

Pointing out environmental factors is not popular with companies although they are one of the few factors they can control or influence. Take the previous example of the graphics artist who had antisocial hours which made it difficult for the rest of the team. He or she may well have said the reason for the hours was that it was more productive when it was quiet in the office than when it was hectic. In this case, how would you deal with the situation?

Open plan offices are common in multimedia companies and the variety of tasks and people needed creates a busy, communication-rich environment. This in turn creates noise. The type of task people have to complete affects the level of concentration. Multimedia is characterized by specialists constructing pieces of the project. Concentration is needed here. There is also a good deal of demonstration and discussion to refine the parts as they are integrated as well as general meetings to communicate both inside the team and to a larger group of company management and clients. It seems self-evident that the environment needs to support contemplative work and communication.

If environmental problems are genuinely affecting the performance of your team, the least you can do is voice your concerns to company management with any suggestions that could help in the short term. Perhaps working from home for a number of days with definite meetings in the office on regular occasions might suit some parts of the project. Perhaps reallocation of members of the team within the building or rooms could help. Perhaps the team themselves could come up with some suggestions.

De Marco and Lister correlated environmental factors with best programming performance in their surveys of programming projects. If the space was quiet, private, large and protected from interruptions, performance was on average 2.6 times better. Of course, this was part of a larger context of research and the ability of the programmers was also taken into account. Their description of how interruptions affect concentration flow is interesting. It takes about 15 minutes for someone to focus at the right level of concentration for intellectual work to flow. If interrupted, it takes another 15 minutes to settle back into the same level. This means that phones ringing, colleagues interacting, and enquiries can be extremely disruptive for productivity. This can certainly affect your project. If there are any strategies that you can use to influence environmental factors, use them.

There are laws governing the ergonomic layout for workstations, the amount of space, lighting conditions and the amount of use of screens. These vary from country to country. There are concerns over issues of eyestrain, repetitive strain injury, the effect of emissions on skin diseases and on pregnant women. As project manager it is in your interest to keep abreast of the regulations to ensure conformity. The health and safety aspects of the environment are the employer's responsibilities but the welfare of your team is yours for the duration of the project.

THEORY INTO PRACTICE 14

Think of the project manager or manager you have admired most. List the functional/technical, decision-making/problem-solving and interpersonal skills he/she had. List any weaknesses. Then list your skills in these areas together with your weaknesses. Finally, draft the same list again but write it from the perspectives of your team members or colleagues, or, even better, ask them to fill the list in for you. What would they consider your strengths and weaknesses in a management role?

Compare the lists and decide on your own development needs from them.

Summary

- The aim is to create a good team culture of cooperation and effectiveness.
- Team leadership means representing the team to management as well as setting the direction for the project.
- As project manager you'll need to employ a variety of management styles to suit different circumstances.
- Research shows that some of the personality traits of teams like multimedia teams can cause problems for performance management.
- The environment can affect the team's performance.

Recommended reading

De Marco T. and Lister T. (1987). *Peopleware: Productive Projects and Teams*. New York: Dorset House Publishing Co.

Katzenbach J.R. and Smith D.K. (1993). *The Wisdom of Teams: Creating the High-Performance Organisation*. Boston, MA: Harvard Business School Press

Belbin R.M. (1981). *Management Teams: Why They Succeed or Fail*. Oxford: Butterworth-Heinemann Ltd

Belbin R.M. (1993). *Team Roles at Work*. Oxford: Butterworth-Heinemann

Phillips N. (1992). *Managing International Teams*. London: Pitman Publishing

Tjosvold D. (1991). *Team Organisation: An Enduring Competitive Advantage*. Chichester: Wiley

Honey P. (1988). *Improve Your People Skills*. London: Institute of Personnel Management

CHAPTER 13

AUDIO ASSET PRODUCTION

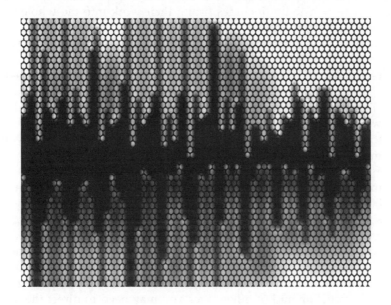

Project manager's responsibilities

■ To book the studio and the artist
■ To make sure scripts are ready
■ To make sure that the recording session is successful
■ To ensure that the material is prepared to the correct specification.
■ To understand the processes involved in producing this kind of asset

Managing asset production

There is some debate about the amount of detail that a manager needs to understand in order to manage the production of assets. In conventional media areas, managers often come up 'through the ranks' and have done the job of the people they manage. In multimedia this is unlikely to happen simply because of its multi-disciplinary nature. A project manager might have worked as a television producer, a trainer, a graphics artist or a computer programmer rather than as all of these. So a detailed knowledge of one area under your control could be counterbalanced by complete ignorance of another. Multimedia production not only integrates these disciplines, it also has to balance them.

In managing the production of assets, and of computer software, you could be working with people in the core team for your project, or you could be hiring in people or facilities for only a relatively small part of it. Your responsibility includes fitting their work into the whole project. This extended team will be less aware of your overall plan and may be less involved and committed. In some cases, such as if you were to hire a video crew for a single day's shoot or book a sound studio for a voice-over recording, they may have very little knowledge of multimedia and its special requirements and idiosyncrasies. Because multimedia involves slightly different technologies to mainstream media there will be occasions when normal practices will not be exactly right and a knowledge, or access to knowledge, of both will make it easier for you to explain your requirements and concerns.

If you, as project manager, know something of the processes involved in creating and manipulating the assets for your project, you are in a much better position to help the asset creator to achieve the result you want. In some cases you might need to be able to unravel technical jargon to do so and you will often find that the level of respect specialists have for you, and their willingness to go that extra mile for you, is influenced by how well you communicate with them and how well they think you understand their point of view. Sometimes you will need simply to point people in the right direction and in other cases you may need to direct them specifically to do what you want. It will depend on their abilities, how well you share ideas and how flexible your vision of the result can be. Experience will make this easier but background knowledge will help you on your way.

In the course of the technically oriented chapters of this book you will be introduced to some of the basic principles and terminologies so that you will be better equipped to achieve what you want. Although it is impossible to cover everything, the aim of these chapters includes pointers to those vital differences inherent in multimedia.

Sound principles

During the course of making a multimedia production there will be, by definition, assets to be created or manipulated which make use of time-based media such as sound and video. In these cases, unlike text and graphics, you are likely to make use of specialist facilities with personnel that you hire to work on your assets. Video will be discussed in the next chapter and this chapter describes the processes involved in dealing with audio from a practical point of view.

The basic idea behind this chapter (and the other practical/technical ones) is to provide you, as a producer or project manager, with enough background on the technical processes to enable you to hold your own in discussions with experts. It will also make your use of specialized facilities more interesting and rewarding. Of course, depending on your background, you might already be an expert in one of these fields. It may also be the case that, in a small development company, you will have the opportunity to 'be' the expert and carry out some of the audio-visual manipulation yourself. So treat our use of the word 'you' lightly since if you hire an external facility to record, mix or edit, it will be an engineer actually carrying out these tasks.

The aim in writing these chapters will be achieved if, next time you go into a sound suite and the engineer asks if you want the sound limited, or what sample rate you want, you can tell him or her, or even discuss it, with confidence. If you hire a facility and an engineer, make use of their knowledge and do not be self-conscious about asking advice.

Before the session

It is most likely that your first use of a sound studio will be to record a voice-over for your program. Music and drama are some other possible kinds of material you might record but this chapter will concentrate on recording a single voice. The basic principles are the same but music and drama have the bells, the whistles and the fairy dust. When you decide to record a voice you need three things: the script, the voice and the studio. You will also have thought about how you want the voice to sound and this will have influenced your choice of voice-over talent.

With a voice-over artist you might have decided to use a famous actor or actress and would like to include their name on the cover. Alternatively your voice-over artist might be a person who specializes in being a voice. In some circumstances you might do it yourself or use a friend or someone in your company who has experience, perhaps as a radio presenter. For the first stages of a project it is not unusual to make a guide voice track yourself which will be replaced with a professional one later.

Unless you know someone already, your route to your voice will be through an agency. There are many who specialize in providing voices, usually for radio advertising, and they will have both famous actors and professional voices on their books.

The voice-over artist will like to have a clean script, probably double spaced so that changes can be made clearly. The artist will often mark in the emphasis to be used when reading. You should send the script to the artist a few days before the recording if you can. The script should be printed out to avoid paragraphs going over a page boundary. The paper should be stiff so that it does not rustle. You should check pronunciations of any unusual words, especially proper names, and if you are producing the session you should be sure about every word in the script. Be prepared to make changes to make the script easier to read. Often the voice-over artist will make very useful suggestions about this. Besides the possible direct benefit, you will be helping to create a good working atmosphere and that will help the artist perform better.

With any luck you will find that your voice-over talent can read virtually anything you put before him or her. Many of these people spend the whole day reading one kind of script or another and can cope with most things. Multimedia, or at least the interactivity part of it, is so different from their usual work of advertising and corporate videos that telling them a little about the project will pay dividends.

You can work out the timings for the speech yourself before you go into the studio. All you need to do is read it at about the right pace and time yourself. A rough guide is about 200 words a minute.

You can find your studio either by asking the professional studio body (such as the Association of Professional Recording Studios in the UK) or from a yearbook. Word of mouth recommendation or a studio you saw credited on another product is also a useful guide. When you book the studio, as with any outside facility, you will need to agree the rate, how overruns are charged, what happens if you under-run and the arrangements for paying. You need to tell them what format you want to take the recording away on and whether you will edit the recording yourself or will ask the facility to do so.

The background

The processes for recording sound date back over a century. Since sound, as we hear it, is the result of fluctuations in air pressure – which cause our ear drums to vibrate and which, if the frequency is right, we hear as sounds – the early methods were mechanical. In the earliest kinds of recorders you spoke, or rather shouted, into a horn and the power of your voice caused a diaphragm to vibrate. A stylus was connected to the diaphragm and this distorted a metal or wax surface over which it moved. To play the sound back you reversed the process and listened to sound coming out of the horn.

The microphone and loudspeaker are still the mechanical components of sound reproduction. They work by detecting or creating the movement of diaphragms and moving air. For the same reasons the microphone and the loudspeaker are likely to be the final components to go digital (if they ever do). To introduce some terminology to help you communicate with the specialists, a microphone is often called a mic (pronounced mike) and loudspeakers are speakers.

In the studio

You will find that a recording studio will almost always be in two parts: the control room and the studio itself. The studio may be called the booth if it is small and used only for recording voices. There will usually be a glass window between the two rooms.

Recording studios are strange places. You might find that no two surfaces are parallel because this stops sounds bouncing between the walls and setting up resonances and standing waves (where the room acts like a big organ pipe). Legend has it that some enthusiastic builders thought that the plans for a sound studio were wrong because the corners were not right angles. So they kindly corrected the error.

The windows, while not being parallel either, will have double or even triple glazing, and the walls, doors and even the furniture will look as if it is either carpeted or designed by someone who likes to hang boxes on the wall. This is to reduce the reflections (for which read 'echo' or 'reverberation') in the room. The difference between echo and reverberation (reverb) is simply in the time between the echoes. Reverb sounds smooth and continuous because the echoes are too close together for us to distinguish them. Unless you want to remake 'Heartbreak Hotel' or set your projects in mountainous valleys you are unlikely to use echo as such. If there is no reverberation around a sound then we say the sound (or the room) is 'dead' as opposed to 'live'. In fact such a room is not usually completely dead (or anechoic) because that would make it almost impossible to talk in. We need some room reverberation around a recording to make it seem natural and something of the sound of our own voice to help us speak. With music, especially rock music, this reverb is normally added afterwards using reverb units (the modern version of the echo chamber – which was simply a room with hard walls). This reverb should not favour some frequencies of sound over others. Reverb that does is called 'coloured' and sounds unnatural. The natural small amount of reverberation in a room, together with any other background sounds, is sometimes called ambience or ambient noise.

To record a voice the microphone is usually placed about 18 inches to two feet in front of the speaker's mouth in a reasonably dead room. If the mic is too close it will pick up lip smacks and other bodily noises. If the mic is too far away the sound will be too live, which means there will be too much reverberation.

When you get close to some kinds of mic you suffer from a phenomenon called bass tip-up or proximity effect. This is, as the name suggests, an increase in the bass component of the voice and it is caused by cancellation of high frequencies when the source of the sound, your mouth, is too close to the diaphragm of the microphone.

In general the positioning of the mic in front of the speaker is crucial in getting a good sound and an experienced engineer will know where to move the mic to avoid popping and breath noises and the notorious sibilance.

The mic will probably be on a stand with a gallows arm or boom suspending it over the table – assuming your speaker is sitting at a table. Some people will sound better, and project more, if they stand up. If the speaker is using a table then be careful about where he or she puts the script. It will probably be under the mic and so you could hear the paper rustling. Less obviously, the relatively hard surface of the paper will affect the acoustic around the voice. The movement of paper, and the movement of the speaker's head as he or she reads, can change the high frequency component of the voice if the mic is close.

There are basically three types of microphone and their names come from the shape of their sensitivity, or polar response curves, as the following diagrams show. The further the curve is from the ball on the end of the mic, the more sensitive it is in that direction. The reasons for the names will soon be apparent. In all these cases you can assume that this curve is the same in three dimensions, a shape turned on the axis of the microphone.

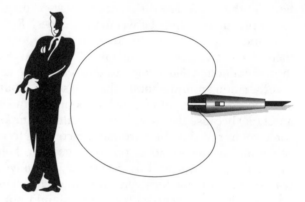

A cardioid microphone.

A cardioid mic will pick up more sound from in front than anywhere else. It is called cardioid because the polar response curve is shaped like a heart.

A figure of eight.

A bi-directional mic is sensitive on two sides, and this is often called a figure of eight.

An omni.

Finally there is the omni, which is equally sensitive all around. Some microphones can be switched between all these response types. You should be able to speak closer to an omni mic than you would with a cardioid.

To record a voice any of these microphone types can be used. A cardioid will have less pick-up from the room but may suffer from popping. Popping, as the name suggests, is the effect caused by blasts of air from the mouth hitting the microphone. In fact it is sometimes also called blasting. This is at its worst with the letter P and a good test is the old tongue twister 'Peter Piper'. If the mic is very close, just breathing out may cause a noise. Most studios will put a wind shield in front of mics to stop this. To a large extent these problems can be reduced by having the mic slightly to one side rather than straight in front and this is called being 'off-axis'.

During the recording you, as producer, will be in the control room. The speaker may, or may not, be listening to the sound of his or her own voice in the headphones. Different people will want to hear themselves at different levels and this can be critical to their ability to read well if they are inexperienced. Giving the speaker a volume control for the headphones is a good idea.

Most people's speaking voices will have quite a wide range between the quietest and loudest sounds. This is called the dynamic range. The engineer can control this dynamic range manually, by adjusting the volume control fader in the control room, or electronics can be used to automatically compress (not to be confused with data compression) or limit the signal. Compressors and limiters reduce the dynamic range of a sound. They are a sophisticated version of an automatic volume control in a tape recorder. A limiter is set to tightly control the volume of sounds that exceed a certain value whereas a compressor operates over a wider range of levels but more gently. It is difficult to describe the effect of using these devices, but you will find some examples on the CD-ROM.

You would choose to limit or compress a voice, and therefore reduce its dynamic range, for a number of reasons.

You are most likely to choose to make the compression or limiting inaudible to the listener, and most often limiting is used to catch and reduce a few bursts of the loudest moments in the speech. In this way you can bring up the level, that is make louder, the whole speech without the few high points causing problems by overloading the electronics. With a digital signal, where overloading causes more distortion than with analog, limiting is useful as a back-stop to prevent accidental overload, especially if you can only do one take.

Both devices, but especially compression, can be used for effect. Because our ear's response to sound is not linear we tend to hear loud sounds with less dynamic range than quiet ones. You can fool the ear into thinking something is louder than it really is by compressing it. This is also useful if you want to put speech over some music and it is important that the speech is heard all the time without sounding shouted.

If your sound is finally going to be played in an 8-bit system then reducing the dynamic range will make the 8-bit playback sound better because there will be fewer quiet parts to disappear into the noise. For similar reasons, anything that will be played in a noisy environment, such as a point-of-information kiosk at a trade show, should be compressed to make it easier to hear.

If you are in doubt about using limiters or compressors, a basic recommendation is to use a little limiting to catch the loudest peaks. If the recording is quiet, with no background hiss or reverb, you can always compress it afterwards. However, you should remember that compression tends to exaggerate reverberation and you have to be wary of this. If there is a high amount of background noise then compression and limiting will noticeably affect this, leading to an effect called pumping. An example of this is also on the CD. If the response time of the compressor/limiter is too slow, you will hear it pushing and pulling the sound as the amplification goes up and down. If it is too fast, it will distort the waveform of the sound.

Volume, otherwise known as levels, has been mentioned already but how do you measure it? There are two kinds of meters in use and they are called VUs and PPMs. VU (pronounced Vee-You) stands for Volume Unit and PPM stands for Peak Programme Meter. VUs are the most common although they do not really tell you anything exact about the signal. However, an experienced engineer can judge the level of something very well with a VU and it arguably gives a good representation of the loudness

VU and PPM level meters.

of the sound. A VU meter will move around very quickly. Even though a VU has a red band at the top (especially if it is a real moving pointer type of meter) you will quite often see it running into the red. This is not necessarily an indication of overload, especially in an analog system.

A PPM is a more exact kind of meter, and was developed by the BBC to control levels being fed into transmitters, although it is also used in recording. What a PPM does tell you is the actual peak signal going onto the tape or into the transmitter. PPMs are designed to have a fast rise time and a slower release. This helps you read them. BBC PPMs also have an integration time (in other words they are not measuring the instantaneous level but an average over a fraction of a second) which means that they will not detect very short peaks. This could be a problem for digital systems but in practice, even though a short peak may be distorted if you look at the waveform, it will usually sound fine because the ear may not hear a very short burst of distortion.

It is more usual to find VU meters and PPMs using lights to show levels but some would argue that a meter with a needle is easier to read. A particularly useful type of PPM is the dual stereo PPM which has two meters side by side, each with two needles. One shows the left and right channels on two coincident needles while the other shows the sum and difference signals for stereo.

Besides level meters and a compressor/limiter, there will be equalization or EQ in the channel of the desk through which the voice passes. This is a glorified bass and treble control and will help the engineer get a suitable sound out of the voice. Because of the ear's sensitivity you can often make a voice sound closer, have more 'presence', by slightly boosting frequencies around 2 KHz.

Working with your voice-over artist

Your recording might be used against a video, a sequence of still images, or in isolation. If you are recording a voice track that goes with a sequence of stills or even over a single image then there will be no problem in recording the voice without any reference to the sequence. This is sometimes called 'wild'. In this case you can work your way through the script, one discrete section at a time, rehearsing and then recording. If the artist makes a mistake (fluffs), all you need to do is ask him or her to go back a sentence and read it again. This is best done as you go along rather than at the end. Anything that will be heard in a continuous sequence should be recorded as nearly as possible in that sequence so as to avoid subtle changes in tone or speed which would be very apparent over an edit. You can mark up your copy of the script with timings for paragraphs and you should also note where any fluffs occur and how many takes it took to get it right.

You can mark takes by using a diagonal line like this / which you mark in at the point you will probably use for an edit, or the beginning of the sentence. If there are two takes you can put in two lines // and you

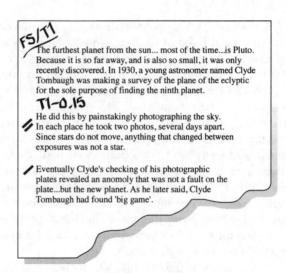

Marking a script.

may also need to note timings by the lines. You can get timings from a stopwatch, or better still from the timer on the tape machine or digital recording system. DAT machines have a built-in time code which is recorded on the tape (optionally with professional machines) and this is very useful for finding takes. A take which only gets through a few words and then falters is known as a false start (FS) and is not usually marked as a take. To assist editing, you should always record a little before where you know you will want to edit, to allow the speaker to get up to speed.

There is another way of dealing with takes, and that is to roll the tape back, play the preceding sentence and switch into record as the artist speaks the lines again. This method avoids editing afterwards.

You might be recording a voice-over that has to be timed to a moving picture. In these cases you could bring in the computer and run the movie or animation or whatever, but an alternative is to record the movie onto a videocassette. In this way you can make use of a facility which has recording and mix to picture capability for TV or films.

Other things to remember about the session: check the spelling of the artists' names for the credits and make sure that you have agreed the appropriate rights. If you have to go back to the artists later to sort out rights, you are at a disadvantage and you cannot assume that because they came to the recording they have granted you the use of the material you require.

What can I ask the studio to do for me?

A recording studio will be able to do far more than just record your voice-over. If you want them to do so they can edit the takes together under your direction (and sometimes without) to produce a finished master. They can take your voice, script and music tracks and mix them together to produce a finished track for your application. Some facilities can even digitally compress the track into ADPCM or MPEG audio for you. It is your choice as to how much you ask the facility to do, and how much you do yourself. This will depend on factors such as your ability and your budget, because the facility will need to be paid and this is an above-the-line cost.

Mono and stereo

A lot of sound in multimedia is mono, which means single channel. This is because mono sound, by definition, takes up half the space of stereo sound. If you have the capability, stereo will be useful to you because, rather like moving images, it helps you build up the effect you want to convey in your application. If you decide to make your application with stereo sound you will need to know whether it might also be used in mono, such as for a consumer application. This is because a little care needs to be taken to make sure that stereo recordings are mono compatible and still sound right when the left and right channels are added together to make mono.

Stereophonic sound means two speakers. We allocate a position to a sound by a combination of time delay – the sound reaching one ear before the other – and level. Using level to give positioning is by far the most common way and in mixing (which we will come on to later) the balance engineer will position sounds between the speakers by changing the amount of the sound fed to the left and right channels. This is known as panning and the control on a mixing desk that does it is called a pan pot (for panning potentiometer). Most of the time this simple panning of sounds will work perfectly.

When recording a real sound in stereo things are a little different. There are three main ways of recording in stereo. They are called the spaced pair, the crossed pair and the M and S pair. The pair refers to a pair of microphones.

A spaced pair will be two omnidirectional microphones positioned several feet apart. For distant sounds, like a crowd at a sports event, this

A spaced pair.

will be fine but the sound will tend to have a hole in the middle since, confusingly, a sound close to the microphones but between them is probably not close enough to either.

A crossed pair.

A crossed pair is also known as a Blumlein pair, after the EMI engineer who invented the technique. You take two cardioid directional microphones and place them as close together as you can but pointing 90 degrees apart. This gives a good stereo image and no hole in the middle. For the best results the microphones need to have identical responses.

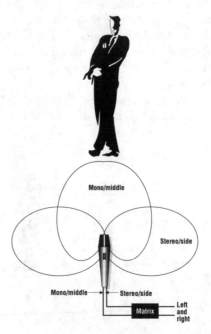

The M and S method.

You can do a simple calculation to show that M (which is mono, left + right) and S (stereo, left – right) can be combined, or matrixed, back to left and right. L is M + S and R is M – S: you can ignore the factor of two here. This method combines a cardioid microphone pointing forwards and a figure of eight microphone pointing sideways. This system has several advantages: mono compatibility is assured; the stereo image is very good, especially at the centre. The microphones do not have to have an exactly matched response. You can in fact buy single microphones which use this technique and yet give left and right outputs as in the diagram.

One additional factor to consider is that, strictly speaking, a sound in the centre will sound twice as loud as one at the extreme left or right when the channels are combined into mono. This should be a factor in the mixing and most panning controls compensate for this. If you want to position a voice off to one side for effect, or to have two voices discussing something, then the best position in the stereo sound field is halfway between the centre and a loudspeaker. This will also give you a good mono signal.

Tricks with sounds

There is a wide range of what are called psycho-acoustical effects which affect the way we hear sound but it might be useful to describe a few potentially useful, or awkward, ones.

The ear's sensitivity to high and low frequencies diminishes at low volume levels. The 'loudness' button on your hi-fi amplifier takes account of this and lifts treble and bass to make it easier to listen at low levels. Another effect of this phenomenon is that if you take two identical recordings and then attenuate (drop the volume of) one, it will seem to lose top, or high, frequencies.

If you want to give a cheap imitation of a sound coming from behind the listener then it can be done by making the sound to the two loudspeakers out of phase. It might be that because we cannot detect a position for an out of phase sound, many people think it is coming from behind them. 'Out of phase' is the exact electrical opposite of mono and is actually difficult to achieve except in a professional sound system. The CD includes an example of in and out of phase sound so you can compare them.

You may be tempted to work with headphones rather than speakers in order to cut down noise leakage and avoid irritating other people, especially if you are carrying out editing yourself in the office. Beware, however, that when it comes to judging sound quality and the balance of a mix, headphones are notoriously unreliable.

One way in which we detect the loudness of a sound in the real world is by feeling the pressure of air on our bodies. For this reason it is dangerous to listen to sound loudly in headphones. The air pressure clue to loudness will not be there and there is a tendency to turn up the volume to the ears to compensate.

Digital basics

Digital technology has entered most aspects of sound recording and editing. The basics of digitization are that the continuously varying sound waveform (the electrical version of the vibrating mic diaphragm) is sampled. This means that many times a second the instantaneous voltage of the waveform is measured. Professional audio is usually sampled at 44.1 KHz, which is the sample rate for compact disc. For reference, middle A on a piano is currently standardized at 440 Hz and when you double the frequency of a sound, its pitch goes up an octave. (This standard slowly changes and in Mozart's time middle A was 430 Hz.)

The highest frequency of sound that can be faithfully reproduced by a particular sample rate is half that sample rate (as discovered by a Swedish scientist named Nyquist) so the range of frequencies, called the bandwidth, of a compact disc is 22.05 KHz.

The 22.05 KHz bandwidth of a compact disc should be enough to reproduce all the frequencies you could hear. Some people, however, say that this is not the case but in multimedia you are unlikely to have a better delivery sample rate to play with. Incidentally, DAT has 48 KHz as its standard sample rate but most DAT machines can also record at 44.1 (after a while you stop saying KHz every time) and, if you have a choice, this is the better sample rate. Any compact discs you include in your mixes will have to be at 44.1 and ought to stay that way. Having said that, it appears that 48 KHz might be the sample rate for the next generation of compact discs.

CDs and DAT share a bit depth of 16 bits. This means that the sound can, in theory, be digitized with a precision of 16 bits, or 65 536 levels. Again, with the exception of the usual sceptics, this will allow you to hear the sound without errors. You can work out the background noise of a digital signal from the bit depth since the maximum error between the 'real' sound and the digitized version of it is half the minimum step in the digitization. Since 16 bit has 65 536 steps and 8 bit has only 255 you can see that 8 bit will be 256 times as noisy as 16 bit. You can hear examples of the difference that is caused by different sample rates and bit depth on the CD.

Fortunately our ears do not respond to sound levels in a linear fashion, which is why a logarithmic measurement, the decibel or dB, is used to measure it. This means that we do not actually hear 256 times more noise. In fact the signal to noise ratio of a 16-bit system is 98 dB (which basically means you will never usually hear it) whereas for an 8-bit one it is 50 dB. Since every 6 dB increment makes a sound twice as loud this means that 8 bit is eight times as noisy as 16 bit. Also the noise only occurs in the sound, not in the silences (unlike analog hiss), but it will be very noticeable on slight noises like rustles, so these should be removed from a recording destined for 8 bit.

With digital audio recording a balance has to be struck between recording at so high a level that you risk overloading, which means clipping the waveform and distortion, and recording so quietly that noise becomes noticeable. Professional systems have now started to record sound with 20 or even 24 bits (24 bits means that the noise is 150 dBs down, which gives the engineers the freedom to record at a safe level without noise). For distribution the sound will be converted back to 16 bit so it can go on a CD.

To convert from 16 to 8 bits the procedure is simply to divide each sample value by 256 and round the errors. From 8 to 16 you multiply the sample value by 256. This will, unfortunately, also multiply the errors that cause noise, so your 16-bit version will not sound any better than the 8-bit original.

The sample rate of a recording can be changed by recalculating the samples and most audio editing and processing software will allow you to do this. There are professional boxes which will do this as well.

For reference, here are bit depths and sample rates that you might come across and where you might find them. The format called 1630 is based on U-Matic tapes and is now used mostly for mastering CDs but it was an original digital audio recording format.

- 44.1 KHz 16 bit – CD, DAT, 1630 and digital audio editing systems. As a rule of thumb this kind of digitized audio takes up 10 megabytes per minute. It is also known as 'Red Book' after the name of the standard for compact discs.
- 48 KHz 16 bit – early digital videotape formats, DAT, digital tracks on LaserDisks and some digital audio editing systems.
- 44.056 KHz 16 bit – digital audio used with NTSC video on 1630 systems but also digital editing systems. This one can catch you out because it is close to 44.1 so watch for it.
- 22 KHz 8 bit (or lower) – personal computer sound.
- 44.1 KHz 20 bit (or more) – some professional audio systems and digital videotape recorders.
- 37.8 KHz 16 bit – intermediate format for production of CD-i ADPCM sound.
- 17.9 KHz 16 bit – intermediate format for production of CD-i ADPCM sound.
- 32 KHz 12 bit – long play DAT.

There are what are termed DASH systems (Digital Audio Stationary Head) which you could come across in a recording studio but these also use either 32, 44.1 or 48 for their sampling rate. Sony used to sell a digital audio add-on for their Betamax video recorders called the F1. This was a 44.1 KHz 12-bit system. Other digital audio formats you will come across are: MPEG audio, which is an efficiently compressed audio format used, with differing names, for Digital Compact Cassette, radio news contribution links down digital phone lines (ISDN); MUSICAM, which is the original name for the higher quality types of MPEG audio; NICAM, which is a 12-bit system used in television for distribution and transmission.

Aliasing

The Nyquist theorem says that in order to accurately digitize a sound of frequency n you must sample at a frequency of at least 2n.

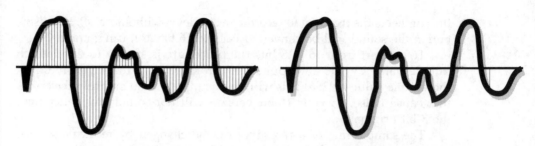

More samples than the Nyquist limit. Fewer samples than the Nyquist limit.

If this rule is not followed strange results can occur. The phenomenon is called aliasing, and the result of this is that the digital signal does not accurately represent the analog original. If there are frequencies higher than n in the signal that you digitize with frequency 2n there will be spurious samples in the result which will usually sound like squeaking.

This aliasing is a particular problem if you down-sample, which is where you take a sound digitized at, say, 22 KHz and shift it down to 11 KHz. You will think you can hear sounds of higher frequency than 5.5 KHz in the result but they are not sounds from the input but aliasing artefacts. For this reason you need to filter before you down-sample. Not all software does this, and you will hear the distortion that results. Down-sampling and aliasing can also introduce other sounds. One instance is if the original recording contains a small amount of television line whistle at 15 KHz. This will be almost inaudible, but if it is shifted down by aliasing to around 7 KHz, which can happen in a 22 KHz down-sampled sound, it will suddenly become audible because the ear is more sensitive at 7 KHz than at 15.

Doing it on hard disk

Tapeless recording and editing systems are now common in audio, and systems are even available for desktop computers. It is possible to record straight onto hard disk, and some audio facilities will do just that for you. These same facilities will edit your audio and prepare the tracks for use in a computer system by compressing them to ADPCM or MPEG audio (or whatever is appropriate).

Where the hard disk systems come into their own is for editing. The general principles are the same but some things are easier and more versatile in a digital editing system.

Editing

Tape editing used to be done by physically cutting the tape with scissors or a razor blade. This process cannot be done with audio cassettes because the tape is not accessible in the machine but quarter-inch tape can more easily be handled. If you are editing yourself then you rock and roll the tape backwards and forwards across the playback head in order to locate exactly the point at which you wish to cut. This is sometimes called scrubbing. Then you mark the back of the tape with a chinagraph pencil and slice the tape with blade or scissors. You join the bits you want together with adhesive tape. The adhesive tape is slightly narrower than the recording tape and has a non-leaking adhesive. A specially machined block is used to align the tape.

Some digital audio systems faithfully recreate the scissors and razor blade experience. In fact one tape format actually allowed you to physically cut the tape. In a hard disk-based digital system the sound is manipulated by working with a representation of the audio waveform on the computer screen. The sound is cut and pasted in much the same way as text in a word processor. One useful feature of professional digital systems is the ability to do a mix across the joins, which can be used to make an other-wise impossible edit work.

Some places are easier to cut than others. You can fool the ear by cutting into a sharp sound, a transient like a bang or a drum sound. By doing this you do not usually notice any cutting off of the preceding sound. In fact the incoming sound is more critical than the outgoing in most edits. For speech some sounds make for better cuts than others; 'p' and 'k' and 't' work well whereas 's' is quite difficult.

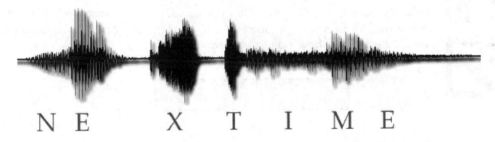

N E   X   T   I   M   E

You should listen to speech patterns to help with your editing. Many people miss out letters from their speech. If you were to say 'next time' you would probably not pronounce both 't' sounds and would actually say 'nextime'. You can take advantage of these truncations to find places to join speech together. You will even find that just looking at the waveform will help you find places because you can easily identify pauses and consonants by the shape of the waveform.

Rhythm is important in speech, and your edits should cut around that rhythm, not across it. Although people do shift the rhythm of their speech, most of the time an edit will feel more natural if a speech rhythm is preserved. Rhythm obviously is very important in editing music, and some of the same rules apply to music and speech. A few milliseconds can make all the difference to a music edit. You can hear an example of 'good' and 'bad' editing on the CD.

It is not true to say that a good edit is joy to hear – because you will not hear a good edit.

Judging quality

Sometimes you will be required to produce assets to a certain quality. This might be specifically mentioned in a contract. It is difficult to define the quality of audio in objective terms. You could say that the frequency response will be one thing and the signal-to-noise ratio another, but these facts will not cover how well a presenter reads a script or how well mixed is a piece of music. The best course, should this issue arise, is to say you will apply 'appropriate' standards or even 'broadcast' standards. You, and your clients or customers, will be able to compare with what you hear on radio and on CDs. It is important for clients to realize, however, that sound heard on a computer will often be of poorer quality than broadcast simply because the computer is not capable of that quality of reproduction, no matter how well the material is prepared. On the bright side, you will usually find that the quality issue can be handled by comparing your results with other similar applications.

THEORY INTO PRACTICE 15

Take the editing practice recording on the CD and, in whatever editing tool you have, try to make the speaker say the opposite of what he originally said. Listen to see how natural this sounds.

Summary

- This chapter has looked at the background to sound recording and explains what you should expect when using a professional audio facility to record voices for your multimedia application. It has outlined the preparation you need to make to prepare for the session.
- The kind of microphone used, the way it is positioned and how the sound is treated will affect the way your recording sounds.
- Stereo positioning is usually achieved by adjusting loudness between the two channels.
- During recording, scripts should be marked up for later editing.
- In digitizing, the highest frequency that can be digitized with a sample rate of 2n is n.

Recommended reading

Bordwell D. and Thompson K. (1993). *Film Art: An Introduction*. New York: McGraw-Hill

Moore B.C.J. (1977). *Introduction to the Psychology of Hearing*. London: Macmillan

Pohlman K.C. (1989). *Principles of Digital Audio*. Indianapolis: Howard H. Sams

Watkinson J. (1988). *Art of Digital Audio*. London: Focal Press

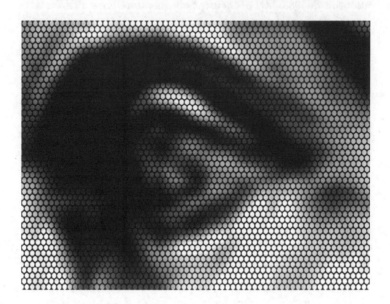

CHAPTER 14

VIDEO ASSET PRODUCTION

Project manager's responsibilities

- To book crews and subjects for recording interviews
- To explain to clients what quality of result to expect on the desktop
- To make sure that the recording session is successful
- To make sure tapes are logged and prepared for editing
- To ensure that the material is prepared to the correct specification
- To choose the most appropriate way of compressing video for the application and make sure it is done to an appropriate standard
- To understand the processes involved in producing this kind of asset

Managing asset production

The previous chapter has explored the production of sound in multimedia, paying special attention to the use of external facilities. For video, similar arrangements are likely to be made. It is possible that the video content of a multimedia application will be shot using a domestic camcorder and edited on the desktop but in many cases the budget will allow a professional facility to be used and the production values will require it.

One crucial aspect of video production is the amount of preparation required. While for sound it is quite feasible for the producer to turn up to interview someone having made the arrangements by telephone a few hours before, for video there is much more that needs to be done and more people to involve. This chapter concentrates on the set up for an interview because that is the most straightforward and, arguably, the most common use of video in multimedia. You might wish to shoot drama, or work on location, but unless you already have experience in these areas you are advised to hire specialist help to direct the shoot and therefore to manage it. Location work is particularly difficult because of the range of permissions you need from people like the police and local authority and because of the vagaries of the weather.

One managerial issue that rears its head in video more than in audio is the question of whether clients should attend the shoot or the edit. There is no simple answer to this but your relationship with the clients should influence you. The main reason why clients should attend is to avoid arguments about changes later since changes in a video are probably the most expensive to fix. This, of course, is a strong argument for making an offline edit and letting the clients see it. If you are completely confident that the clients respect your abilities then you might not need to involve them but if you think later changes are likely, and if you have agreed a fixed price for the project, then invite them. You should emphasize the costs associated with changing video after the edit.

Moving pictures are a recent entrant into computing, although computers have been a part of video for a long time, at least on the professional and broadcast television side. Engineers have been devising ways to manipulate and create images for broadcast television for a long time, starting with graphics and control of equipment. Today computers play a part in every aspect of broadcast television production.

Just as video is starting to take over as the dominant medium in the multimedia mix, so multimedia is beginning tentatively to make its way into television. Video on demand is essentially a multimedia database system for the home, and prime time television programmes are using desktop computers to generate graphics as part of the editing process.

Television itself dates back to the 1920s, and moving film goes back into the 19th century. John Logie Baird devised a mechanical system of sending moving pictures down a wire, and through the airwaves, at a time when radio itself was in its infancy. Electronic scanning took over from his wheels and cogs and the BBC launched the first regular scheduled television service in 1936 to a handful of very rich viewers in the southern part of England. A television set then cost more than a family car.

This chapter deals with the way in which a television picture is made and how you might record and manipulate it on its way into the computer. Some background on the way a video signal is built up, and the differences between the various formats and standards, will help you work with video. As with the last chapter on audio it will concentrate on the kind of equipment and techniques that you, as a multimedia professional and practitioner, will come across when you make use of video.

Basic principles of video

Because our brains are easily fooled, we see a rapid succession of still images as a continuous stream and, with the right images, we see movement. The movies work like this, by showing us tiny slices of reality 24 or 25 times per second. The frames of a movie are those slices of reality. Television slices the reality a slightly different way because each of the frames in a TV signal is made up of hundreds of lines.

As a compromise between resolution (in pixels), the rate of change of the picture (in frames per second) and the amount of radio waves that a television signal would occupy (bandwidth), the engineers who designed television made each frame out of two fields. The first field only covers half the picture by missing out alternate lines of the image as it scans down the screen. The second field fills in the gaps, like this:

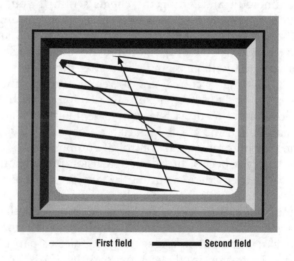

——————— First field ■■■■■■■■ Second field

The beam that 'paints' the picture on the television screen starts at the top and scans from left to right at a very slight angle downwards. For the first line only, the beam starts in the middle rather than at the left. When it reaches the right it flies back to the left hand side and starts again, a bit lower down. Eventually, after doing this a few hundred times, the beam reaches the bottom right of the screen and promptly flies back up to the top left and starts all over again. This time it will be scanning in between the lines it laid down last time; eventually it will reach the middle of the bottom line and fly back up to the middle of the top line, and the whole process starts again.

So there are two comb-like scans, interleaved with each other, making up each frame, with each consisting of half the number of lines in the whole picture. Each is called a field. The complete picture will be refreshed only 25 or 30 times per second, which keeps the bandwidth down, while the apparent flicker of the picture is at the rate of the fields, which is twice as high and so is less noticeable. A neat trick; but, as will be shown later, this system of interlaced fields causes no end of problems when we get onto the computer.

Composite video television standards

These are the three main systems of colour television. They are known as composite video because the brightness and colour information is mixed together into a single signal. The oldest still in use is NTSC, which is used mostly in North America and Japan. The main European system is PAL, also used in places like Australia and South Africa, and there is also SECAM, used in France (whence it came), Eastern Europe and the Middle East.

For NTSC a constant frequency signal at 3.58 MHz, called the colour subcarrier, is superimposed on the picture to carry the colour information. At the start of each line of the picture there is a short burst of the colour subcarrier. The colour at any point in the line (this is analog so the concept of a pixel is not strictly valid) is determined by the relationship between the subcarrier at that point and the reference burst.

There are 525 lines per frame in NTSC. In broadcast 487 lines have picture on them: half in each field. In multimedia practice NTSC is considered to have 480 active lines rather than 487. In its earlier black and white incarnation, American television used 30 frames per second, but for colour it changed to 24.97. It was supposed to be 30 but obscure technical reasons to do with the subcarrier frequency changed all that.

PAL has a subtle, but significant, difference from NTSC in the way that the colour information in the subcarrier is encoded. NTSC suffers from colour shifts due to minute timing changes during a line. PAL compensates for this by switching the colour encoding between alternate lines and so 'averaging' out the errors. PAL also has a higher frequency subcarrier, at 4.43 MHz. PAL has 625 lines in a frame, of which 576 have picture on them: half in each field. PAL shows 25 frames per second exactly.

SECAM, the French-devised third system, uses a totally different method for transmitting the colour (it sends the two colour components alternately with each line) but is otherwise the same as PAL, so if you fed a SECAM signal into a PAL monitor you would see a black and white picture. SECAM is reputed to really mean 'System essentially contrary to the American method' or Système en couleur avec mémoire. Although SECAM is still used as a transmission system, and gives very good results, it has problems for production, mainly because you cannot mix or fade a SECAM signal out because of the way the colour is encoded. Incidentally, NTSC is reputed to stand for 'Never twice the same colour' but actually it is National Television Standards Committee.

There are some variations, particularly a South American variation of PAL called PAL-M which is basically NTSC timing with PAL colour. You will sometimes see PAL-I and PAL-BG referred to, but these are different only in the way they are transmitted; the videotapes are compatible even though the televisions and VCRs are not, mainly because the sound is transmitted on a slightly different frequency and that is why a European PAL television will not usually work in the UK and vice versa.

On European videocassette machines you may see a form of NTSC called NTSC 4.43 or Modified NTSC. This is a special version of NTSC and it happens because the colour information on the videocassette is stored in a different way to the original composite signal. When the VCR plays back the tape the colour signal is put back in its 'proper' place. On some PAL machines, NTSC is rebuilt with the subcarrier at the PAL frequency. It saves having two sets of circuits for the colour in the VCR and the monitor. However, this modified NTSC will appear as black and white if you feed it into a real NTSC monitor or a digitizer card which expects real NTSC. This can also happen with Y/C systems like S-VHS and Hi8. You will not come across this problem with broadcast videotape machines, and it is not applicable to the component systems we come on to next, but it is the most likely cause of mystery colour disappearances when using NTSC video-cassettes on multi-standard VCRs.

A single video cable can be used to carry a composite video signal since the colour information is encoded in with the luminance and the synchronization pulses are usually kept together with the picture information. Some equipment labels composite video CVBS.

Component video

In recent years professional colour videotape has become either digital or component, or both. Component video means that the colour (chrominance or chroma) and brightness (luminance) information are kept separate, having been mathematically derived from the red, green and blue (RGB) signals received from the camera imaging tube or chip.

The luminance part of a component signal is referred to as Y. The true colour components are Red-Y and Blue-Y. Red and Blue signals are smaller in value than green so they make for larger (and therefore less noisy) components. Often the components are referred to as YUV (in PAL) and YIQ (in NTSC) but these are not strictly equivalent.

Sometimes you will come across the letters U and V in computer graphics. For example, one of the colour modes in CD-i is DYUV and here the Y, U and V are the colour components. The D stands for Delta and means that the picture is coded using information about small changes, or deltas. (Strictly speaking there is no such thing as an NTSC or PAL component but people do sometimes refer to component systems by their related composite system names in this way.)

Using colour components this way is useful for TV for two reasons. Firstly the luminance signal is exactly the same as the old black and white signal and so the video is backwards compatible and easy to view on a monochrome monitor. Secondly, because we do not see as much detail in colour as we do in brightness there is no need to have as high a definition for the chroma as for the luminance. This saves bandwidth. Photo-CD makes use of the same phenomenon.

Component video offers better quality than composite because the colour information is kept separate from the luminance. It is possible for a colour television decoder to mistake some of the fine detail in the luminance information in a composite signal for colour, causing spurious coloured patterning. This means that luminance information of similar frequency to the colour subcarrier will be missing from the composite picture.

Another advantage of component video is that PAL and SECAM tapes are the same. Connectors for component analog video are the same as for professional composite, only there are three of them. The sync pulses are usually carried on the Y line.

Halfway between composite and component video is S-Video as used in Hi8 and SVHS. This has two signals, one being the Y and the other a combination of U and V usually referred to as C. So a connector for S-Video might have Y/C written on it. An S-Video connector is made either from two BNC or phono connectors or from a four-pin mini-D type, like the Apple desktop bus connector. Sync pulses are carried on the Y line. There are only two forms of S-Video since, once again, PAL and SECAM are the same at this level.

Blanking and time code

Besides the image information, making up the visible part of the lines, there are elements of the signal which tell a television set, and other equipment, where the lines, fields and frames begin and end and provide reference information about the colour. The places in the television signal where the picture does not exist, but these signals do, are called horizontal (for lines) and vertical (for fields) blanking. This is because they are blank, although the vertical blanking interval (VBI) has become home to such things as teletext, vertical interval time code (VITC, pronounced Vit-see) and test signals.

Time code is very likely to be useful to you. When you look at a video-tape to select extracts for digitizing, time code is the way to specify the sections you want. Every frame of a television signal can be allocated a unique number divided into hours, minutes, seconds and frames (of the form hh:mm:ss:ff, for example 05:46:35:19). This time code signal is recorded on the tape along with the video and audio.

Time code is sometimes referred to as SMPTE (Society of Motion Picture and Television Engineers, pronounced 'sempty') although, strictly speaking, SMPTE time code is for NTSC video only and the PAL/SECAM version is EBU (European Broadcasting Union).

'Burned in Time Code' (BITC) or 'Time code in vision' is a system where a character generator superimposes the numbers of the time code on the frames to which it refers. This is invaluable in choosing extracts and editing. Since a time code number can refer to either field in a frame, some readers will add a field indication to the number you see because most video tape machines show you a field rather than the whole frame when the tape is in still 'frame'.

With NTSC time code you will see the term 'drop frame' used. Because NTSC does not have a whole number of frames every second the time code has to be adjusted every so often to keep it in step with real time. This is just like the extra day in February in leap years. In the case of NTSC a frame is dropped, hence the term. This is fine when it is important for the time code to show time-of-day, as it is called, or to know exactly how long a programme is, but you need to remember that some time code numbers will be skipped. For everyday video editing it is more straightforward to use non-drop-frame time code. You should know which type of time code your NTSC tapes have otherwise you will miscalculate the actual duration of your video. In PAL there is no need for drop-frame time code as PAL has exactly 25 frames per second.

In the studio and on location

You might use only a small amount of video in an interactive application but its use can be very powerful and effective. One common form is known as a talking head. This is where all you see on the screen is a single person talking. If you have a famous presenter for your application then you might see him or her a few times like this. Even if most of the time you only hear the voice, it is nice to show your viewers what the face behind the voice looks like.

The talking head might be recorded in a studio or on location (meaning not in a studio) and he or she might be positioned in front of a real scene (a bookshelf is a common one for a subject expert) or against a single colour. A single colour is useful because, in some circumstances, you can decide on the background later and add it in the edit suite or on your computer.

Since a human face does not contain any blue, blue is commonly used. Television people call this chroma-key or colour separation overlay (CSO – hence CSO blue to denote the colour). Film people call it a matte (if it moves it is called a travelling matte – and yes, it was used for flying carpets in Arabian Nights films – and now you know the origin of the name of that character in Fraggle Rock). Another name for this technique is 'blue screen' although other colours can be used: the BBC often use green and the traditional colour for movies was the light of a sodium discharge lamp.

Colour separation overlay.

Although in film making a travelling matte works using totally film-based methods and some clever work at the time of printing, in television an electronic circuit detects the blue and switches the signal to another source wherever there is blue. This substitutes the other image for the blue.

Common problems occur due to spillage of the blue light onto the person's face, shadows on the blue backcloth, and difficulties in coping with the fine detail in hair. The most sophisticated colour separation systems, like Ultimatte, can solve these difficulties but, in any case, good lighting helps avoid them.

Sometimes it pays to shoot against black. This can be very effective to isolate the person speaking and emphasize their role as a specialist, and it can be less distracting than the ubiquitous rows of books. Black does not spill onto faces and, if you are careful, you can overlay onto black just like blue or green. In this case you need to watch out for shadows, especially under the eyebrows.

Although these are film and television techniques, the use of colour separation overlay extends easily onto the desktop, and video editing and manipulation programs usually allow you to clean up and replace coloured backgrounds in this way.

The simplest way of lighting a single person uses three lights. One will be a spotlight on the face, one will flood the scene to lighten the shadows and the third will be positioned behind to both light the blue screen (if you have one) and backlight the person to help lift them from the surroundings and give the scene a three-dimensional look. The spotlight in front needs to be high enough so as not to make your speaker screw up his or her eyes but not so high as to cast shadows in the eye sockets. As usual, good lighting will look so natural on the screen that you will wonder just what you have paid for. The lights have names, and a redhead refers to a one-kilowatt lamp while a blonde is a two-kilowatt one. The lights will need to be set up but it is bad manners to inflict this on the speaker who will be under the lights for long enough later. One of the crew will stand (or sit) in for the speaker while the lights are moved and adjusted. Find someone the same height as the speaker. Also, you should make sure the speaker does not wear clothing containing the colour of the background, if you are using overlay.

For a professional and hassle-free video shoot you should avail yourself of an experienced cameraman and crew. The smallest crew will be one that only consists of a cameraman and you, the director (so get yourself a chair and a megaphone). You should seriously consider having a sound recordist, who will also help the cameraman to set things up, and a PA (production assistant) who will take notes and carry out the little administrative chores and free the director to. . .direct. You can reasonably expect the crew to bring their own equipment and videotape (referred to as 'stock').

If your application needs more substantial shooting, such as some drama or location documentary filming, then you will probably need to bring in a specialist director. If you have the experience to direct this kind of material, you probably do not need to read this chapter anyway. Crews for drama shoots can be very large and include workers with colourful names like the gaffer, best boy and grips.

The kind of camera used for professional video is similar to a domestic video camcorder, but it is physically bigger with a better lens and will give a much better picture. The cameraman will probably connect up a monitor for you to see the picture. For an interview, don't put the monitor where the speaker can see the picture.

Your speaker will need a microphone and you will probably not want to see it. For this reason a common microphone used in filming is called a rifle mic, or hypercardioid. This is a long and thin microphone although you will usually see it in a wind shield or wind sock. This makes it look like a big furry hot-dog held on the end of a pole by the sound recordist. Alternatively a very small microphone can be clipped to the person's tie or jacket collar. These are usually omni-directional and it is not unusual to position them upside down to avoid blasts of breath.

Shooting an interview

Although an interview seems to be one of the simplest forms of television shooting it is still difficult to direct well. Part of the problem is that you will want to edit what you record for inclusion in the finished application. With a sound interview you can cut almost anywhere as long as it makes sense, but with video you have the added difficulty of having the picture to cut along with the sound. It is highly unlikely that two similar pictures will cut together. In the case of a person speaking you will see the join as a jump, which is quite disconcerting. To hide the jumps you can do one of two things ... but you need to have recorded the material to do so. Firstly you can cut to a different view of the person who is speaking, known as changing the angle, or zoom or move closer (in) or further away (out). To disguise a cut, a zoom will work better than a simple change of angle but ideally you should combine both.

Changing the size of the shot has a curious side effect. Zooming in on a person speaking, either as a real zoom or as a cut to a closer shot, makes what he or she says seem very dramatic, as if confiding in the viewer. Zooming out has the opposite effect.

The second method of covering an edit is known as the cutaway. You can cut away to anything relevant. This might be some footage of whatever the person is describing. Alternatively the cutaway can be to something as simple as a shot of the person's hands as they move to emphasize a point. Of course, while you are cutting away from the speaker's face you can edit the sound to your heart's content.

The shorthand for describing the amount of the speaker you can see in a shot is roughly like this:

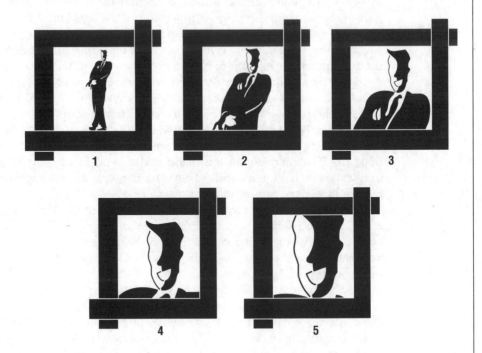

(1) Long shot – you can see the whole person and maybe enough of the surroundings to see where you are.
(2) Mid-shot – you can see most of the person speaking, including his or her hands.

(3) Medium close-up (MCU) – you can see the top of the person, from the middle of the chest upwards. This is sometimes called a 'head and shoulders' shot and is the basic shot for an interview or statement to camera.

(4) Close-up – you can see little more than the head.

(5) Big close-up – very close (tight) on the head, cutting off the forehead.

Incidentally, women who wear strapless dresses are difficult in interviews because the MCUs and close-ups make them look naked. This may not be the effect you want.

A very useful technique for interviews is to turn them into statements. This is used a lot in television documentaries, and basically means that the interviewer is neither seen nor heard in the edited result. This means, of course, that one place to which you cannot cut away is a picture of the interviewer nodding sagely (these shots are known as noddies). In this case it is important that the speaker never actually answers a question directly, and you should ask the interviewer to say things like 'tell me about your adventures up the Limpopo river' rather than saying 'was it fun up the Limpopo?' A common tactic is to ask the interviewee to repeat the question as the first thing he or she says in reply.

It is possible that you might be conducting the interview yourself, especially if you are not including the interviewer in the final edited footage. Part of your role is therefore as much to put the speaker at his or her ease as it is to ask anything meaningful. You will nod encouragingly, but never say anything while the interviewee is speaking. Some subject experts are so used to appearing in front of a camera that they will respond accurately to a request like 'tell me about Jupiter's red spot in 30 seconds' with consummate ease. Subject experts like that can be worth their weight in gold.

For the speaker, it is possible to work from a script but not appear to be reading. This kind of technique with half-silvered mirrors has been of benefit to politicians everywhere since Ronald Reagan showed it to Margaret Thatcher, but in television it has been in use for decades. It is used extensively in news and current affairs programmes where the presenter has little opportunity to learn a script.

Prior to the interview you should run through the topics you want to cover, and you should have given the speaker time to research the answers, even if it is his or her specialist field. Rehearsing can reduce spontaneity, but retakes are always a possibility. You can change the shot for retakes to make editing between them possible.

If you have a PA with you, he or she can make notes of questions to set against the time code which can usually be read on the side of the camcorder. You should resist the temptation to use time-of-day time code or drop-frame time code in NTSC and start each new roll at a new hour on the time code. This way you can easily judge which roll is which (they are still called rolls even though they may be videocassettes) from the time code numbers. So the time code 04:23:01:10 is on roll 4 and 13:21:10:00 is on roll 13. It is vitally important that the time code always goes forwards as you work through a tape and that the code never passes through midnight. This is simply to make it possible for the editing system to know which way to spool a tape to find a number, and unfortunately 23:59:59:24 reads as being after 00:00:00:00.

Preparing for editing

The tapes from your recording are known as rushes, from the time when they were shot on film and were rush-processed so that you could see the results the next morning. They will be dubbed onto videocassette, usually VHS, with burned-in time code (BITC) so that you can equate the time code to the parts of the material you are viewing. A time-coded transcript of the rushes is a useful first step in editing and can help you choose which parts of the interview you want to use.

There are usually three stages of videotape editing, although in the multimedia world you may not actually do any of them in a dedicated facility since more and more video processes can be carried out on the desktop. The first stage of the process is to prepare for the edit. This will involve looking through the recording in the cold light of day and choosing which parts of it to use. The odds are that you will have recorded much more than you need for the final application. The result of this stage is a list of extracts, probably marked on the transcript with their time code numbers.

Offline

The second stage is the offline edit. Offline editing was originally introduced because of the high cost of editing equipment. Early offline systems used videocassettes but offline editing was the first application of non-linear desktop video. The offline session is like a rehearsal for the online. Edits would be tried out, again and again, until the editor and the director settled on the ones that worked. The result of this stage was a list of the edit decisions.

The edit decision list can be taken into a 'real' edit suite and the edits carried out on the tapes. If this process is done automatically it is called auto-conforming, and this technique came back into fashion in the early days of digital video tape machines because of their high cost.

Today an offline session is as likely to take place on a computer, using a system like AVID or Lightworks, although the basic principle is the same. Quite a substantial industry has grown up around these non-linear systems, as they are called. Non-linear is another way of saying random access. Some non-linear editing systems are designed to seem familiar to video professionals while other systems are more computer-like and so are not as popular with video editors but have their fans in the multimedia community because they feel familiar to them. Non-linear systems started as offline edit systems although they are migrating upwards in quality and are passing through news broadcasting on their way to full acceptability as a high quality editing medium.

An edit control room. Photo by Vassilis Skopelitis courtesy of JCA Facilities in London.

Online

A professional edit suite, like the sound studio, was likely to be in two parts. The videotape machines, with their whirring motors and fans, were kept in another room, called the machine room. This is sometimes still the case but with the quieter videocassette-based systems used today, the machines are now often kept in a rack next to the desk. In some facilities it is common practice to have a central pool of machines and allocate them to suites as required, rather than having machines dedicated to a particular suite. So you may not even see the machines being used for your session.

You, as the client, will be in the control room of the edit suite (Figure 14.4). There will be a bank of television monitors in front of you, with a control desk and a vision mixer. It is one of the standing jokes of the video industry that, in 'Star Wars', when the denizens of the Death Star zapped a planet, they controlled the destructor beam with a Grass Valley vision mixer, common to many videotape editing suites around the world. (Computer people get their laughs from Scottie trying to use a Mac Plus in the Star Trek movie about saving the whales.) The staff of the suite will probably be two people: the editor and the tape-operator, also known as the tape-op. Almost without fail a character known as a runner will come in from time to time and offer you coffee or toast.

The editor's skill is in working out how to cut your material, to your specification, so that it flows and so that the edits do not jar. There are little tricks, such as cutting just before a movement in the incoming picture, which distract the viewer's attention momentarily and can be used to disguise the cut. With an edit, the material you have before the edit is called the outgoing shot, and that after the edit is called the incoming shot. The edit is adjusted by tightening it (making it happen earlier) or loosening it (making it happen later).

The editor will be editing sound and video. Often the sound will be mixed across an edit even if the video is cut. This is done to soften the impact of the cut. If the sound is heard before the vision cut it is said to be leading it. An edit where sound and video are cut at different points is said to be split (a split A/V). Sometimes you will continue the sound and come back to drop a short cutaway shot to replace some of the video.

Online videotape editing, in a broadcast suite, is still a linear process. You start at the beginning of the programme material, edit shot onto shot, and finally reach the end. This means that you need to be satisfied with each edit as you do it since you do not have much option for changing it. Hard disk systems allow you to edit in any order and you can go back to an earlier edit to change it if you want to. Eventually this method of editing will be the prevalent one. It is important that you are satisfied with the edited material when you leave the edit. The last thing you do should be to view the material all the way through to make sure it is cut to your satisfaction. Then you can arrange for a high quality safety copy to be made and for a viewing cassette to show, perhaps, to your client. Do not transport the main and safety copies together. The idea is that the safety copy can be used if the main copy is lost or damaged.

Just as audio studios have signal processing equipment for echo and delay, so a videotape edit suite will have its equivalent. The computer graphic and compositing software used in multimedia have their equivalent in such devices as the Quantel Paintbox, for television still graphics. One very common piece of equipment is the digital video effects unit, or DVE. With a DVE attached to the vision mixer, the video can be processed to make it change size, appear to move with 3-D perspective and even be wrapped around shapes. Such devices have a variety of names and manufacturers but one legendary name was for a piece of BBC hardware, never marketed, which was called TIPSE. This stood for Technical Investigations Picture Shuffling Engine.

One important thing to remember about digital processing of television pictures is that, without exception, the picture will be delayed as it passes through the device. Usually it will be delayed by one frame, which in PAL is 40 milliseconds. This delaying of the picture will eventually make the sound lose its synchronism, so it is usual to delay the audio to match and edit suites have audio delay lines for this purpose. There are many opportunities for sound and vision to lose synchronization so this is something you should watch for. If the slip is constant, it can easily be fixed by re-editing the audio onto the videotape in a slightly different place.

Videotape machines

It is possible that you will come across a variety of videotape formats, depending on the kind of work you are doing. Some of them will only be used now for archive footage but it may be useful to know what the terms mean. Unless otherwise stated these machines can be found in PAL and NTSC formats, although component formats should be referred to as 525/60 and 625/50 (for lines and fields) or simply 525 or 625. SECAM and PAL are the same at a component level so there is no difference between a Betacam-SP tape recorded in France and one recorded in Germany or the UK. Similarly SECAM SVHS is the same as PAL SVHS as far as the recording on the tape is concerned.

The oldest tape format still used, even if only for archive material, is 2-inch Quad. Originally the American company Ampex developed a system called Quadraplex, which used 2-inch tape, in 1956. Other companies also made 2-inch machines for this format. Long-established broadcasters, like the BBC, have archive material on 2-inch and it lasted until the seventies so it includes colour. Some stock deteriorated over time due to physical problems with the tape itself and the quadraplex system was relatively violent, spinning four heads rapidly across the width of the tape, so it is possible for playing a 2-inch tape to damage the tape, especially if the edge of the tape is already damaged a little. If the owners will still let you use this material, and they allow it to be played despite the risk, then it should be copied onto a more recent format as it is first played. Oxide from the tape can easily clog up the tape heads and sometimes engineers will use a piece of card or even their thumbnail to remove oxide from the heads as the tape plays. The basic rule is to leave 2-inch to the specialists and, in any case, very few facilities will handle it these days.

There was a 2-inch helical scan system which was used by some broadcasters. This is incompatible with the 2-inch quadraplex machines. A well-aligned 2-inch recording can be of extremely high quality with a sharper signal than later analog formats.

After 2-inch came 1-inch. This was a helical scan format, which means that the tape heads are on a drum that moves in almost the same plane as the tape path. Videocassettes are helical scan as well. The main manufacturers of 1-inch machines were Ampex and Sony (who made C format machines) and Bosch (who made B format machines). Almost all 1-inch tapes in the UK and USA will be C format but some countries, like Germany and Austria, used B format. The essential thing to know is that the two are incompatible.

The 1-inch tape was in use from the early 1980s until the early 1990s, by which time cassette-based formats like Betacam-SP had replaced it. Sony developed Betacam as a derivative of their ill-fated Betamax VCR system. There is a difference between Betacam and Betacam-SP and although most engineers will use the words interchangeably (or just say 'Beta') you should always specify Betacam-SP if you mean Betacam-SP just in case the video library also handles the older Betacam format. This is mainly a problem in the USA rather than Europe, where PAL Betacam never really caught on.

Betacam-SP is still very much in use. It is a very handy system to use with small cassettes being used in camcorders (with 20 or 30 minutes of tape time) and larger tapes in console machines. Video quality is good and, being a component system unlike 1-inch or 2-inch, the pictures are better suited to digitization. There is another component cassette format competing with Betacam-SP and that is M-II (M-Two). Beta machines come from Sony, Ampex and Thomson and M-II from JVC and Panasonic.

As far as sound goes, 2-inch tape carried a single mono track with reasonable quality, although it suffered from high-pitched whine caused by the video tracks which lie at right angles to the sound track. The orientation of the tape oxide was also suited to video and so in the wrong direction for audio. The 1-inch C format has either three or four tracks, depending on configuration. The performance is good but Dolby was often used to improve the signal-to-noise ratio.

Betacam-SP has four sound tracks. Two are very high quality but cannot be used during editing since they use the video track. So in practice the other two lower (but still good) quality tracks are used most.

Cassettes

Although virtually all professional videotape formats are now cassette-based rather than reel to reel (also known as open reel), there are video-cassette formats which are regarded as domestic or industrial. There had been domestic and industrial open reel videotape formats, notably from Philips and Ampex, which became available in the late 1960s but the price was far too high for domestic use.

Videocassettes first came onto the market in the 1970s with the 1500 format from Philips and U-Matic from Sony. U-Matic is still with us and has high quality (Hi-Band and SP) versions. It is also used for digital audio as the Sony 1630 format. However, you are unlikely to find U-Matic tapes used in high quality video today since Betacam-SP and S-VHS/Hi8 have taken that niche. U-Matic cassettes use 3/4-inch tape and are sometimes referred to as the 3/4 inch format. One serious disadvantage of U-Matic is that the maximum tape length is 74 minutes. (Coincidentally this is the maximum duration of a compact disc.)

The most common videocassette format for domestic and industrial use is VHS. The picture quality of VHS is relatively poor with particularly fuzzy colour performance. Hi-Fi sound tracks have been recently added to VHS and achieve very high quality even though they are analog. S-VHS uses cassettes of the same size as VHS but with different tape. S-VHS gives much better results with higher bandwidth resulting in sharper pictures and better colour. S-VHS machines can usually play and record VHS but not vice versa and both systems use half-inch tape. JVC developed a higher quality version called Professional-S.

Video-8 is Sony's successor to Betamax and boasts the smallest cassettes in video. There is a high quality version, analogous to S-VHS, called Hi8. These formats sometimes have digital sound. The tape width is 8 mm, hence the 8 in the names.

There are industrial versions of Betacam-SP with a lower price and a lower, but still very good, quality. The gap between S-VHS and Betacam-SP is also narrowed by the high quality version of S-VHS available from JVC. One advantage of the industrial Beta systems is that they are compatible with the full spec. version.

Videodiscs

John Logie Baird actually sold 78 RPM videodiscs in the 1920s but it was not until the 1980s that commercially viable videodisc machines came onto the domestic market. In Europe the domestic market for videodiscs never really caught on although there is a niche for film fans and classical music enthusiasts. Even this market may disappear when high quality digital video from a CD arrives.

Interactive video, which uses videodiscs with computer control, was the precursor of multimedia and you are unlikely to be working with videodiscs (in any case that is outside the scope of this book). However, you might use videodiscs as a source for video and audio for multimedia and there are a few points to bear in mind.

PAL LaserDiscs can, if they are older, have analog soundtracks. In any case PAL discs can only have two tracks, analogue or digital but not both, whereas NTSC discs can have both and often do. If you are trying to digitize from an NTSC videodisc, check whether your player outputs real or modified NTSC.

There are two types of recordable videodisc in use today. Like the older recordable discs they are incompatible with each other but are nonetheless interesting and may be useful for time-lapse photography or animations.

Sony produced a WORM videodisc which records component and is considered to be of broadcast quality. This system is used by some television stations to hold station identification sequences because of the random access and lack of deterioration (unlike tape).

Pioneer produced a magneto-optical recordable/erasable videodisc which also has two separate head assemblies which can be used independently for playback. This is also a component system.

Both these machines exist in PAL and NTSC versions.

Digital formats

In the 1990s digital tape formats began to replace analog ones. First there were D1 and D2. D1 is a very high quality component digital system developed by Sony but unfortunately the cost of machinery and tape stock made it popular only with advertising agencies, film companies and video research. D2 was a derivative system which recorded digitized composite signals (PAL or NTSC). As a result it could be easily integrated into existing systems and was more popular. Neither D1 nor D2 compressed the data used to record the video or audio. However, it was the advent of half-inch digital systems that brought digital video within the cost range of the majority of broadcasters.

D3 is a composite digital system, D4 does not exist, and D5 is a component digital system without compression. There is a mode for D5 which supports high definition pictures with some compression. Digital Betacam is from Sony (of course) and uses a little compression in the signal. Some Digi-Beta machines can play Betacam-SP tapes, which makes for versatility in editing. It is also possible to get Betacam-SP machines with digital inputs and outputs, but these are not Digital Betacam.

There had been some doubt as to whether Digital Betacam's compression, small though it is, would have an effect on pictures which were to be compressed further using MPEG. In practice this does not seem to be a problem after all and Digital Betacam is a popular format for multimedia work.

Even though there is a digital output from these tape formats, the usual way of copying the pictures into a multimedia system is by digitizing or grabbing the analog output. This is partly because of the high data rate of professional digital video (270 megabits/second) and partly because of incompatibilities in the shape of the pixels between computers and the international standard for digital television.

At the time of writing, Sony have just introduced a digital 8 mm format for the consumer market. Similar digital systems from other manufacturers will follow. It is currently unclear if these digital systems will allow direct copying of data into a computer system or whether the signal will still have to be grabbed from an analog output.

Copying tapes for use in multimedia

Since it is extremely unlikely that you will be allowed direct access to a master videotape it will be useful to outline some suggestions for formats.

If the master is composite then your working copy can be either composite or component. Since, as I will explain in a moment, it is better to digitize from a component source, in most cases you will want to ask for a component dub of the master. If you can work with a digital source then you should ask for a component digital copy.

It is possible that you will be editing and possibly processing the video to make a new master tape. This might happen if you were to be encoding material for MPEG and wanted to prepare a master of your own first. This might include video noise reduction and re-editing. In this case a digital composite dub would be recommended (such as D2 or, more likely, D3).

This way the decoding of the composite video to component can be done as part of your processing and you will have more control over it.

Film should be dubbed from telecine onto a component format.

Under no circumstances should you get a composite dub of a component tape; neither should you digitize from a dub on videocassette such as VHS, S-VHS or Hi8 unless you really have no alternative. Incidentally, you can save money by asking the facility house to dub a VHS with burned-in time code in vision, for your viewing, as they dub the master.

Finally you should not standards convert a tape between PAL/SECAM and NTSC or vice versa. Your copy should be in the same standard as the original.

Digitizing video for multimedia

Digital video in multimedia can mean partial screen or full screen, full motion (that is, 25 or 30 frames per second) or partial motion (down to 10 or fewer frames per second). The details of digitizing from a video source are very much down to the particular equipment in use, but there are some general principles.

'Recording' the video into the computer is called frame grabbing and this grabbing should, if at all possible, be done full frame and full frame rate. It is possible to frame grab uncompressed but this requires very fast digitizing hardware and local storage. Broadcast equipment like the Abekas digital videodisc uses a special type of hard disk where data can be written to all the hard disk's heads (they have more than one) simultaneously in order to achieve the necessary throughput. The kind of hard disk used in a desktop computer cannot work this fast unless several are joined together in an array.

In order to play the video back on the computer it will have to be compressed and probably shrunk in size but this is better done 'at leisure' rather than in real time. From a practical point of view high quality JPEG can be used during the grabbing process to save disk space and to reduce the cost of the necessary hardware. The results from this will usually look very good.

One important point about frame grabbing is that the frames you store on your hard disk will be either component or RGB, they will not be composite. This means that if you are grabbing from a composite source the grabbing board will need to convert (decode) PAL or NTSC into component or RGB. This will involve filtering the incoming signal to separate out the colour from the luminance. Unfortunately, the cost of a good filter to do this would be much higher than the cost of the rest of the equipment put together so the filtering in a commercially viable grabber board has to compromise on quality and some artefacts may be noticeable.

Firstly the luminance bandwidth may be compromised by the filtering out of the colour subcarrier if the video input is a composite one. Many filters (including those in most television sets) remove the higher frequen-

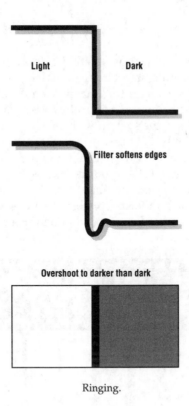

Light   **Dark**

Filter softens edges

Overshoot to darker than dark

Ringing.

cies of the luminance signal, those above the subcarrier, as well as the subcarrier itself. Secondly filters 'ring' and this has an effect on vertical edges in the picture. A sharp vertical edge has high frequencies in it. The sharper the edge the higher the frequencies involved. Passing such a signal through a filter can have a detrimental effect on the shape of the edge and the signal can overshoot and ring (just like a bell). What you see is a dark band between a bright and a dark part of the picture, darker than the dark part. Now if the dark part is black this results in a small part of the picture that is blacker than black, which is possible in an analog television signal. For this reason, amongst others, black and white in a digital television signal are not set at 0 and 255.

A good filter can avoid these kinds of problems but a better way is to avoid filtering altogether and always digitize from a component source, such as Betacam-SP. If the signal has to be converted from composite, because it was originally recorded that way, then a high quality broadcast filter can be used during a dub from the original tape or a digital composite copy of the original tape to a component tape.

Taking a movie film and recording it onto videotape uses a machine called a telecine and the process of putting the film onto tape is called a transfer. For digital video in multimedia this telecine transfer should be done into a component videotape, and preferably a digital one. The film should be clean to avoid dust and for top quality transfer the imaging gate on the telecine machine can be submerged in a liquid with the same refractive index as the film base. This is called a 'wet gate' and produces excellent results.

Video digitization should be done from the original television standard and not from a standards converted videotape. This is because standards conversion changes the image, even if only slightly. In any case, for digital video, the computer controlling the playback is generating frames at its own rate and the system will cope automatically with the input frame rate. Unfortunately it will do this by attempting to read out a frame when it needs one, even if there is not a new frame available. In this case it repeats the last frame. (The opposite may occur where frames are dropped.) There is nothing you can do about this, but you would make it worse by digitizing from a standards converted source where this process, or a sophisticated version of it, has been gone through already.

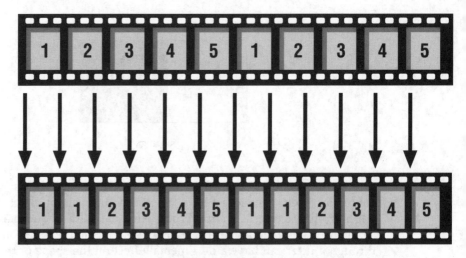

To read out six frames where five are available means one frame is repeated

A television standards converter will interpolate new frames, or combine old frames, in order to avoid the jerkiness that this basic 5–6 conversion has, but a computer display does not do this. This may suggest that if you have the freedom of choice, you might actually use NTSC, rather than PAL, for your video even if you are in Europe, because the NTSC frame rate is more like that on the computer.

Another set of problems are caused by the television signal being interlaced. When a television camera captures motion during a frame it does so in two separate slices of time, a 50th or 60th of a second apart. The moving object will have changed position between those two slices, the fields. When this is played back on an interlaced television screen there is no problem because the output display is interlaced with two fields per frame in the same way as the input camera. This does not happen when the full frame is displayed on a computer screen because a computer screen is not interlaced and writes the picture in one sweep from top to bottom, left to

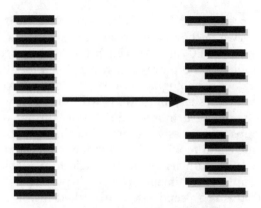

Alternate scan lines were recorded later and so are displaced right on the computer screen

Combing.

right. The result is that horizontally moving objects can appear to break up like a comb. Vertical filtering, also known as convolution, can be used to correct this fault; it does not occur when the camera was a film camera because a film camera exposes the whole frame at once.

This situation will also only occur if the video on the computer screen is the same size (has the same number of pixels) as the original video grabbed. If it has been shrunk to half size, for example, to make a quarter-screen image of 320 by 240 pixels, then the result will be a slight horizontal blurring rather than a comb effect.

Some computer systems will allow the computer display to be set up to be interlaced but use of this is rare unless the application is going to be shown on a television monitor. Using an interlaced display with a computer causes flickering of fine detail in the picture (called twitter) and filtering this out reduces the effective resolution of the image.

When shrinking an image, whether it is movie or still does not matter, new pixels should be calculated from combinations of the old ones, rather than by sub-sampling (that is, dropping some of) the old pixels. If this is not done then near-horizontal lines will 'staircase' and also appear and disappear with movement of the picture, as they go from 'visible' pixels to 'no longer visible' pixels and back again. This process is called filtering and vertical filtering, to blend together information from the fields, is very important when dealing with television pictures in the digital domain.

Compression

Video in multimedia is, by definition, digital. For practical reasons it also has to be compressed because it is impractical to handle the high data rate used by raw video. Broadcast technology is able to handle this, but at a price. For multimedia we have a choice of various 'standard' methods of compression, and the choice available increases as time goes by.

Two of the international standards that are applied to video compression are JPEG and MPEG. JPEG, which is discussed in the chapter on graphics, is a compression system used for still images. JPEG is attuned to work with photographic images, which have smooth gradations of tone rather than sharp lines. JPEG works in only two dimensions: the height and the width of a frame. MPEG adds further data reduction by comparing groups of successive frames. Since not all of an image changes – frame by frame – in a movie, this redundancy can be used in the compression.

With sufficient data bandwidth available, from a fast hard disk for example, JPEG images can be displayed fast enough to become a movie and this is a pseudo-standard called M-JPEG. MPEG uses less data but is more difficult to decompress (and compress). Both of these standards, when used for movies, require hardware or a very fast processor. MPEG actually encompasses three variations with MPEG-1 being the version designed for use on compact disc at 1.5 megabits per second. MPEG-2 is a higher quality, higher bandwidth version and MPEG-4 (currently under discussion) is aimed at low-bandwidth applications and interactivity.

Several software video compression systems exist, making use of operating system architectures like Video for Windows (particularly Intel's Indeo) and QuickTime (with Cinepak). Although these give poorer quality for their bandwidth than MPEG-1, they need no hardware to display and will run on medium powered processors. The CD includes some examples of video compression, of various qualities.

In fitting movies into an operating system environment, the manufacturers (such as Apple and Microsoft) define standard interfaces for control of the movie with VCR-like controls for play and fast forward and rewind. A progress bar, to show how far through a movie you are at any moment, is also a standard part of such an interface.

QuickTime and Video for Windows both can work transparently with a range of video compression systems since the operating systems present a consistent interface to your application. This means that you can switch from using, say, Indeo to using MPEG-1 without changing the application as long as the two videos have the same resolution.

With the movie come sound and stills, since an audio file is basically a movie with no pictures and a still is a movie consisting of only one frame. It is MPEG that currently offers the best set of these features since MPEG audio and MPEG stills are of extremely high quality and are very efficiently compressed.

Judging quality

The points outlined in the previous chapter on quality as it applies to sound also apply to video. However, it is usually very difficult to achieve broadcast quality with video on a multimedia system and your client should be aware of this. Again, use of the term 'appropriate' to describe the quality may be the best option. Some of the quality issues are less tangible. The quality of editing and the camerawork are independent of the technical quality of the desktop video, and in these cases you should aim for a quality threshold similar to broadcast television. Explaining early on that the multimedia video will not look as good as TV, and showing the client some examples, will avoid this becoming an issue, but you should be prepared to explain why, especially to a client who has experience of corporate video or broadcasting.

THEORY INTO PRACTICE 16

One of the ways of building video skills is by watching. Look carefully at what you see on television. See how people are framed by the camera and watch particularly how faces usually look into space within a frame. Look at how a movie is cut and think about why a cut might occur in a particular place. Watch for the way the incoming shot often starts with an action which will distract your attention from the edit itself.

Summary

- Moving pictures are a very effective way of conveying information in multimedia.
- You need to be aware of the different broadcast television standards that you might encounter and of the difference between composite and component video. NTSC and PAL are the main forms of composite video and each has a component equivalent.
- For a variety of reasons component video offers better quality than composite and is more suited to multimedia digitizing.
- Time code is a numbering system used in videotape recording which will also be useful to you. You can use it to show tape numbers as well as time.
- Shooting a video interview is one of the most likely kinds of video you will undertake. The subject can be separated from the background by shooting against blue or black.
- The stages of editing video are preparation, offline and online. New technology and non-linear editing systems using PCs are blurring the distinction between online and offline editing.
- Options for compressing video so that it can easily be handled on the desktop include moving JPEG, MPEG and software systems.

Recommended reading

Ozer J. (1995). *Video Compression for Multimedia*. London: AP Professional

Quantel Limited (1994). *The Digital Factbook*, 7th edn. Newbury: Quantel Limited

Watts H. (1984). *On Camera*. London: BBC Publications

CHAPTER 15

GRAPHICS ASSET PRODUCTION

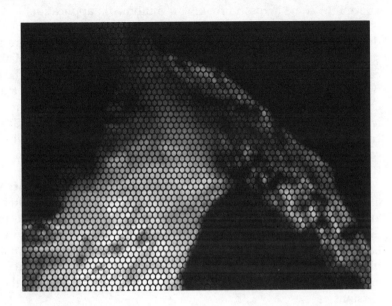

Project manager's responsibilities

- To assemble the necessary graphics team
- To ensure that the project definition is in a form that adequately briefs the graphics team
- To monitor the development of the graphics and liaise between the client and the team over changes and misunderstandings
- To make sure that 'proofreading', the checking of any written material in the graphics, is carried out
- To make sure that the source graphics are archived at the highest reasonable resolution, no matter how they are displayed in the application
- To understand the processes involved in producing this kind of asset

A picture is worth a thousand words

No matter how innovative your interface design, how sophisticated your programming, the public face of your multimedia application and the major make-or-break factor is going to be your graphics. Your potential customer will feel able to make an instant judgement, for better or for worse, on the basis of that first impression on the screen.

Just as with software, the creation and manipulation of graphics is a complex business and the purpose of this chapter is to provide some general background to the techniques and systems that you might wish to use in your multimedia application and to outline some of the problems you might come across in making a multimedia application.

The two key parts of managing the production of graphics are the definition of the task and the selection of the personnel. There should be some definition of the approach to graphics in the project plan. In some cases a graphics artist or art director will have taken part in the definition of the application. On the basis of the graphic requirements a team will be chosen. It may be that you are working in an organization that has graphics artists on the staff or a pool of freelancers. This situation is more common for graphics and programming than for sound or video. In this case you might find that the project plan evolved to fit in some way with the abilities of a particular graphics person.

There are many kinds of process that go to make up art work and after a brief explanation of terminology for colour, this chapter will look at the differences between them and how the way they are made may impact upon the management of a project. This will apply to two stages because you should work with your images in the highest quality possible and then convert down if necessary to the standard required for delivery. Archiving should also be done so as to include the highest quality versions.

Colour

A colour image on a computer screen is made up of red, green and blue dots which are very close together. Red, green and blue (R, G and B) are what are called the primary colours for any colour displayed with light. (For pigments, like paint and printing ink, the primaries are red, yellow and blue.) You will find an example on the CD of how a colour image is built in this way.

For this reason we refer to a colour image on the screen as an RGB image. Almost any colour can be produced by mixing the three primaries and, in a full colour image on the screen, each picture element or pixel is built up from varying amounts of red, green and blue light. Shades of grey are produced by making the amount of red, green and blue in the pixel equal. For black there is no light and for white the light is 'full on'. In digital terms there are 256 shades to each of red, green and blue in a full colour 24-bit image.

With fewer than 24 bits there will be fewer colours but it is possible that each of the colours that can be shown can be predefined from the full range, or palette, of 24 bits.

Drawings

This word has a double meaning. To the person in the street, drawing is taking a pencil and creating a freehand work of art. Drawing, like painting, is the essence of fine art.

In computer terms a drawing is an image that consists of distinct segments or shapes, called draw objects. It is sometimes referred to as line art but this term could be ambiguous, sometimes also referring to an image on the screen that is made up of only black and white pixels.

The classic draw objects are lines, rectangles and arcs together with a range of wavy lines called curves of which Bezier curves are perhaps the most familiar. The important thing about a drawing is that the objects in it retain their separate identity, so that they can be manipulated independently of each other and even if, in the image as seen, the object is partially or completely hidden behind other objects.

Each object has characteristics which can be changed. Drawing applications will allow you to rescale an object or a group of objects. The width of a line, and the pattern with which it is drawn, called the pen, can be changed. If the object has an 'inside', it can be filled with a colour or a pattern. A polygonal shape or a curve can be altered by moving the corners or changing the controls on the curve.

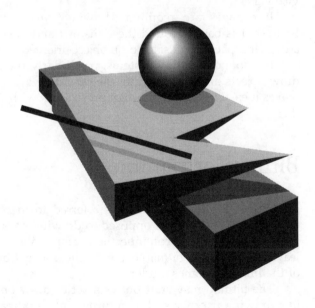

Changing one object has no substantial repercussions on the other objects. If the circle in the diagram is moved it would reveal the polygon behind it. The image only becomes a pattern of dots on the monitor when it is displayed or when you choose to 'fix' it. By definition the drawing does not have a scale and can be expanded or shrunk or distorted as

required with no ill effects as seen above. An exception to this scale independence is the thickness of lines since that tends to be fixed. As a result you might wish to increase line thickness as the size increases and vice versa.

If changes are required, drawings are relatively easy to modify. Because it is based around these distinct and almost unconnected objects, a drawing package is said to be object-oriented.

In some computing systems, particularly the Apple Macintosh, these draw objects are supported by the operating system at a low level, which makes it easy for different programs to work with them and even exchange them.

Bitmap or painting

In contrast a bitmap, sometimes referred to in computing as a painting (hence paint packages as opposed to drawing packages), only exists as the patterns of dots. To continue the example above, if the ellipse moves it leaves a hole. If the bitmap expands, the dots get bigger and the resolution of the image becomes cruder.

The bitmap may start out as a set of draw objects. It may be created in a drawing package and then turned into a bitmap 'fixing' the pattern of lines and shapes. It could have been scanned in from a photograph. Scanners are devices which take a 'real' image such as a print or a slide or transparency or even a photographic negative and scan across the image, from left to right and top to bottom, to produce a stream of dot information about the image which can be stored in a computer file and so make its way onto the screen.

Making changes to a bitmap, such as changing text in the image, could have serious implications because of the holes left when parts of the image are removed. One way around this problem is to use a painting package which allows control of layers of an image and the way they are combined, or composited, together.

Composites

The addition of alpha channels and layers into paintings has helped to bring some of the advantages of draw objects to the world of the bitmap. Separate bitmap objects can be combined into a composite image. Even though changing a bitmap object itself is still difficult, the relationship between objects can easily be changed. Text (one object) over a photographic background (another object) can easily be changed. Each component of the final image is known as a layer and the alpha channel determines how the layers blend with each other.

An alpha channel is a graduated mask. It is essentially a fourth channel after red, green and blue and it determines how much of the RGB image layer is shown at any point of the composite image and how much of whatever is underneath shows through. For most of the image the mask would be 'white' showing that all the RGB was visible and none of the underlying layers. Outside the image it would be 'black' showing that none of the RGB was visible there but the underlying layers were fully visible.

At the edges of the image, where it would be designed to blend into its surroundings, the alpha channel would gradually change from white to black and the depth of the 'grey' at any point would determine the visibility and mixing at that point.

In a montage, where there might be several small images grouped together over a background, each of the small images would have its own alpha channel and would exist in a separate layer. In this way changes can be made to each of these elements independently of the whole composite image. A further refinement of this technique would allow layers to be completely transparent or translucent. A reflection in a window would be transparent, with the image behind the glass being opaque behind it.

As a result of using layers in this way an image becomes easier to change under some circumstances. Let's use the example where a final image consists of a photograph with some text superimposed on it. If there is no layering to the image in your archive then to change the text you will have to find the original image of the background and build the image again from scratch. With layers you can change the text, which will be in the foreground layer by itself, without having to touch the background.

Paint packages can be biased towards creation, retouching or both. For many multimedia artists Adobe's PhotoShop defines the retouching package (although it is not alone), especially once it became available on the PC platform as well as the Apple Macintosh.

3-D modelling and rendering

Quite often an application will have illustrations and montages which have a three-dimensional look. This may or may not include an animation such as a smooth movement of the viewpoint through a group of objects. 3-D packages are usually object-oriented like a drawing package. You can build a solid object using techniques analogous to building with bricks, using a lathe to turn or extrusion (like squeezing toothpaste). Just as two-dimensional draw objects have become part of low-level operating system tools (sometimes called primitives), in time three-dimensional objects will join them. This will make the creation of 3-D objects easier and cheaper because, again, programs will be able to make use of the operating system's objects rather than having to define their own.

Once the scene is designed and the objects in it built and positioned you can choose the surfaces for the objects. This can include texture mapping where a bitmap is spread over the surface of an object, bump mapping where the object is given a bumpy surface, and setting the reflectivity or opacity of the object.

Then the lighting conditions can be set up with a balance of ambient (general) lighting and spot and flood lights and the viewpoint chosen. All these parts of the process are part of the modelling.

Finally the scene is rendered to produce the final image or images. Unlike other graphical processes which work more or less in real time, rendering can be very slow. A single image can take minutes or even hours to be rendered as the computer works out the view. The end result can be quite stunning, and can be genuinely referred to as photo-realistic. This is one reason why 3-D modelling is such a popular technique.

3-D images can take a long time to render partly because of the time taken to work out the shadows and reflections in a scene. One very popular technique for determining reflections is ray tracing. In this case every ray of light in the view is traced as it 'bounces' from the light source, the objects in the scene and the viewers eye. Ray tracing is very computationally intensive and an alternative is environment mapping, where a view of 'the world as seen by the shiny object' is computed and wrapped around the object itself.

Three-dimensional modelling, like illustration and animation, are special skills somewhat distinct from general graphics work and you are likely to find artists who specialize in one or more of these areas.

DPI and bit depths

In computing terms you define an image in a number of ways. For a bitmap the most obvious defining parameter is size. In printing, graphics artists are used to defining an image by its size in inches or centimetres, and then saying what the resolution is. This means that if you have a scanned image that is two inches across, with a resolution of 150 lines (or dots) per inch, there are 300 dots across the image. Print is defined in this way because print has a fixed size: the size of the image on the printed page. Computer displays are not necessarily like that and television screens are definitely not like that. In these cases the size in inches is not important, but the size in pixels is. So the computer person will give the image size as 300 pixels across and not really be worried about its physical size in inches. Note that to a printer, a screen is part of the process by which an image made of continuous gradations of colour, like a photograph, is turned into something that an ink-based printing press can actually reproduce. This book uses the word screen to mean the image seen on the computer display.

Certainly a computer display has its equivalent of the printer's screen. Dots per inch is the usual way of defining a computer screen output as well. This is usually 72, 75 or 80 dots per inch (dpi) and each dot is a pixel. For a computer display of 75 dpi, the 300-pixel image will be four inches across. You need to be clear in your mind about the relationship between the size of an image in pixels, in inches and the connection between the two, which is its dpi. If the image on the screen is to be two inches across again, instead of four, then it can be shrunk by half in a paint or photo-retouching package.

There is a third dimension to computer screen images, which is the bit depth or colour depth. The number of bits in the screen display determines the number of colours or shades that can be shown. For a fixed size of image in pixels, the size of the file needed to store it doubles for most of the stages below.

1 bit gives you two colours (black and white)
2 bits give you four colours
4 bits give you 16 colours
8 bits give you 256 colours
16 bits give you 65 536 colours
24 bits give you 16 777 216 colours

Usually, when literature refers to 32-bit colour (as on the Apple Macintosh), this refers to 24 bits of colour information and 8 bits of alpha channel or mask which is used for compositing. Also a 16-bit system often gives five bits each to red, green and blue and uses the sixteenth bit for a one-bit mask. Another technique is to give green more bits than red and blue because our eyes are more sensitive to green.

The CD includes examples of an image stored with different bit depths.

There are occasions when you will see a reference to colour of more than 24 bits which is really just that. Colour scanners increasingly scan at 10 or even 12 bits per colour, making 30 or 36 bits. This is because the colour rendition of the object being scanned will not usually match that of the computer and it is handy to be able to adjust the scanning to compensate for this. The difference usually shows in the darker and lighter parts of the image. This becomes especially true when working with photographic negatives, which have a particularly wide latitude (the film equivalent of dynamic range or bandwidth).

Of course you can substitute 'shade of grey' for colour. It is generally assumed that the eye can distinguish fewer than 256 shades of grey which would suggest that you could represent a smooth gradation from black to white with 256 shades. Unfortunately this does not always work because our vision is extremely sensitive to the transition between very similar shades. However, 256 grey levels is reckoned to be far and away good enough and it certainly works for everyday images. For colour images the boundary lies between 16 bit and 24 bit.

Although 24 bits are best for a colour display, you can make do with fewer bits if the individual colours are chosen carefully from a 24-bit palette of colours, to match the colours in the image. Very few images run across the whole 16 million colours and so using a custom palette, as this is called, is a useful way of getting the bit depth, and also the size of the file, down. Often you can go down to 256 colours with a custom palette and the results will be virtually indistinguishable from a full 24-bit image. Unfortunately a custom palette is not always a practical idea, especially if several images with different custom palettes, and even the windows on the screen, are expected to share the same screen display and the screen is not a 24-bit one. The result will, at best, be an attempt by the operating system to reconcile the different palettes but, at worst, some of the images will turn psychedelic.

The basic rule of reproduction, and this applies to print as well as computer displays, is that you can trade spatial information for bit-depth information, which you could call colour resolution. This means that you can group together pixels and use the group, averaged between the individual pixels in the group, to show more colours than an individual pixel can. The group of pixels acts like a larger pixel which is capable of showing more colours. This technique has versions like half-toning and dithering which you can use as well as or instead of a custom palette. It is even possible to dither a one-bit image to make it look almost photographic, if the screen resolution is high enough and you do not look too closely.

Dithering.

As an extreme example, the illustration shows a grey-scale image of the Matterhorn which has been dithered from eight bits (256 shades of grey) to one bit (black and white). This is called a diffusion dither. You really have to squint and imagine really hard to see this as a grey-scale image, but the basic principle of dithering is there: groups of dots simulating greys.

Using what when and why

For the designer of a computer-based application there are times when you will need to think very carefully about how your images are stored and reproduced.

In an ideal world, apart from special effects, you would always use 24-bit images in your multimedia applications. However, you could run into problems doing this for reasons of display incompatibility and file size. If the display of your target delivery system is not 24 bit then you need to know how it will react when fed a 24-bit image. If it does not gracefully degrade it by, for example, dithering it, you would be better off dithering the images yourself. If there are palette problems, common in applications using windowing interfaces because of differing requirements of the windows on the screen, this can make your images look poor to the point of being psychedelic when their window is not active.

Custom palettes present a difficulty in that, when switching from one picture to another in a sequence, the palette may not switch at the same time as the picture. This can lead to a brief flash of weird colours on the screen as the palette settles down. There is a brief moment while the beam scanning the image onto the monitor switches off as it moves from the bottom of the screen back to the top, called the vertical blanking interval or VBI. The VBI allows a short period during which both screen image and palette can be changed so that the palette flash is not seen – as long as the necessary changes can be made quickly enough.

File size is important for reasons of capacity and loading time. As well as taking up three times the space of an 8-bit image on your hard disk or CD-ROM, a 24-bit image takes three times as long to load. This could be crucial if you are expecting very fast response times.

You should also think carefully about whether you want to use 24 bit if it is available. It may be that some of your images will work very well in eight bit and so you should consider using them this way. This is particularly true of animations where you might need to reap the benefit of smaller file sizes, or even use simple but fast compression methods (run-length encoding, for example) to avoid having to move too much data too quickly.

Even though your final delivery may not be a full 24-bit colour image, you should carry out all the retouching and compositing operations in 24 bit. Working on an 8-bit or a 16-bit version of an image will never give as good a result as working on the 24-bit original. This argument also extends to the archiving of graphics, and they should be kept at the highest reasonable quality as well as in their final form.

Anti-aliasing

Although text is essentially a one-bit image, there are circumstances when you would want to display text with more bits. It is all part of that trade-off between spatial and colour resolution. When converting from an object (such as text or a drawing) to a bitmap you have to fit the edges of the object to the pixels on the screen. If you do this and set the pixels black or white depending on whether the majority of the pixel is covered by the line or not, you get jagged lines on the screen, known as jaggies or stair-casing.

The alternative is to colour the pixels along the edge different shades depending on how much of them is covered. This will disguise the jaggies and usually renders them invisible. The shades are blends of the foreground and background colours.

Because the effect of the mismatch between the real line and the 'quantizing' caused by trying to fit it onto the pixels in the image is known as aliasing, the kind of rendering which puts the grey pixels around the edge to smooth it out is known as anti-aliasing. Anti-aliased text, particularly, has become

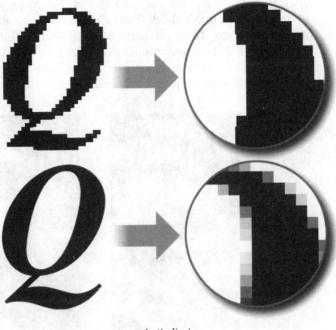

Anti-aliasing.

very popular with computer typographers and designers because it looks more like words on paper and less like a screen bitmap.

Some computer operating systems can render text to the screen in an anti-aliased fashion in real time but in other cases the text needs to be built into the image as a graphic. However, even if the operating system is doing the anti-aliasing, it will be slower than simply printing non-anti-aliased text.

There are some occasions when you should think carefully about using anti-aliased text. This is especially the case when the text is small because the grey wedges around the edge tend to make small text look fuzzy. This problem increases with the reducing of text size because the 'grey' pixels around the edge have a fixed size and so become a bigger proportion of the text size as the text shrinks. In some cases, more careful alignment of the text on the screen will optimize the appearance. The worst case scenario is where the text is small enough, and misaligned enough, that some of the strokes of the characters are almost completely grey. In this case they just look out of focus. Making the size of the characters such that their top and bottom edges lie exactly at pixel boundaries reduces this effect, but few characters have straight lines at their edges. Basically you have to check the images carefully.

Look before you leap

Any graphic should be checked on the delivery system. It is going to cause substantial problems if a whole series of graphics are produced on, say, a

Macintosh in 24 bit, for use on CD-i in one of its idiosyncratic graphics modes, and you don't check them at an early stage. Reducing the bit depth of an image can have all sorts of undesirable side effects, particularly quantization. This is sometimes also called posterization or contouring. It is the result of taking a smooth transition from one colour to another and replacing that with a series of discrete steps.

Posterization.

In this image, as an example, you see an extreme case of posterization. There is a risk that the 24-bit image on the left (subject to the vagaries of reproduction in print), which has 256 shades of grey in it, would come out looking like the one on the right if that computer screen could only display four levels of grey.

Unfortunately you can only be sure of this kind of compatibility if you have checked your image on every screen format.

Taking less space

You will usually need to reduce the size of graphics files. This can be for reasons of space, for example on a compact disc. It can also affect the time it takes to access the files, whether from a CD or from a network.

One way of reducing the size of a graphic is by degrading it. The size of the file, in pixels, can be reduced. A 640 by 480 file could be shrunk to 320 by 240 and blown back up on display. This will lead to a dramatic reduction in quality. The colour depth of the picture can be reduced. One quite effective way is to change from a 24-bit image to an 8-bit one with only 256 colours. If the palette for the picture is carefully chosen a 256-colour version of a 24-bit picture can be a very effective substitute. This is known as an adaptive palette.

Recently an international standards group developed JPEG, which compresses photographic images substantially by losing the less visible elements of the picture. JPEG at relatively low compression rates, such as five to one, will usually be indistinguishable from the original. This means that JPEG is even more efficient than eight bit with an adaptive palette.

Compare the two images below.

JPEG Matterhorn.

JPEG artefacts.

The first image was compressed using a high quality JPEG compressor but if we subtract this image from the original, and the range of brightness in the result is expanded so that the changes are easier to see, a mosaic pattern becomes visible.

In the second image, the finer the dots are, the more detail has been removed by the JPEG algorithm. The reduction achieved by JPEG here is a factor of three. If the image was colour the difference would be greater. You can find these images on the CD.

Reducing the size of a file reduces the time it takes to load that file from a CD or a network. If the image needs to be decoded, as a JPEG image would, then you have to take account of the decoding time. Despite this, on a multimedia system you will probably find that the time taken to download and decode a JPEG image is still less than the time taken to download an uncompressed version.

Computer graphics and video graphics

If your graphics artist has a background in video, he or she may suggest that you work with video graphics equipment. In general the kind of facilities available on such equipment is similar to that on computer packages but more powerful (unless your computer is really high end). The main differences are that television is a 16-bit system, making use of our relatively poor colour resolution of vision, it is interlaced and it has a set image size. On the plus side, this kind of television equipment (Quantel is a major manufacturer of such systems) has dedicated hardware and so can operate very quickly, often blindingly so. There is a large pool of experienced video graphics people. Also, if you are actually manipulating images from video, the facility will be able to handle this for you in an integrated manner.

Asset management

It is likely that the number of graphics files you will have in your application will be large. It could be the largest number of files and, if you take into account versions, sections of composite images, and animations then the number can easily run into thousands.

For this reason it is vital that from the beginning you adopt a known system of naming files. This is especially difficult with filing systems that do not allow long names, such as DOS. It is tempting to use paths in your directory structure to identify files but this has risks since files can become separated from their directories. Some kind of coding is probably going to be the only safe solution to this problem, with a short code identifying the image and its status. A suffix or extension should be reserved for the file type since some filing systems recognize files only by this extension. The resources in Apple files are potentially very useful and very detailed information about a file can be put there as a special resource, but this does not help you if you are working on a PC. Also you will have to consider the problems of recognizing files from lists including lists in archives.

In particularly complex cases a database may be required to handle the assets in an application and several software companies have been addressing the problems of handling an image database of this kind. You may wish to write a system of your own which can be used for different applications.

Image compatibility and quality

Since it is possible to display a photographic quality image on a 24-bit display, you will need to take care that any compression does not noticeably degrade the image. In agreeing quality standards with a client you will need, as with audio and video, to align your quality with what the delivery system can display. However, there may be times when the delivery system will encompass a range of displays, and under these circumstances you will need to check how the images look on all the platforms and try to make sure they degrade gracefully as the platforms' capabilities decline.

From a practical point of view the days of image standards for still pictures being incompatible are almost over, since there are a number of good conversion packages which can take an image in one format and convert it to another with no loss. You should be aware, however, of differences between uncompressed, compressed but lossless, and compressed with loss (or lossy).

An image which is compressed without loss, such as one compressed with run-length encoding, will be the same as an uncompressed one when the latter is expanded. Lossy systems are more unpredictable but the good ones, such as Photo-CD and JPEG, can be used as if they were uncompressed as far as delivery of the image is concerned.

There is a caveat. If you are going to manipulate an image you should start from an uncompressed or lossless-compressed image. Exceptionally, Photo-CD can be used for origination as the compression system used for it is visually lossless, even though it does lose some information. This loss amounts only to information that we do not see since our eyes do not resolve colour as well as the brightness information.

Proofreeding!

In software they say that 'there is always one more bug' and the typo is the graphical equivalent. It will be important to check for any errors in the graphics, just as you will do with any voice-over script. Any text on screen should be checked for spelling and consistency of presentation before it is passed on to the graphics team for display on the screen. However, even the most experienced typographer can make a mistake, and if proper names or foreign languages are involved, extra care is needed.

Proofreading is a skill and, in any event, should not be carried out by the person who wrote the text because they will sometimes see what they expect to see rather than what is really there. You cannot rely on spell checkers because spell checking does not usually pick up misused words or typos which are valid words such as 'if' for 'of' or 'reed' for 'read'.

THEORY INTO PRACTICE 17

The CD-ROM contains examples of images with different resolutions and bit depths. You should familiarize yourself with the effects on different kinds of material and, using whatever image manipulation software you have, experiment with changes in the number of colours.

Summary

■ There are two basic types of image, one which is object-oriented and known as a drawing and can be changed relatively easily, and one which consists only of the exact dots displayed on the screen. This is a bitmap or painting and is less easily manipulated.

■ Working with a composite image in a package that uses layers and alpha channels can give you the best of both worlds because you can separate the sections of the image and work on them independently.

■ Unless you are working with photographic images (usually 24-bit colour), you will have to select a range of colours carefully for representation of the image. This is known as the palette.

■ In transferring a 24-bit image to a smaller palette, say eight bit, there are compromises that have to be made. However, the resulting file will also be smaller.

■ Reducing the number of colours in an image is not the only way of shrinking the file since JPEG compression, which is an international standard, can achieve a shrinkage with less visible artefacts.

■ Whatever you do with images, it is vital always to check how the image will look on the delivery platform. And don't forget to proofread any text.

Recommended reading

Foley J.D., van Dam A., Feiner S.K. and Hughes J.F. (1990). *Computer Graphics, Principles and Practice*, 2nd edn. Reading, MA: Addison-Wesley

CHAPTER 16

INTEGRATION

Project manager's responsibilities

- To assemble the necessary software engineering team to implement the application
- To ensure that the project definition is in a form that can be implemented in software
- To monitor the development of the programming and liaise between the client and programming team over changes and misunderstandings
- To define the testing to be carried out and oversee that process
- To understand the basics of programming logic so as to better understand the problems facing the programmers

Multimedia fusion or confusion?

Multimedia can be said to gather the best, and the worst, aspects of both computing and the audio-visual industry and they have to be fused

Fusion or confusion?

together in the core stage of multimedia development. This is the integration of the application. Here the underlying computer software is applied to the assets and this is often the first time that anyone, including the designer, sees the jigsaw fitting together.

Managing a team in software development has much in common with the general principles covered in Chapter 12, Team Management Principles. The software team involved in an application can range from a single person upwards, although for multimedia your team is unlikely to be larger than four or five. If you have a single person working on your project it will be beneficial for that person to have contact with other programmers so that any sticky problems can be sorted out. Within a team you may wish to have one person who manages the team's work. Software is often written on a modular basis, with separate but self-contained parts of the application being written by different people. It can be necessary for someone with software knowledge to distribute the work and make sure the modules fit together.

The choice of people to program your project will depend on how it will be carried out. Different software engineers will have experience using different languages and tools. Ideally you will have enough experience, or be able to get suitably impartial advice, to choose the environment and therefore know what kind of programmer to recruit.

A second part of managing software involves the specifying of what needs to be done and ensuring it is carried out. Taking advice from a programmer during the early stages of the design can avoid problems later and can help you to describe the application in ways that a programmer can clearly understand. When specifying an application there will be input from every part of your team and from your client. For a consumer product your client could be replaced by information on what customers want, but the basic principle remains the same.

The purpose of this chapter is to give an overview of the software aspects of multimedia but it does not set out to show how to actually carry out the programming. Just as in the audio and video chapters, this chapter aims to help non-programming specialists to understand the processes and problems that arise in multimedia software development.

A computer program is a series of operations and decisions. Something happens as a result of the user carrying out an action, and the software will respond. It is the designer's task to decide what that response will be and the software engineer, or programmer, who implements this as code. The software engineer will write the software that carries out this integration by using either an authoring tool or a programming language.

Authoring versus programming

There is no hard and fast rule about what constitutes authoring as distinct from programming. Packages with which you can write multimedia applications range from graphical packages like Hypercard where you can build basic interactive structures with a few clicks of the mouse button and a few pulled-down menus, through scripting languages with a language not unlike English, to the hard stuff, such as C and C++. In general the versatility and performance of your application will increase as you move towards a full-blown programming language like C, but it will be more difficult to implement.

On the other hand an authoring package often lends its own look and feel to the application and experienced authors can sometimes look at a program and say 'Oh, that was developed using Macromedia Director' or 'That's a typical ToolBook application'. This is partly the result of early users of such tools making good use of the facilities the tools provide – a package-led approach.

As time has gone on the desired functionality has become more of a driving force than the obvious abilities of the tools. It must be said, however, that authoring tools do have their limits, especially when it comes to performance.

So, how do you choose between the different options? In the end some kind of risk–benefit analysis needs to be done to compare your options but there are a couple of underlying factors which you need to take into account.

As a general rule, the lower the level of coding you undertake, the longer it will take. This is partly because the code will take longer to write, but it will also be more prone to bugs that are difficult to track down. To counter this, if you have software engineers working in your team who have experience of lower-level coding then they may program very quickly. You, or your software team, should be building up a set of routines or libraries for multimedia programming. This is particularly true if you are working in C or C++. You can incorporate these libraries in future projects as well. This is the main reason why it is a good idea for you only to license your code to your clients rather than grant them all rights. Otherwise you will find it difficult to make use of your basic routines from earlier projects.

Besides the inherent abilities of the team at your disposal, you will also be judging the requirements of the particular application. In some cases it may demand low-level coding, for instance if there are any gaming elements, but for less responsive and more asset-led applications an authoring tool may be very appropriate.

The authoring tree

A good graphical authoring package or structure editor will have an underlying scripting language and a good scripting language will allow you to build new commands with a lower-level language like C. At the bottom of this pile, rather like the court of ultimate appeal, the low-level language could call routines in machine code for speed. Machine code written as part of an application is common in games but much less so in multimedia.

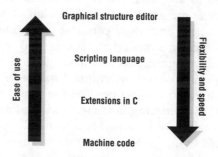

A graphical structure editor, or similar, lets you define the flow of an application's logic by drawing it on the screen in some way, often just like a flow chart in traditional logic. Examples of this kind of authoring package include Icon Author and Authorware.

Alternatively the flow could be predetermined as in a card-based hyperlinked system where you define hot-spots or buttons and then have a new card which is displayed as a result of activating the button. The buttons can also trigger other things besides jumps to other cards, and you can trigger events on opening or closing cards as well. Examples of this kind of system include Hypercard and ToolBook.

A third kind of authoring system uses a time line onto which you put events. The hyperlinks in this kind of system jump around on the time line. Macromedia Director is an authoring system of this kind.

Although these are, in fact, three different kinds of authoring systems, what they have in common are that you can build a simple application or define the outline of a more complex one without typing in any commands. In almost every case, these authoring tools have scripting languages underneath such as Lingo with Director and Hypertalk with Hypercard.

There is no real hard and fast rule about an authoring or scripting language as opposed to a programming language. One definition is that a scripting language is a special type of computer language in that it usually appears to be in English. Scripting languages can also offer intuitive variables like 'it' so that when you 'get the time' the value of 'the time' is held in a variable automatically called 'it'. Then when the next command is 'show it' the value of the time will be displayed. Since the script reads 'get the time, show it' the script reads like English.

This definition falls down partly because well-written code in computer languages can sometimes be as relatively easy to read as English. Also C++, which is a very powerful programming language, has a variable 'this' which always refers to the current object. Some scripting languages, such as Script-X and CD-i Talk, are decidedly cryptic and yet are called scripting languages.

Another definition is that a scripting language will only be able to carry out a defined range of tasks, whereas a programming language is versatile. This one is closer to the truth but still not accurate. As long as a language can carry out basic arithmetic and logic it can, in theory, be applied to any task. But that may be the key. In practice, most scripting languages are good at some tasks but very inefficient in others.

To help with their core task, scripting languages for multimedia will have built-in support for sound and video which would have to be specially programmed in a more general-purpose programming language.

Because of the hyperlinked nature of the HTML (Hypertext Mark-up Language) documents used on the World Wide Web, you could argue that HTML is a scripting language and the kind of programs that read HTML, the so-called Web browsers, can handle pictures, sound and movies. It is possible to use HTML as a simple form of multimedia authoring. HTML is designed to work in a distributed system, namely the Internet, and distributed multimedia is becoming increasingly important.

A final analogy for programming versus authoring: you might be able to use a screwdriver (a low-level and versatile tool) to dig a hole in the road, but would you want to do so? The jackhammer or pneumatic drill (a rather blunt analog of the authoring tool) is better suited to the job, but less versatile than the screwdriver. Conversely, think about trying to turn a screw with a jackhammer.

Stages

There is some confusion as to the stages of software development, since some of the terms mean different things to different people. In practice, because of the diverse backgrounds of people working in multimedia, a strict software-oriented development cycle might not be followed or indeed be appropriate, as has been discussed earlier in Table 2.1. It is up to the development team as to how they manage their programming, but some clients will expect some of the more formal elements of software design.

To help understand this, what follows is a brief outline of a more software-oriented procedure and may not be at all appropriate for your multimedia application.

In addition, the quality standards (such as ISO 9000) which can be applied to any process lay down definite meanings. One common software approach is to write a user requirements document and a functional specification. The proposal to the client may well have covered some aspects of this since the application structure might have been outlined. Ideally someone from the software team would have been involved in this process or else the structure would have been based on previous work and be a structure that is, to a large extent, tried and tested.

User requirements

User requirements is an ambiguous expression and, if it is mentioned, you will need to be sure of what is actually meant. There are two meanings both of which are useful and you might consider including both in the software process.

The first meaning is 'what are the needs of the user that the multimedia application can satisfy?' In this way the user requirement of a word processor is basically the ability to write and manipulate text and this kind of information follows from the scoping of the project when the needs and objectives of the user are determined.

This is a very general interpretation and allows the design team to lay down the functionality of the software in a general way. Sometimes this stage is called a user specification and, in order to help a potential client or sponsor understand what the application will do, it could include short scenarios which describe (hypothetically) what it would be like to use the application.

The second meaning is 'what does the user require of the application?', which is a much more specific question. Here the answers are things like 'a user-friendly interface', 'spell checking', 'automatic saving of work on a regular basis'. It may be that your client will have very specific requirements that the complete application must fulfil, and a strict user requirements list like this is a good way of expressing those. The software team use the list as input saying what needs to be done. It is their task to work out how to do it, which leads to the functional specification.

Functional specification

Whereas the user requirements outline what needs to be done, the functional specification gives much more detail about how a task will be carried out. At its fullest a functional specification will list the outcome of every action carried out by the user and will say how that is to be achieved.

For a major software project, the functional specification will be a very large document and will be carefully researched and written. It can take many months to write the specification and it is the document that defines the application. If clients have a software background, they may ask for such a document. Otherwise, the programmers will perform the same sort of task adapted to the constraints of multimedia but clients will not necessarily be given it as part of the documentation because its use to them without a programming background would be minimal. If clients have requested a functional specification, then once this document is agreed and signed off, any changes have to be similarly discussed, agreed and signed off as change requests. A change request can then be evaluated in terms of its impact on time, quality and budget as discussed in Chapter 5.

There is a basic difficulty in applying a strict functional specification of this type to multimedia which is why its use is intermittent in the industry. This results partly from the audio-visual nature of multimedia. A lot of the content of the application lies in the assets, and they can be very difficult to specify since, at the start, they will not have been researched. Also, time-based media are notoriously difficult to specify since the performance of the integrated application depends on so many factors, including the exact nature of the time-based asset itself. We are not yet at the stage in multimedia where our clients and viewers can take as read the quality thresholds that apply to assets in the way they can for radio or television. The concept of broadcast quality cannot yet automatically apply to multimedia simply because of the variety of display systems on people's desks.

A second problem with the functional specification lies in the difficulty of writing down what is a very dynamic process. For this reason many developers use prototypes, or demonstrator applications sometimes also called animatics, to define the task to be carried out. Even then there is an acceptance that not everything intended can be achieved. This would never be the case with a piece of accounting software. Sometimes for multimedia the only accurate definition of an application will be the application itself.

Finally, a recent trend in software design has been to forego a functional specification altogether. With object-oriented programming, where distinct modules of the program are defined carefully so that they operate as independent objects and just communicate with each other, the important thing to define is the way the program will work. The exact detail of how the objects are coded is left to the software engineers.

For these reasons any kind of functional specification, and also the user requirements, are likely to be internal rather than external documents in a multimedia development. Their primary purpose is to help the software team to build the application rather than to define the application for the client. As a result the documents may even be called something completely different but would fulfil broadly the same purpose.

Alpha and omega

The actual development, as distinct from the talking about the development, also has names. Again, there is some variance as to what the terms really mean, but this is one set of meanings. Software people will sometimes refer to stages of a project in terms such as pre-alpha, alpha, beta and golden master. A wider approach to testing than a pure software approach is discussed in Chapter 18. Using this as a reference, the point at which you would put your application out for external testing is what would be referred to as a beta version by software-oriented developers.

An alpha is more for testing internally in the team, and you might not even show it to the client. To extend the meaning of alpha into multimedia you might say that an alpha is structurally complete but does not have all its content in place, only enough to test functionality while you are waiting for the complete content. This is part of the type of testing referred to as developmental testing in Chapter 18.

The golden master is the one which is really going to be sent for replication and distribution. It is fully tested and has survived all the testing you, and possibly your client, has thrown at it. The application is signed off or gets final acceptance.

As the software team gets bigger, the difficulties of keeping track of the development increases. In multimedia the problem of version control or version tracking, as this is called, increases as well because most of your assets will be going through changes too. As part of your version control you will need to devise a numbering scheme for everything you do, including the documentation. Here are some suggestions:

- Anything that is unfinished has a version number smaller than one, for example 0.3 or 0.99 (for 'almost there'). You can have more numbers after the decimal point to show very small changes but this is a rather subjective concept.
- A more complex numbering system, such as 1.2 B 24 would denote that this is the beta version of version 1.2 of the specification and this

is the 24th build of the application. The term build implies a compiling process or some process that takes the software in one form and turns it into another.

■ An odd or an even number beyond the decimal point could indicate whether the change from the last number was due to new functionality or a bug fix.

In a modular piece of software a version number should be given to every module, especially if different people are writing different modules. Use comments in code freely to explain what is going on, including the basics of what the module does. Images built as montages of other images will also require version numbers.

Bugs

Computers are, at best, very stupid but very logical. They never know what you mean, they only know what you say in your programs and this can be extremely frustrating when something goes wrong with a program and it has to be investigated.

Legend has it that the use of the word bug, meaning a problem in a computer program, dates from Admiral Grace Hopper who was one of the very early computer pioneers (and sometimes credited with inventing the software computer program). A big computer failed and the cause was an

insect (bug) which had crawled onto a logic module and died as a result of the heat or voltage. The logic module used a valve or vacuum tube.

There is a saying in programming – 'There is always one more bug' – and unfortunately, the reliability of complex systems decreases geometrically with the number of component parts. Since a computer program does not wear out like a car engine, its reliability is better defined as correct operation under all conditions. Things the user is not supposed to do – like illegal keystrokes – should be catered for during software development. But, reliability tends to decrease with the increasing complexity of the program. It now seems to be accepted that a complex computer program can never be tested for absolutely every eventuality.

This can be difficult for clients to understand. If they come from an area where seeming absolute quality is achievable they might overreact to a bug. The onus is on the software team, and the project manager, to test as thoroughly as possible, bearing in mind cost and time constraints.

One option is to allow the client to use the software in anger for some time and delay final acceptance until that period is finished. If you are going to do this then it is vital that the schedule and cost allow for it and that this has been agreed up front, not as an afterthought. See Chapter 18 for how to specify a full testing strategy.

If it is of any consolation, even long-established software can have bugs, some known and some unknown. One very common microprocessor, which was for a long time a mainstay of 8-bit computing, had a low-level addressing bug which was never fixed. If a bug is known about, and software works around the bug, it is possible the bug will never be fixed because fixing the bug would affect the existing programs working around it.

The demo factor

In many organizations and projects there will be pressures to demonstrate applications. This could be for the client, or other clients, or the board, or at a trade show. The demo factor brings two major implications to the development of the application.

Firstly, and this is a negative factor, the timing is likely to be such that you will have to assemble a special version for demonstration. This is very likely to be the case if the demo is taking place early in the development of the application.

Secondly, and this is a positive factor, a demo can be a very good bug finder. There is something about letting a member of the company management demonstrate the software which brings the bugs out from the woodwork. Of course this means that the demo should be 'scripted' so that nothing untoward happens. Unfortunately people demonstrating applications do not always follow instructions. The author was involved in a project where the demonstrator was warned that under no circumstances should he do a certain thing because it was known to crash the program.

He, of course, did just that – at the beginning of his demonstration to the Chairman of the multinational company for which he worked.

However, that is a lesson you learn very quickly the hard way, and it is a lot easier to lose a client than to gain one. The best approach is not to be pressganged into giving demos too early.

The only other solution is to make sure that even a demo is solid enough to continue working and not crash completely. Do not have buttons that call a routine that crashes; rather, make them 'blind' and not do anything. It takes minutes to restart most multimedia systems.

The jigsaw

Software engineering is becoming more and more like a mix and match jigsaw puzzle. Programs are made up of objects which interact with each other and can be reused in other applications. Multimedia applications will have three main sections which need to be fitted together.

The user interface is the means by which the user controls the program. It may or may not include assets of its own.

The program logic runs behind the user interface and carries out the tasks the user interface requests, and will possibly have an agenda of its own if, for example, the application includes any simulations.

The assets are the audio-visual components of the program which the program logic will choose and activate, usually on the instructions of the user interface.

Even if the application does not easily break down into these three sections, there are reasons why you might wish to separate them from a logical point of view. The user interface may run remotely from the core program logic in a networked application. Assets will need to be proofread or otherwise checked, which is their equivalent of debugging, and replacing assets is easy if they are not inexorably entwined in the software. Program logic is less platform-dependent than the user interface and so is easier to port from one platform to another.

Risky business

There is a wish in most software teams for them to be exploring new territory and not continuously reworking the same old routines time and time again. It is considered a matter of pride to be asked to beta test some new software tool or operating system extension.

Against this is the risk that 'pushing the envelope' can be a dangerous business. The envelope is your current level of expertise and when you push the envelope you try something newer and more challenging. To build an application you need to be able to plan and move forward through the development cycle, and if the sands shift beneath you because of bugs in the tools or changes in their functionality then you are in trouble. There are few things worse in computing than chasing a bug for months only to find eventually that the problem lies in the operating system or the language or some other third-party software such as a low-level driver.

Of course there always has to be a first time to use a new tool, so you can never be completely sure. The message is to think very carefully of the implications of using something new and to allow for extra time for the learning curve in your planning.

The time when you use a new version of a tried and trusted tool or of the operating system can also be problematic and, as a general rule, upgrading should not be carried out in mid-project unless there is no alternative.

It is also possible that using a previously untried feature of familiar software can cause difficulties. Unfortunately it is not always possible to rely on documentation since a complex program, by definition, is very difficult to document fully. And as already mentioned, there can also be bugs in even long-established software and even the operating system or processor.

The link between software and the client

The project manager's dilemma.

More so than in any other area of multimedia development, the project manager or producer has to be able to act both as a buffer and as a translator between the client and the team. As project manager you have to trust your team to truly represent the status of the software. Sometimes they will give you what seems completely counter-intuitive advice as a result of some esoteric way the compiler or authoring tool works or because of a known problem with the delivery system. The risk is that the client, if not familiar with software engineering and programming, will sometimes think that there is no substance to the real problems you will face. You are the liaison between the team and the client and you need to be able to understand the problems the software hits in order to explain such things. There is a fine line between explaining a complicated problem to clients and blinding them with science and where that line is depends a great deal on your relationship with the clients.

THEORY INTO PRACTICE 18

Talk to people you know who have programmed multimedia applications and ask them what they liked and disliked about the process and about the tools and languages they used. You should take any opportunity you have to try new tools and you will find demonstration examples of some on the CD-ROM and on the Internet.

Summary

- Integration is the core stage of multimedia development, where assets and software are fused together to make the application.
- Choosing the software package, programming language or authoring system is key to this stage. Multimedia authoring systems will have built-in support for different kinds of asset.
- You will need to define names and numbering conventions for the different stages of your development and testing.
- Testing and fixing bugs in complex code will be time consuming and it is essential to avoid the possibility of bugs in tools and operating system routines as they will confuse the testing.
- 'Pushing the envelope' is risky.
- The software development in multimedia is likely to be the least understood part of the process for a client.

Recommended reading

Apple Computer Inc. (1987). *The Apple Macintosh Human Interface Guidelines*. Reading, MA: Addison-Wesley
Vaughan T. (1994). *Multimedia: Making it Work*. Berkeley, CA: Osborne McGraw-Hill

CHAPTER 17

RIGHTS, COPYRIGHT AND OTHER INTELLECTUAL PROPERTIES

Project manager's responsibilities

- To ensure that all assets used in the application are cleared for the correct use
- To avoid the rights status of the whole application being compromised by uncoordinated rights issues
- To consult expert opinion if there are any doubts

Rights and wrongs

Suppose I came round to your house for dinner one evening, and you showed me a beautiful model boat you had made. It had taken you several weeks to build it, and you had lovingly fashioned every plank on the deck and every line in the rigging yourself. It was well made and I liked it. To quote the Bible, I coveted it. So on the way out of your house I hid the boat under my coat and I walked away with it. Is that theft?

Once I had reached my house I took your boat and put it into a machine that made copies of it: each copy indistinguishable from the original. I took those copies down to the market the next day and sold dozens of them and paid you nothing. Have I done anything illegal or immoral?

Suppose I came round to your house for dinner one evening, and you played me a beautiful song you had written. It had taken you several weeks to compose it, and you had lovingly fashioned every nuance in the melody and every line in the lyrics yourself. It was well written and I liked it. To quote the Bible, I coveted it. So on the way out of your house I remembered your song. Is that theft?

Once I had reached my house I took your song and sang it into a machine that recorded it and then made copies of it. I took those copies down to the market the next day and sold dozens of them and paid you nothing. Have I done anything illegal or immoral?

In law a copyright is as much an object as something you can touch. It can be traded and it can be passed on to your heirs. Unfortunately it is also intangible. You cannot actually touch it and so it does not match our usual understanding of a property.

Copyright is one important aspect of what is called intellectual property (IP). This chapter has two aims. Firstly it will provide some background to copyright itself, and why it is important, and secondly it will outline some of the rights models used in the media to see whether they can be applied in a particular multimedia application for the licensing of IP and assets. There is a caveat. Intellectual property is a complex area of the law, and expert advice should always be sought if there is any doubt. It also differs from country to country and even the basic philosophy behind rights differs between countries. This chapter is only intended as an introduction and not as a user guide.

In the beginning

Copyright as a concept in English law has its roots in new technology. In the second half of the fifteenth century the invention of printing made it possible for books to be mass produced and, as a result, unauthorized copying was a possibility. The book printers, the stationers, formed themselves into a guild and were granted a royal charter in 1556. Under this charter lawfully printed books were registered with the guild and the guild had powers to act against unauthorized copies.

The first copyright act dates from 1709 and gave the 'sole right and liberty' of printing books to authors and whoever they assigned rights to. Protection was for a period of 14 years from publication but could only really be enforced if, as before, the book was registered with the Stationers' Company.

Later revisions of the law widened the net to include other creative works such as engravings and music. Eventually the emphasis on copying had to be extended to embrace rights of usage for performances of music and drama and eventually sound recordings, cinematograph films and broadcasting joined the fray: the concept of what is still called copyright extending to embrace new means of distributing intellectual property.

From this beginning has come international agreement on the protection of intellectual property. This covers inventions, copyrights and, to a lesser degree, designs and a recent addition which is moral rights. To a great extent the introduction of moral rights into English law reduces some of the differences from, say, French law. The English approach has been that protection of copyright is protection of the material benefit of exploiting that right. This is why English law protected the rights of printers. The French and Belgian perspective is that copyright is in some way a recognition of the artistic achievement of the author. In fact in French it is not copyright that is protected, but *droit d'auteur*.

Getting a copyright

In US, UK and European law a copyright is created at the same time as the copyright work. The situation used to be different in the USA where you had to publish using a particular notice of copyright, or in some cases register a copyright for it to be in existence, but this situation was anomalous and recently changed. Timing is important since the only infallible test of having a copyright lies in being able to prove possession of the copyright work before anyone else. In other words, you have the original. A common, and cheap, method of achieving this is to mail yourself a copy by registered post, which fixes a date to the copy in the envelope as long as it remains unopened. (Time travel will play havoc with all this, as Douglas Adams has pointed out in *The Hitch-Hiker's Guide to the Galaxy*.)

You can have copyright in a work of art (painting, drawing, sculpture, and so on), literature (prose or poetry – even the source code of a computer program), music (more on this later) and in a photograph or movie or television programme. There has to have been some effort exercised to create a copyright so that by photocopying a drawing you do not create a new copyright – you only risk infringing the original one. This condition, in English law, is sometimes called 'sweat of the brow' and is less demanding than US law which requires creative effort.

The advent of electronic reproduction has confused the copyright situation and the law keeps changing to cope with it. Until the 20th century there was no need to recognize that there could be copyright in a photograph or sound recording and as time has gone on whole new issues have been added to intellectual property such as 'look and feel' (can you protect the way your user interface works? – Apple and Microsoft have been battling over this issue for many years) and recently an important US court held the menu commands of a leading spreadsheet to be uncopyrightable.

International agreement on copyright has been based on a series of conventions that are ratified by governments. Since the distribution of intellectual property is an international business it is only equitable that a country should expect the same kind of protection for its citizens' work in a foreign country as it gives to its citizens itself – or indeed gives to citizens of foreign countries. Needless to say, some countries have taken a more lax view of this kind of protection than others as any visitor to certain parts of the Far East may have found.

Although copyright protection is automatic in the UK, it is considered a good idea to assert the copyright by printing a notice such as © 1996 Elaine England and Andy Finney. Other phrases such as 'all rights reserved' and 'if you copy this we will send the boys round and sort you out' or the prominent FBI shield that you see on American videos are arguably a bit over the top. The reason for them is to remove any possibility that a defendant in court could claim he or she didn't know the material was copyright. This is, of course, no defence to a primary infringement, but it could be considered to be mitigation since ignorance of copyright is widespread. Primary infringement is the initial production of an infringing copy. In cases of secondary infringement, ignorance can be a defence in the UK. This would happen if, for example, you imported an infringing work or licensed the work and were reasonably sure that the person who provided the material had cleared the rights. Even if an infringer acknowledges that 'copyright infringement is theft', as they say, there is also an attitude that copyright owners are rich and would not miss a few bucks. But we all have the potential to be copyright owners and deserve not to be ripped off.

When you produce a copyright work as part of your employment, the copyright usually rests with your employer. Similarly, in the UK, but not in the USA, when you commission a freelancer to produce it for you, the ownership of the copyright will usually rest with whoever commissions the work or pays the person who produces it. But this is not always so and a discussion of this problem is beyond the scope of this chapter.

Photographers, for example, retain their copyright under English law even if they are commissioned.

If you have to decide about copyright ownership you should think of it in terms of future use. If you as creator will have no further use for the work then you lose nothing by assigning copyright or granting an exclusive license. Assigning your rights means that they are no longer yours: you have sold them and an assignment is always exclusive.

As commissioner you have to be able to use the work for its intended purpose, which may or may not require you to own the copyright. (Code is a special case which is discussed later in this chapter.) Beyond these issues the copyright in something is as much a part of the deal as the money paid and can be negotiated since the copyright has a value in itself that is distinct from ownership or use of the work itself. It is also unrelated to the time it took to create the work since a Picasso sketch remains a Picasso sketch whether it took him ten days or ten seconds to draw it. To be safe all copyright assignments and licences should be in writing. In fact, under English law, an assignment of copyright can only be made in writing.

Moral rights

Moral rights are a relatively new addition to intellectual property in English law. This provides a method in law for you to be credited for your work (called paternity) and for your work to be used only in ways of which you approve and without unauthorized changes (integrity). Given the interactive nature of multimedia, moral rights are quite significant, especially integrity. It is worth noting that you can do anything with a work if the author consents. In the USA, moral rights are narrow and usually only apply to visual arts.

The composer of a piece of music has a moral right for the music not to be edited. You should not cut out the verses to leave just the chorus or change the order of the verses. If you design an interactive application which allows the user to do things like this then you risk infringing the moral rights of the composer. For this reason most music publishers will not allow you to include a song in your multimedia application under circumstances where the user can change the music because they do not have the permission of the composer to do so. Music will be discussed in more detail later.

When a graphics artist builds a montage of images from many sources there is a risk of infringing moral rights. A particular photographer might take exception to having something excerpted from the image or having the image cropped. Juxtaposition of one image with another might be problematic for reasons other than copyright because it is possible to libel someone by publishing an unwisely montaged picture, so great care should be taken with this. Is it real or is it Photoshop? An extreme example would be to build a photograph of a notable teetotal politician drinking a glass of water into a montage so that he appears to be drinking in a vodka distillery.

Because moral rights are new to English law there is less guidance on what can and cannot be done than there is with more established areas of copyright. One possibly contentious area arises because the author or authors of a computer program have no rights of paternity or integrity. This is because computer programs are often written by large teams. But does this also apply to multimedia? As a creative person your future depends on people recognizing your past work and it is important that credit is given where it is due. There will be instances where, as a multimedia developer, your client will attempt to deny you a credit. Your only straightforward way of achieving your just credit is to insist on it in your contract with the client, rather than by relying on the law. Conversely, many commissioning contracts will include a clause waiving moral rights.

Exceptions

One problem with copyright, if taken to extremes, is that while the owners have their rights, the rest of us should also have some leeway to enable life to go on; and the concepts known as fair dealing (fair use in the USA) and insubstantial portions come into play. In law, and in the right circumstances, these are two important exceptions to infringement. A critic reviewing a book has the right to quote from it without asking permission. A student studying the works of an artist has the right to photocopy illustrations to include them in a research paper. You can quote a small (insubstantial) extract from a literary work.

In the USA there are also exceptions for parody, news coverage and so on; even some commercial use may be fair if it does not injure the copyright owner.

Unfortunately we cannot always benefit from these exceptions in multimedia production. Recently, in English law, it has been ruled that some of the exceptions to infringement do not apply if you are making a commercial product, and a multimedia title for sale would be commercial. The term 'insubstantial portion' does not necessarily mean that anything short is OK, and two obvious exceptions to this are the denouement of a mystery novel and a line of poetry. The test is always one of degree and there are no hard and fast rules about what constitutes an insubstantial portion. Importantly, this kind of exception only applies to literature, not a film or a piece of music for example, so you cannot argue that a four-second sample from a hit record is fair game because it is an insubstantial portion.

Alongside the exceptions included in copyright legislation, there has to be an element of common sense. It is very difficult to judge whether a photograph will work in a montage without trying it out. Here, technology is actually making things more difficult for us. In the old days, to make a mock-up of a page of a magazine, you might cut out copies of photographs from the colour supplements and paste them onto a piece of paper. That does not infringe copyright in the photographs. Doing the same thing on a computer involves scanning the photographs, and so you infringe the copyright unless you already have permission to scan the image into the computer. In this case the intention is the same but changing the means by which you carry out your intention has led to a possible infringement.

One very constructive idea to get over the mock-up infringement problem has been implemented by some stock photo libraries who give you a blanket permission to reproduce their images for mock-ups.

Music

One area of copyright that causes confusion is music and it is worth going into this rights situation in some detail. The confusion arises because there are several different rights in music which have grown up in custom and practice over the years.

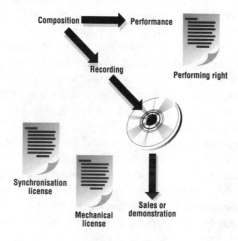

Music rights.

Once you write a tune it is copyrighted, and you have the exclusive right to exploit that tune which you might do yourself, or by assigning the rights to a publisher who then 'works' the tune on your behalf for a fee. Once upon a time music was 'plugged' by a song 'plugger' going to the office of a band leader and playing the tune on a piano in the hope of the band performing it. Today a 'plugger' is more likely to be taking a disc jockey out to lunch.

If you grant permission for someone to perform your tune in public, that is, logically enough, called the performing right. In the UK performing rights in music are administered by a body called the Performing Rights Society (PRS) and they collect money from radio stations, concert venues and the like. In the USA the equivalents of PRS are ASCAP, BMI and SESAC. In multimedia you are unlikely to have to deal with the performing right although, because of the similarity of wide area network distribution (for which read Internet) to cable, PRS have gained a foothold here. If one of your multimedia productions is played at an exhibition, and it contains music, then permission is needed otherwise the performing right is infringed. In the UK it is usually the responsibility of the venue to cover any fees due for public performance of music and they probably have a blanket licence for this purpose, as do many bars and shops.

If your tune is recorded another permission is required covering what is called the mechanical right. This right, administered in the UK by the Mechanical Copyright Protection Society (MCPS) and by The Harry Fox Agency in the USA, is quite distinct from the copyright in the recording. If you include a record or CD in your multimedia application you will need permission and a licence covering the music, which will come from a music publisher, and a separate licence for the use of the recording, which will come from a record company. This need for a dual licence has led to some publishers setting up special libraries for use in film and television – and now multimedia – where all the rights are controlled by the publisher so they become a one-stop shop for music. Using these recordings is always cheaper so library (sometime called production) music should be your first choice for music in multimedia.

With library music the licence is usually called a synchronization licence because the music is mostly used synchronized to images in films and television, and generally does not attract a royalty payment, just a fee based on duration used. You and the library publisher can also negotiate for reductions, royalties or whatever you jointly agree.

Another significant benefit of library music is that it is provided specifically for you to tailor to your needs. The publisher will expect you to edit it to fit your requirements. This will not be the case with a commercial gramophone record where you would normally have to explain in some detail just what you want to do with the recording before permission is considered. The British Musicians Union also considers that interactive multimedia is a different usage compared to sale on a record or CD and might require that you pay another session fee; this fee would be in addition to a licence from the record company and the publisher. The session fee is the fee paid to the musicians for playing the music at the recording unless they were members of a regular group, in which case they would probably receive royalties from sales.

When you license a music recording from a record company, the company may have to pay royalties to the principal performers from your usage, depending on the contract between the record company and the artists. In many cases, use in multimedia would not be covered by their contract and the record company would have to negotiate for the right with the artist before being able to license it to you. This may be impractical and so the record company would have to refuse you a licence.

Alternatively you could get the music specially composed and recorded and a surprising number of multimedia projects do this. On the one hand this ignores what a good library publisher can offer but it does ensure that you have original music, which might be very important to your application. If you do commission music, you should make sure you take further exploitation rights. This would enable you to use the music in a sequel, or to release a record if your games theme was a hit.

The public domain and clip media

Copyright does not last for ever. As the concept of copyright in law developed, so the time for which a work was copyright grew. At the beginning of the 20th century copyright only lasted for the greater of 42 years from the date of publication or seven years after the death of the author. In the following hundred years the period has grown to allow the heirs of the author more time to benefit from the work until the period reached 70 years after the death. This was 50 years in the UK until copyright was harmonized within the European Union.

In the USA the duration is much more complex than in Europe. Pre-1979 works are protected for an initial period of 28 years, renewable for a further 47 years. A work which first expired after 1963 was automatically renewed but complex rules govern who actually receives the renewal rights. Currently the 50-year expiry term applies in the USA as it did in Europe, but a pending bill would raise this to life plus 70 years.

Any assumption that a work is out of copyright is fraught with danger and you should seek professional advice, but in general a literary or artistic work is in copyright in Europe until 70 years after the end of the year in which the author died. This becomes more complicated for a translated work where the translator has rights too and similarly for illustrators and engravers.

In Europe, a sound recording expires 50 years after publication. So if you have an original 78 rpm gramophone record from before 1945 in your possession – an old Caruso recording, for example – then the recording is no longer in copyright. The tune, however, could well be in copyright since its copyright lasts for 70 years after the death of the composer. Similar arrangements apply to photographs and to movies – known as cinematograph films – the situation is complicated since performance in public was not seen to be a publication. So some movies have surprisingly long copyright lives. The situation is not simple and undoubtedly you can imagine the complexity of rights in a production containing multiple media forms each of which has different copyright terms and needs world rights.

Incidentally, you should assume that a transcription onto CD of an old recording is copyright, especially if the sound was cleaned up in the process. It is possible to fingerprint digital files to identify the source, so if you wish to use an old record, you should clean it up yourself.

So now we come to the Mona Lisa. Since Leonardo da Vinci died over 70 years ago, the picture is out of copyright. It is so old that copyright did not even exist at the time. Therefore you might assume that you can include an image of the Mona Lisa in your application without permission. Unfortunately this is not the case and the reason will become clear if you consider how you would acquire an image of the painting – stealing it from the Louvre is not an option.

If you owned the Mona Lisa you would have the right to control access to it and as a result, to control reproductions. This is true of any collection of out of copyright works, usually in the hands of museums or art galleries. They will grant permission for reproduction, for a fee, as if the work was in copyright and they owned the copyright. The agreement you sign with the gallery allows you to use the image for a specific purpose. If you use it for another purpose you are not in breach of copyright but you are in breach of the contractual agreement. There will be a copyright in the photograph you receive from the library as well.

Going to the gallery or museum and photographing the picture yourself would not infringe copyright but the museum would presumably only allow you entry on condition that you did not take photographs, or that if you were to do so, they would not be for publication. This is a contractual obligation on you, but it could be invalid if it was not brought to your attention before you bought your entry ticket. The Van Gogh museum in Amsterdam has a more straightforward approach. They do not allow anyone to take a camera inside. Incidentally, if you were able to take a photograph through an open window, you would not have infringed copyright or any contract. Whether the resulting image would be good enough to publish is another issue altogether.

In general the terms 'out of copyright' and 'in the public domain' are used to mean the same thing, but they are not exactly so. Copyrights expire after a time, but the owner has the right to give them away before this time if he, she or it (because an organization can own copyrights) so desires. The owner can also allow people to exploit the work without payment with or without conditions attached. This is known as placing it in the public domain. However, just because an author places something, like a piece of software, in the public domain does not mean that it is out of copyright. Often conditions are attached – so read the small print or the 'read me' file. The copyright on something placed in the public domain in this way will expire at the usual time.

NASA, like other US government agencies, places its material in the public domain. This means that you can use images from the space probes free of charge (apart from paying to get the picture itself). However, NASA does state that you cannot use the images in such a way as to suggest that NASA endorses your product. So there is a condition, albeit a relatively small one, attached. Since 1978 works of the US government have not had copyright protection at all (Section 105 of the US Copyright Act) but this was not intended to extend outside the USA, which raises the question of European use and even of export outside the USA of finished works incorporating such material.

Some companies produce libraries of assets which are supplied 'royalty free' for you to use on paper or in multimedia applications. This is clip art, or clip media. This material is often still in copyright and it is not really in the public domain either because you pay for the book or CD-ROM which contains it and your use of the material is restricted. There is probably a restriction to make sure that you do not produce more clip media discs from their clip media discs, and you might be restricted to a certain number of images in a single production. But you do not have to pay anything else to use the material in as many productions as you like.

CD-ROMs of clip media range in price from tens to hundreds of pounds/dollars. You can even buy clip art in books, and the Dover Books series of clip art and design are a notable example of this. They often reproduce illustrations from Victorian books and magazines because they are, in themselves, out of copyright. If you own or have unrestricted access to hundred-year-old copies of the *Illustrated London News* or *Strand Magazine* (with its original Sherlock Holmes stories and illustrations) then you could exploit their contents because you have the actual out of copyright originals, assuming that the author and illustrator died long enough ago.

As a multimedia developer you must think not only of the rights you take in assets you license but also consider the rights you can take in any work you commission. You could be commissioning art work from a graphic designer, photographs, music or scripts. There is even the software written by your programmers.

As a rule of thumb you should explicitly acquire rights in any work done for you by your staff or freelancers. This would be included in the contract for the work but, to be sure, has to be a contract with the person doing the work, not an agency or subcontracting company. If you are acquiring rights from a freelancer or subcontractor then he or she must be able to pass on those rights and should indemnify you against any claims should that not turn out to be the case. You can acquire rights in future work if it is appropriate, and it is important to obtain moral rights as well.

Rights models

In order to make use of someone else's intellectual property in a project you have to get permission, and this will result in the granting of a licence for the use of the copyright material. It can be difficult to describe the rights involved, so one approach is simply to describe what the project is, how it will be used and who will buy it. In some forms of media a number of specific rights have grown up which define the uses you can make of the material you have licensed. For example:

- All rights
  As it suggests, this type of agreement gives the developer all the rights for exploitation of the material. In practice this might be the kind of right taken in a small interview or script rather than a substantial contribution to an application. In the case of small contributions this kind of agreement might attract only a small fee, or maybe no fee at all. However, since an all rights contract with no residuals (residuals being payments for further use of the material beyond the original purpose) are rather biased in favour of the producer or publisher rather than the contributor, they should be used with care.

- Non-theatric
  In audio-visual publications, a non-theatric right is one which excludes broadcast, home video and theatric rights. This sounds a little back to front but basically broadcasting is usage for radio or television transmission (and possibly cable), theatric is performance where the public pay to see the material (as in a cinema) and home video is where the public pay for the material. Non-theatric covers use in training, business, education, conferences and exhibitions. This is the case even if the public pay admission, because they are not paying specifically to see the material.

- **Home video**
  This right, applied to videos, allows you to sell or rent the material to the general public. The equivalent for audio is the Gramophone right whereby record companies pay musicians to include their contributions on records.

- **Interactive right**
  This is a term that has recently been applied to a permission to use material in any interactive form such as CD-ROM or, possibly, Interactive Services on Demand (but this last example overlaps with cable). It is platform independent but has definite implications for moral rights if the viewer can modify the assets.

- **Flash fees**
  Stills, when used on television, are sometimes paid for on the basis of the time they are on screen. The common, but essentially impossible, question from picture libraries for multimedia is 'How long is it on screen?' Music will usually have a rate dependent on duration, but you do not 'still frame' a piece of audio. However, you could repeat a loop of music under a menu, for example. In this case you should negotiate a special rate for the use.

Split market.

The terms used above are some that you might come across, and they are not platform specific. There seem to be two schools of thought regarding the licensing of assets for multimedia. The first says that the licence should relate to the market for the product. Terms like non-theatric apply to that method of licensing. The second school of thought says that the method of delivering the material is more important than the market and will want to license differently for analog and digital, for interactive and linear, and for MPC or CD-i. It is unclear at the moment which way the licensing model will go but the author's preference as a developer is for the market-led approach.

Unfortunately, in an immature market – and for immature read also 'small' – it could be considered restrictive for a developer to have to renegotiate if they want to port an application from one platform to another. If you make a single disc that will play on any computer platform this becomes totally impossible. To get around this you might ask for a licence for all platforms.

Similarly you have to consider whether a foreign language translation of an application which otherwise remains the same should require renegotiation of the licence for pictures or music. MCPS, on behalf of library music publishers, are quite clear on this and count translations as part of the original licence as long as only the voice track has changed.

One model, adopted by at least one major multimedia developer, is to acquire rights for all versions on all platforms for the life of the product. The 'life of the product' is a vague term which has, as yet, remained untested, but probably allows revisions but does not allow the material to be used on a disc on another subject.

Licences are also granted for territories. These may be language specific (such the amusingly named GAS – Germany Austria Switzerland) or regional (North America or EU) or historic (British Commonwealth). World rights used to be considered to be all-encompassing but the advent of satellites has led to a Solar System or Universe territory.

One usage issue which is exercising some multimedia developers is the question of contribution. 'Just what is the contribution of this asset to my application?' This is obviously a question you should be asking when you assess a fee but it can also become a negotiating point. Does an image that is only seen if the viewer navigates his or her way down through five levels to a particular screen of explanatory detail carry as much weight as an image in the main menu?

The risk of following this path of argument is that, rather than lowering the fee for the less-seen image, it raises the fee for the one in the main menu. The question has to be judged on the basis of what is actually being bought. In practice it is the right of reproduction of the copyright image, related to the intended use, which is being bought. Trying to quantify how likely it is that a viewer will see the image is akin to differentiating between different pages in a book.

The already confusing rights situation in multimedia is compounded by different asset owners applying different models. Picture and music libraries work differently and two picture sources may operate in different ways as well. Since there should be a known status of rights for the whole multimedia application it is important not to risk one asset compromising the others in terms of such things as the duration of a licence, or territories the application can be sold in. Not paying attention to this can result in the rights in the whole product being affected by the lowest common denominator of rights in its individual assets.

Because of possible ambiguity and misunderstanding, it is dangerous to rely on terms like 'non-theatric' or 'interactive' instead of a clear specification, in a licence, of exactly what media, platform and so on is actually meant. A licence should also say who owns rights not expressly granted.

Royalties versus buy-outs

Should you pay royalties or pay a one-off fee for use of material? And if you buy-out rights, what multiple of the standard fee should be used?

Although a creator has every right to share in the profits from his or her work there are compelling reasons why a buy-out can be a fair offer. In a small market it might be a very long time before a royalty stream amounts to much. A buy-out on the basis of an estimated number of sales may lessen the opportunity for making more money in the long term but it does give the asset owner 'money now', which may be much better than 'maybe more money much later'. Look upon it as repositioning the risk and consider the interest earned by investing the extra money instead of waiting for a royalty trickle.

From a practical point of view it can be difficult for multimedia developers to administer royalties if they are small companies. Often the applications are made for clients who pay the developer a fixed fee for the development and the developer may not get any royalties, which does not provide a basis for any downstream royalty payments to asset owners. Clients may not be willing to undertake to pay royalties because they had no control over the negotiations.

In more mature media, such as books, television and records, companies have whole departments that handle royalty tracking and payments and in time multimedia publishing will probably follow this model.

Rights in code

The situation for rights in computer code is a little different from rights in assets because of the way code is written. It is often built up of fragments, libraries and routines which were written for other projects to carry out certain tasks such as drawing a picture to the screen or synchronizing sound and pictures.

It is custom and practice for software not to be sold but to be licensed. If you produce a multimedia application for a client you should not assign the copyright in the code to the client because that will make it difficult for you to reuse that work. Clients ought to accept this but it does mean that you need to state it explicitly in the agreement with your client. You will, of course, have to grant a free licence to use the code otherwise they cannot make use of what they have paid for, but they will not own it.

As a developer contracting software from a programmer you will have the opposite point of view and will probably want to make continuing use of any code written for you. This means that you will have to explicitly take the rights you need from the programmer. If you have contracted a company rather than a person you need to be sure that they can assign you these rights because they have taken them. Should you ever want to license rights in code to your client then you have to have the rights yourself first. It's a basic rule – you cannot license rights you do not have.

How to negotiate

There are no hard and fast rules but a few guidelines would be helpful.

- Be fair and honest. Few rights holders are going to cheat you, they are just after an honest income. Similarly you have a right to pay a fair price.
- Set yourself a target price, based on experience, but don't be unreasonable or inflexible. The more you do this the more you will have a feel for costs.
- Accept that some rates are just not negotiable because the owner does not want to negotiate.
- Be prepared to say 'sorry, I cannot afford your rates' – but make sure you have time to change your plans for the application.
- Remember that the asset owner who has only one asset to sell may want more money than a library.
- If you run into trouble with an asset after the application is 'finished', never admit that to the asset owner. Balance the cost against the cost of changing the application (plus a new asset) rather than your original target price since paying an extra hundred for the picture will cost you less than paying two hundred to go back and change the application.
- Be consistent in your description of the usage to be agreed. This is much more important than worrying about one picture costing too much since one asset that cannot be used in Japan means your whole application cannot be used in Japan.
- If the man with the big cigar says that the voice-over fee is $20,000, accept that he is really trying to say 'Go Away!'.
- Build up working relationships with asset owners, partly because it will make the negotiations more convivial, but also because buying in bulk can be cheaper.

■ Don't confuse the technical cost (such as dubbing the film or photographing the picture) with the licence fee and make sure you know which you are paying and when.

■ If you can, offer to return a picture to a photo library quickly. They might lower their fee as a result. For a bulk deal you could even scan the images on their premises with your equipment. Don't forget to ask for permission to digitize images as part of the process of deciding what to use.

The rights check-list

Can we administer and pay royalties?

What is our target fee for any particular kind of asset?

What computer platforms are we licensing for?

Is excerpting for promotional editorial or advertising of the application included?

What is the duration of the licence?

What territories are covered?

Are foreign language versions covered?

How do the agreements relate to my expected pattern of sales in these territories and languages?

Are further editions of the work covered?

Are bug-fixes covered or would they be considered new editions?

Are derivative versions covered?

Have the asset providers indemnified us against claims for infringement should they not have true title?

...and finally, patents and data protection

You cannot copyright an idea, only the form in which the idea is expressed. The idea that a television transmitter and receiver could be put in an orbit so high above the earth that it appeared to be stationary, and could then be used to relay television signals, cannot be copyrighted. It could be patented – or could have been in 1944 when Arthur C. Clarke wrote his famous Wireless World article on the subject. The article itself, being the expression of the idea in literary form, was copyright and indeed will be for at least the next 50–70 years since, at the time of writing, Mr Clarke is still very much alive.

A patent is a document given to you by the government giving you the exclusive right to exploit and control exploitation of a process for doing something. You have to be able to describe the process in such a way that any reasonably capable person could carry out the work from your description; so you cannot be vague and, say, patent time travel without describing how to do it. The process must not be obvious (patently obvious?) since there has to have been an inventive step in the process that you have seen but others have missed. Finally you have to have done it first. If you were beaten to the idea by someone who can prove it then your patent will not be granted or could be declared invalid, even if you genuinely knew nothing about the other idea. This is called 'prior art'.

In most countries you have to keep quiet about your invention since disclosure can invalidate the patent as well. So do not be tempted to give a learned paper on the subject too soon. Timing is critical and swear everyone you discuss it with to secrecy – that is, 'non disclosure'. To paraphrase Mr Micawber: 'Your rival is one day later than you and you have happiness – one day before you and you have misery'.

Prior art can come from the craziest places. One, possibly apocryphal, instance tells of a patent examiner who was trawling through literature to see if a particular new idea had been described before. He finally found a reference, but it was not in a scientific journal or a PhD thesis: it was in a comic book.

If you have been granted a patent, you have the right to control use of your idea for (in most countries) up to 20 years from the date of filing. A patent does not actually have to be taken out by the inventor. Often employers will take out patents based on work done by their employees. The employee will be the inventor but the employing company will have the patent rights if the work is done during the course of the inventor's employment.

The process of getting a patent is both time consuming and costly. It is important that a patent is carefully worded so that it can stand up to scrutiny for inventiveness. A particular kind of lawyer called a patent agent should be involved in this process. Currently there is no such thing as an international patent. The patent will have to be applied for in every country for which protection is required. This should be the countries in which your product would be used or manufactured. You have the right to stop both sales and manufacture of an infringing item – or to negotiate a royalty payment.

A final point is that in the process of granting you the 'letters patent' the government will also publish your invention. This will even happen if you decide not to pursue the patent.

As the inventor you have the choice of patenting your invention. If you decide not to patent it you should consider finding a way of establishing your 'prior art' by publicizing your idea. If you do this, someone else trying to patent the same process later on will not be able to gain a patent and so stop you making use of your 'own' invention. Altruistically, publishing your idea allows other people to make use of it. It is the equivalent of shareware.

Although you cannot copyright an idea, and many ideas cannot be patented or would not be because of the cost and time involved, you can protect your idea by contract. If you need to discuss your idea with anyone you should get them to sign a non-disclosure agreement (NDA) in which they agree not to disclose your idea. That will afford you a measure of protection and, along with terms and conditions of trade, every company should have a stock NDA.

Data protection is only occasionally going to be an issue with a CD-ROM. Basically, under English law, anybody who uses data relating to living people may have to be registered under the Data Protection Act. The definition of a data user and a data subject are carefully set out in the Act and in the guidelines for registration. People who operate data bureaux also need to be registered.

If you produce a database on a CD-ROM, which contains personal information about living people, you are a data user and must be registered. Your customers, if they are not able to change the data on the CD-ROM, are not data users and so do not have to be registered. If you give them the power to change the data then they may become data users as a result. Any company or person who uses a computer may have to register. Although simple use of mailing lists and word processing are excepted from registration it is worth noting that use of email is not.

Data protection is not dealt with in the same way by every country but within the European Union there are further steps being taken to harmonize legislation. There is no such thing in the USA.

THEORY INTO PRACTICE 19

On the CD-ROM you will find some licence agreements used by asset providers. These are worth studying and will give you a basis on which to consider your own negotiations.

Summary

■ Copyright is a property like any other and, as such, should be respected. A copyright is automatically granted when certain kinds of work are produced, including artistic and literary ones. In some countries, besides the copyright, by which the owner controls reproduction, there are moral rights which protect integrity and paternity.

■ Any asset you wish to use in multimedia is going to have copyright implications but music is perhaps the most complex of these with composer, publisher and sometimes recording company having a stake in the exploitation.

■ There are exceptions which allow some limited use of copyright material without the need for clearance but usually, free use is possible only when the work is out of copyright.

■ Ideas cannot be copyrighted, only the expression of them. If you have an idea for a process for doing something then a patent may be the appropriate course of action.

Recommended reading

You should always take careful legal advice on rights issues but it is useful to have some basic background. Most of these books are based on English law. When reading books on copyright, make sure that they are up to date. The last major revision in UK legislation was in 1988.

Holyoak J. and Torremans P. (1995). *Intellectual Property Law*. London: Butterworths.
This book is aimed at students and gives substantial background on all aspects of IP including patents and copyright. Some international issues are covered as well.
Henry M. (1994). *Publishing and Multimedia Law*. London: Butterworths.
This book covers more law than IP. It is fairly expensive but includes 52 sample contractual documents on paper and PC disk.
Philips J.J., Durie R. and Karet I. (1993). *Whale on Copyright*, 4th edn. London: Sweet & Maxwell.
Strong W.A. (1993). *The Copyright Book: A Practical Guide*, 4th edn. Cambridge, MA: MIT Press.
This is a guide to US law for non-specialists.
Wall R.A. (1993). *Copyright Made Easier*. London: ASLIB.

The American Information Superhighway initiative has produced some useful documents with a background to American rights law. They are available as of early 1996 on the Internet at http://www:uspto.gov/web/ipnii. The report can be found under 'Speeches, Testimony and Documents' in the 'Documents' directory.

The Chartered Institute of Patent Agents (Staple Inn Buildings, High Holborn, London WC1V 7PZ) publish information leaflets which explain the functions of a patent agent.

The Office of the Data Protection Registrar publishes guidelines to data protection as it is implemented in the UK. Copies are available from the Information Services Division, Data Protection Registrar, Wycliffe House, Water Lane, Wilmslow, Cheshire SK9 5AF.

CHAPTER 18

TESTING

Project manager's responsibilities

- To match testing methods to the project
- To devise a testing strategy in conjunction with the team and the clients
- To create enough time and budget for the testing to be carried out effectively
- To manage the acceptance testing process in order to get final sign-off for the project

Multimedia and testing

There is a good deal of confusion about testing and multimedia. Is it necessary? Does testing have to be done by people outside the team? Should software testing techniques be applied to multimedia applications? How much does it cost? What's the value?...and this list can continue *ad infinitum*.

There is also fear of testing probably linked to the dread of examinations from everyone's school years. It is a subject that is generally avoided in multimedia circles but hopefully this chapter will show it is essential to have a testing strategy for each project and to make clients fully aware of the extent of the testing outlined in the strategy.

The confusion of terminology doesn't help either. 'Testing' and 'evaluation' are the main culprits. They are both to do with making improvements which is why they are difficult to separate. However, the main difference appears to be that testing implies matching a prescribed set of quantifiable criteria against performance to find errors. Evaluation is wider in that it is not looking for specific errors but improvements to the design during development or when the program is finished. Validation is another term that causes confusion. The problem here is that the interpretation of the term changes depending on the context where it is used. In evaluation, validation means checking that the methods used are ones which will provide the type of data that is wanted. If one of the needs specified is detailed user reaction to the concepts, it will be invalid to select internal testing alone as a test method, for example.

The subject of testing is complicated because there are so many types that can be applied at every stage of a project. Also, the mix of disciplines in multimedia means that different approaches to testing might be employed. Concept testing with focus groups, prototypes, peer review either within the project or with external review of the design documents, usability tests, field trials and acceptance tests are some of the varieties that could be employed.

The type of data collected with any of the processes veers between quantitative and qualitative, objective and subjective, formative and summative. There are arguments for and against all the different methods and you will have to decide which approach serves the project's requirements, time, cost and quality constraints.

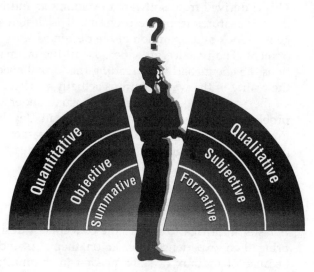

Testing data categories.

You need to become acquainted with the varieties so that you can devise a testing strategy that will serve your projects. You'll need to understand how to cost the different ways and also consider subcontracting the specialist forms of testing. This whole area can be a specialism in itself.

As a brief introduction, the varieties mentioned above will be summarized but it is worth you taking time to explore this area in greater depth with further reading.

Concept testing

This approach comes from marketing. It means trying out the main project ideas on selected groups of people representative of the intended user group. The ideas may be presented in a paper walkthrough or through discussion. This is conducted very early on so it would be prior to any prototype stage of development. The project may not have had complete agreement to proceed and the findings may influence further agreement. A facilitator opens up discussion around the concepts, perhaps relating them to competitive products. The aim is to check out if the predicted reactions to the new product match the wishes of the users. This is done early in development so that the design can be adjusted in line with the findings and so that there is more confidence that the intended direction will be successful. Concept testing is also known as Focus Groups. This is a commercial approach to checking out predictions about a product with prospective customers against competing products in the market.

Prototyping

This is derived from software development and is a mock-up of several of the key features from the program. It is designed to get feedback on the general look and operation of the design as early as possible during development. The practice grew because of the mismatch between the expectations the clients had from reading the formal specification documents, and the reality of the way programs actually worked. This was often explained as the gap between written and visual understanding. The gap caused problems of redesign at a late stage in development and was costly. Prototypes can also be used with users to gather their reactions to the main operations at a stage where changes in the design can be made efficiently.

Peer review

A faster approach to testing the concepts of design is to get colleagues to bring their experience to bear on them. As indicated, this is important because of the mix of skills needed in the multistrand design. However, this relies on prediction according to factors that have been identified and prediction is not a science. Experience gives insight but multimedia is relatively young. External peer review can extend the range of experience and insights, particularly if the reviewers are selected for their experience in the respective multimedia application area. The aim is to refine the design at an early stage to help faster development.

Usability tests

These are rigorous tests applied usually when the project has been integrated and is ready for release. They originated in software development as a method of proving that the program met the needs of the users. Often the tests are carried out in specially adapted usability laboratories which simulate the workplace. The users are monitored electronically with cameras, microphones and records of key-presses. They are observed through one-way mirrors. The very large amount of data is analysed to determine where and why the users experienced difficulty so that redesign can take place. Multimedia projects do not usually employ these to the extent of computing application testing, but research projects where data on user reactions is needed, or market-led projects like applications which are meant to sell products, may have some requirement to apply these rigorous methods for market research.

Field trials

Here the application is tested in situ with the users. They are observed and interviewed. There are a number of different methods of observation and interview that can be employed. The users may also be required to fill in questionnaires. The data is collated, analysed and the recommendations for redesign given. Again, this is not as common with multimedia as with software applications, but in some cases, like accredited multimedia training programs, the accreditation body might need to see that the application conveyed the correct level of information with a certain number of trial users. Some retail applications might also require proof of use in the field.

Acceptance testing

If there is a clear specification of what is required, then testing can be carried out to prove that the application conforms to the requirements. This relates more to the operation and functional performance of the code and is derived from software development.

We are going to concentrate on developmental and acceptance testing as they indicate categories of test related to the stage of the project rather than specific methods which will have to be agreed with your clients. Developmental testing means the numerous checks that are carried out during the course of development to ensure that each part of the project meets its specifications. Many developers have come to use the terms alpha test and beta test in the same sense as developmental and acceptance tests are defined here. These are referred to in the integration chapter (Chapter 16) since that is concerned with the influences from software development. This chapter tries to provide an umbrella for the whole issues of testing that can be met during projects by amalgamating insights and methods from different disciplines.

What is testing?

Testing means examining the project performance according to the specifications that have been agreed. This will include the robustness of the code, the structure and content of the program, the interface, the interactivity, the look and feel. It is obvious once this is stated that unless you have the specifications agreed, you cannot prove that your application passes the final test. You will not be able to draw a line to show that you have completed the contractual agreements. The lack of understanding of what constitutes completion of the application is a risk that you need to control to ensure that final sign-off runs smoothly.

Developmental testing

Another point that is self-evident once stated, is that testing the program against specifications is a continuous process during development. Each of the sign-offs that have been suggested is part of the process: the overall structure, the video, audio and text scripts, the video and audio edits, the look of the graphics, the look and feel of the navigation. This is not always recognized as part of the testing process but it is. A lot of testing occurs during project development. Each of the people on the team is concerned to produce a professional product so they care about their own performance. If it is a good team, they'll monitor each other's performance in a constructive way. But however much they pool their expertise to predict how the users will react, how the code should operate, there will always be weaknesses.

Many of the weaknesses will be spotted and corrected. Some will be noticed and left. This might appear a strange admission, and you will not find it stated in much of the literature, but it will be true of the majority of projects. Some design errors will be impossible to change because of the repercussions on the whole of the rest of the project. They need to be spotted very early in the project to be implemented without adverse effects on other parts of the application. Sometimes clients insist on certain features that you know will be detrimental in release – remember the drastic changes to the video sequence caused by an executive in Chapter 12, Team Management Principles.

Acceptance testing

Sometimes design defects only become apparent in use. One or two factors might show up where what appeared logical from past experience does not apply well in new circumstances. The main problem in trying to get final sign-off is to find what is acceptable for both parties. This can be any point on a scale between impossible to use and perfection. Even the most frequently used and maintained programs, like word processing software, undergo evolution from the first release to maturity and beyond. Sometimes they are released with a statement as to 'known bugs'. Complex multimedia applications will naturally be able to sustain improvement if there is a proper allocation for an improvement cycle. Now, this is not granting the right for developers to abdicate their responsibility on the quality of the delivered product. It is just trying to establish what is fair and equitable in an unsettled set of circumstances.

The program has to operate without failing. That is the first standard that will not be disputed by both parties. This will drive the acceptance test. But, even this becomes problematic. I know of at least three projects where a bug in third-party code in the development software had a severe knock-on effect on the operation of an application. This is actually more likely to occur with multimedia because the level of use of code has been limited in the emerging market. This means that the more obscure problems in code occur even when software has been around for some time and appears stable. Use in a new set of circumstances will tease it out. What happens in this situation? Is it your responsibility? Is it the clients'? Is it the original developer's? Here, your own developers fall foul of the problems others face in trying to reach perfection in software. Remember to include a limited liability clause in your contract to cover this risk. See Chapter 10, Contract Issues 2.

Defects in the program will range in severity, knock-on effects and frequency. You need to identify the problems, the severity and the effects on the robustness of the program. This will include correcting any data that is wrong, whether it is a typing error, words in the wrong place, text layout and so on, as well as code defects – wrong sequence, failure to operate a navigation path, corrupted screens, for example. Your aim is to present an application that will work efficiently and perform correctly within a span of correct use. If the specification did not mention it needed to be 'hacker' proof, you do not have a responsibility to test it under the most extreme circumstances. However, users do have a knack of using programs in ways that are not logical. So a span of unexpected use should be tried out as well as expected normal use.

All these points should indicate that acceptance levels should be specified in advance and that testing has to be systematic and thorough to prove robustness across a span of use.

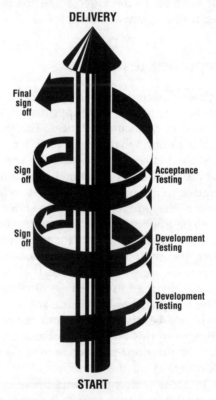

The test cycle.

The test phase is cyclical. Developmental refinement occurs to ensure each sign-off stage. The assembly of all the parts according to agreement leads up to integration of the pieces and acceptance testing. It sounds as if there should not be too much to do at the end if all the pieces have been approved. That is rarely so with multimedia because the integration can have repercussions on previously agreed pieces. The size of text approved in isolation may be illegible because of encoding deterioration, overpowering graphics near it and so on. The colours may shift and in turn affect the legibility of text or clarity of the graphics. A module that worked perfectly on its own falls over when you try to activate it from a subroutine. The development platform might be different from the delivery platform specification and someone might have overlooked some of the issues of transfer from one to the other.

Systematic testing has to be done once all the parts are assembled and integrated. A testing plan should be drawn up to ensure that all paths will be explored, all data checked for accuracy, all interactivity operates as expected, the right data appears in the right sequence, and any records that the user builds up during use are faithful and accurate. Each application will have its own features so these are examples of the more generic aspects that might need systematic testing.

If an application is complex, and extensive use will be made of it by a range of users, then it becomes more important to use one or more testers from outside the team at acceptance testing. During production, the team will have developed patterns of use for themselves based on their experience of the program. It becomes increasingly difficult for them to predict use from a naive perspective. An external, experienced tester will help draft a test specification to simulate a variety of experience while checking the accuracy of all the data. It will be necessary to use formal test sheets to keep records of the errors and the sequence of actions that caused them and to have some code of severity to help decide where correction time will be best deployed. Then, because the error needs to be retested to prove it has been corrected successfully, the person who corrects it should initial and date correction and the retest should be initialled and dated. See the sample acceptance test sheet.

The sheet may seem over-bureaucratic and it should be adapted or discarded depending on the type of project at the discretion of the project manager and depending on the level of testing required by the clients. For more complex projects the sheets can help because there is a tendency for revisions to the code to cause knock-on effects. Retest after retest can take place, gradually whittling away the errors. Because there are retests, it is easy to work on the wrong version so dating and version numbering become more important. See Chapter 16 on Integration for a further explanation on versioning.

What is a testing strategy?

A testing strategy sounds complicated but it isn't. It means stating in writing what measures will be taken to ensure the final program meets the

Sample acceptance test report sheet.

Project name:			Version number:		Programmer's name:			Platform description		
Tester's name:					Date:					
Retester's name:					Date:					
Machine no./spec.										
No.	Error description	Priority code	Programmer's comments		Status: Fixed/ Left	Initials	Date	Retest status	Initials	Date

clients' requirements. This will include noting the number and type of sign-off stages, the responsibilities of the team members to meet the technical and functional requirements at each stage, the analysis of the users if applicable, a peer review process if applicable, the building and trialling of a prototype if necessary and whatever other methods you decide to employ during the development stages.

The developmental testing is part of the testing strategy. You can indicate that prior to and around sign-off points for the project, the team will be testing to ensure that each part of the application meets the specification that has been agreed for sign-off.

If you have agreed to carry out any of the specific tests that occur early in the project like focus groups and prototyping, these will form part of the development testing strategy.

The acceptance test description should be as detailed as you can make it so that it is clear when your team has discharged their responsibilities. If you have had to build a multimedia presentation for an executive, it is straightforward for the individual concerned to try it out and approve it. But if you have a kiosk application with items for sale to the general public, then it is time consuming and far more difficult to collect the data to prove its usability.

You may decide that one internal round of testing, record error, resolve error and recheck until satisfied will be enough. On the other hand you may decide on this and then an external round of testing, perhaps done by nominee(s) from the client company and/or by external testers. Your decision will be based on the complexity of the project, the time and cost of the testing agreed and the wishes of the client.

Any of the specific tests like usability and the use of an external tester which occur in the latest stages of the project will form part of the acceptance testing strategy.

A word of warning here about nominees from the client company – often they will ask several others to try the program out and even set up a small sample of use with the target audience. This is laudable only if that is exactly what you understood was going to happen. If the clients expand the testing specification spontaneously then the risks increase against them signing off.

The wider the acceptance testing, the more likely that insights about the users will emerge and point towards design rather than code changes. This is normal in emerging fields where user reaction and use is guessed at. Clients need to recognize this and accept that their application may not be perfect in every detail but that you have faithfully tried to achieve the best given the constraints. Both you and the clients will learn from the process and be able to assess the user needs better for future applications based on the reactions. Until multimedia markets have matured and sound analysis of user likes and dislikes has been carried out, this will be the situation. It is unfair of the clients to expect more, so you need to state and re-state their responsibilities and the risks that they are taking with the possible consequences spelled out.

You can agree that all text will be spelt correctly and that the screen layouts will conform to the agreed specification. You can agree that the program will function as specified, saving code errors in third-party software and hardware. You can agree that the final product will be tested for robustness according to a testing plan that will ensure that all functional paths are tried and that a normal span of use, accounting for differences in the users, will be tried out. All these would constitute an acceptance test strategy that both your team and the clients would find acceptable.

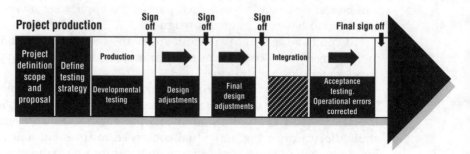

Stages of testing.

So, it is prudent to explain in the strategy plan that design defects are picked up during development and operational errors are the main focus of the acceptance phase of testing. If the client is concerned to refine the design, you can offer several alternatives during the development stage, like a prototype trial, but it must be the client's decision to bear any time and cost implications or sacrifice adjustments to the design. If this is clearly stated and agreed, you will have done your duty both to your client and the team so that the level of expectations is set. For example, if there was no agreement for a user trial with end users, and then modifications to the application made on the results, any request for this would clearly form an extension of the original project in terms of time and cost.

Prediction of use can be based on experience, but actual use will differ. Unless user testing and redesign have been part of the project specification, your part of the contract is to use your knowledge and experience to guess use. The clients act on the users' behalf to vet your specification. If there is no needs analysis as such built into the project plan, the clients' responsibility is to act on their users' behalf in good faith, to allow a proper user trial, or to accept tests designed to test robustness of the application.

Your testing strategy should be written up as part of your detailed contract documents and should be alluded to in the scoping document.

Very often the cost of extensive testing and redesign is left out of a multimedia project specification because to do them properly adds so much to the nominal cost of development that a developer fights shy of them. Multimedia is still a difficult market, so any means of pruning project costs is used to arrive at a proposal cost that will make it competitive. But to ignore this completely by pretending that the development stages of multimedia run smoothly is, in the great majority of cases, not the case. The final sign-off will then stand more risk of getting into a never-ending loop.

This can cause dreadful problems for a project manager just at the time that everything seemed to be sewn up. Some projects spin out of control right at the final stage mainly because of re-adjustments. The clients refuse to sign off until these are completed; the developer is certain the adjustments are extras that should be paid for. Small adjustments can be absorbed but often there will be one or two seemingly small changes that have large repercussions. It's also likely that your team will be in the process of being disbanded or reallocated onto other projects at this stage so it becomes far more problematic to implement even small changes.

It is at this point that early decisions taken in the project acquire significance. Did you suggest a structured testing plan as part of the project plan? Did you suggest user trials with prototypes? Did the clients reject it? Did they understand the significance of saving money on these items at this time? Did you explain?

If you take the time to plan the testing strategy at the beginning of the project and, if necessary, refine it with your clients during development, mindful of time and cost factors, it will pay dividends at final sign-off.

Insights into software testing

Acceptance testing in multimedia is the closest to pure software testing because it addresses the code underlying integration. Some of the problems, like third-party software bugs and corruption of data that was stable, have been mentioned but some of the insights from pure software testing should be noted.

Testing is a black hole and the project manager cannot accurately predict how much time and effort it will take to make the program robust. Usually, the deadline for how much time can be devoted to it will be forced on the team by the amount left prior to the release date or handover date to the clients. This is why it becomes important to define the priority of defects so that best use can be made of whatever time is left.

There are problems inherent in the nature of changing code and effectively, this is what happens when the programmer addresses the errors found in tests. There is a 20–50% chance of introducing another error. So, it is possible for retested code to end up displaying more errors than on first testing. This is not automatically a reflection on the programmer. Testing is like diagnosis; it spots defects that can be symptoms. The programmer may ease the irritation but may not cure the main infection. Other symptoms can then occur which, when studied, show a coding problem that may warrant extensive rework.

Experienced programmers recognize that the more original code is changed, the more likely the integrity of the overall logic will suffer and break down. Another lesson from their experience shows that there are different ways of treating errors. You might be asked if you will take the risk on a 'patch' or 'quick fix', or negotiate an extension from the clients, because to address the error in depth might jeopardize the delivery date. You will have to take the decision.

It will help if you recognize that despite the acceptance test being the final test phase for the project, it is the first full test for the integration. So, in effect, the integration stage has a development stage of its own where it needs time to shape up. Depending on the complexity of the application, you should create enough time and space in your project plan for a few test cycles. You might decide to call the first cycle Integration Testing to allow the recognition that this is the first chance to address the robustness of the integrated code, and then call the retest Acceptance Testing.

Testing and error correction have traditionally been handed over to more junior programmers. There are dangers in doing this and you need to make sure your original programmers are involved to the end of the project. It has been found that other programmers don't have the overview of the project and address the errors in isolation. They cannot link the symptoms to a main cause as effectively as the original code writers. Fixing errors can therefore take longer for them. Also, there is more likelihood of the introduction of new errors from inconsistencies between the original programmer's code and the new code.

It should be evident that the end of the project is a vulnerable time for the project manager. There are pressures from the team, the clients and the management. These are over and above the pressures from the diminishing time and budget factors.

Final sign-off

If the acceptance test is prespecified and understood by all parties, then final sign-off will follow smoothly. It is important to have this agreement in writing just as with other sign-offs. This will act as the end of your team's and your responsibilities to the clients so that final payment can be claimed.

Your specification for the acceptance test can form the basis for the components listed for sign-off but you should add a sentence or two stating that this sign-off concludes the project and that your company has carried out all its obligations according to the agreements.

THEORY INTO PRACTICE 20

Which of the symptoms of a poorly defined testing strategy have you known? Tick all that apply.

Symptoms of poor testing strategy

1. Clients asking for extras before final sign-off.
2. Clients refusing to sign off the project.
3. Poor version control re-introducing errors which had been corrected.
4. Never-ending testing and error correction cycles
5. Little testing done because the project ran out of time
6. No original programmers left to correct errors

Are you clear now on how to avoid these problems in your next projects?

Summary

- Multimedia does not have a strong tradition of testing. It has not developed a clear relationship with the methods of testing from other disciplines and has not devised its own.
- There are many forms of testing. Each has its strengths and weaknesses in relation to the needs of an application.
- The project manager has to balance the needs of the application with time and cost factors to devise a testing strategy.
- The clients have to agree to the strategy in the full knowledge of what it includes and what it excludes so there are no last-minute recriminations.
- Developmental testing is the combination of sign-offs of the completed parts of the project as well as the natural refinement of the individual assets during the development process.
- Acceptance testing takes place at the final stage of the project to predefined criteria specified in the testing strategy. The integrated code is tested and the robustness of the project is scrutinized.
- Final sign-off agrees that the team has met its responsibilities and the application performs as specified.

Recommended reading

Brooks F.P. Jr. (1982). *The Mythical Man-Month. Essays on Software Engineering.* Reading, MA: Addison-Wesley

Dumas J.S. and Redish J.C. (1994). *A Practical Guide to Usability Testing.* Norwood, NJ: Ablex Publishing Corporation

Humphrey W.S. (1990). *Managing the Software Process.* Reading, MA: Addison-Wesley

Roper M. (1994). *Software Testing.* London: McGraw-Hill International (UK) Ltd

CHAPTER 19

CLOSING THE PROJECT

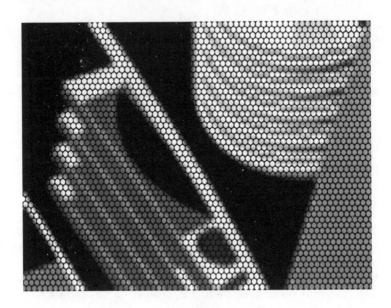

Project manager's responsibilities

- To build into the schedule enough time to archive effectively
- To carry out any company policies for archiving projects
- To rationalize all documentation, assets and budget information

Archiving: The rationale

If the project has been a large-scale production then there are lots of ends that need to be tidied up. This can seem like bureaucracy running amok, but once you have been caught out by clients requesting individual graphics from their application for marketing purposes, clients returning after several months to do an update that had never been mentioned, your colleague wanting to see the budget breakdown to help in costing another similar project, another colleague wanting the name of the voice-over artist and agent, your management dealing with an enquiry from the corporate client company's inspectorate about exactly who had signed off

Chaotic archiving.

the content in the project a year earlier, an enquiry from the musicians union about the 15 seconds of a record used, a museum insisting that they are one slide short and claiming four months' penalty fees, and so on, then the value of the time put into archiving in a structured way pays for itself.

What needs to be archived?

Companies may have their own policies for archiving their projects. Many have different systems and locations for storing text, audio tapes, video tapes, code and graphics. There will be different versions of the assets from different stages of the project and during production you will have held on to them all because quite frequently you revert to parts of an earlier version as the project progresses. Keeping the different versions also allows you to keep a check on how much is changing and whether you could absorb the time and cost or need to renegotiate.

Once the project has received final sign-off, all the assets need to be sorted to ensure cover in all aspects for any further requests. This is an onerous task which usually falls on the project manager and/or admin. assistant as the only ones left working on the project. If no archive check-list is provided by the company it will be in your interest to draft one because it is easy to forget one or two major items – like getting the master tape back from the encoding company, if you used one. They often hold on to them in case of any rework needed.

You need to make sure that you have scheduled enough time for yourself to archive the project after final sign-off. It will take three to four days of initial administration for a commercial, large-scale project. The amount of text material that will have been generated might fill most of one filing cabinet. You may have a few boxes full of offline tapes, copies of the master tapes, voice-over tapes, music tapes, photos, slides, a stack of worms from testing! You will be pressured to get the graphics and code off the system to free space for other projects.

So it will help to have a systematic approach to archiving. The paper from the project can be split into formal documents, scripts, and budget information. There may be a set way of boxing the files or a separate store room with filing cabinets devoted to archiving. As electronic archiving becomes increasingly popular, and the need for automated multimedia documentation increases, the archiving of projects will become easier. There may be a coding system according to the project number or name so that any assets stored in any location will need to be cross-referenced with them. If there is no system, it will be wise to cross-reference by name anyway.

Formal documents

These will include all contractual documents such as the final proposal document, any terms and conditions agreed as per the firm's policy, any agreement to ways of working, all sign-off documents for the intermediate stages and the final sign-off. It should also include all confidentiality agreements from the team members if this was a condition accepted from the client. Copies of all contracts drafted for subcontractors or freelancers should be held with the formal documents. All rights agreements for the video, audio and graphics assets should be sorted and filed accordingly. You'll need an index of what the files contain for quick access later. Finally, a list showing where assets like video master tapes, audio tapes, and code backups are being held is necessary for a full formal record to be complete.

Scripts and assets

Text copies of the final scripts for all the components should be held with their electronic files. This will mean sorting out the versions and updating any of the scripts with the inevitable last-second changes that were probably written in on copies. All assets that belonged to the client should be returned. Make a list for the archive files and date it showing exactly what was returned when.

If you had to use external assets from picture libraries or museums then a similar list should have been compiled for those. Many of them should have been returned and recorded during the course of the project but there are often quite a few of the more important ones left over in case they were needed again. Whoever was managing the rights and clearances for the project should have made good records showing what has been returned and what is outstanding and why.

The company may have a policy to recycle the video offline tapes for other projects or may choose to archive them as well. The masters may well be held off-site for security purposes so these will need to be clearly marked in an appropriate way for easy identification later if necessary. There may be packaging guidelines for off-site storage that you need to conform to. Wherever the audio, video, graphics and code are held, you need to make sure their location and date of transfer is recorded for the formal set of documents.

Budget information

During the project you will have been monitoring the actual time and cost against the predicted time and cost as stipulated in the final proposal agreement. These are important records so detailed files are essential. If your finance department has been collating the team's time sheets against tasks or sign-off points, and costing according to the internal and external rates you gave them, then you should already have a file with their printouts. They should be able to provide you with a detailed printout for the complete project soon after final sign-off. However, for many reasons this rarely seems to happen, so often you have the best understanding of exactly where the project stands in relation to the actual expenditure. Record your understanding.

You need to rationalize the details that you hold with those that the finance section holds. For example, you will have the detailed breakdown of numbers of assets cleared from each source so it will probably be easier for you to arrive at a final cost for asset rights clearances than the accounts section. You will then be able to match the figure against the predicted figure to see where the project stands on this. You should have been on top of this type of equation all through the project, so that refining the information should be relatively easy.

It is a good idea to write a budget report to put with all this information comparing the predicted and actual spend and the predicted and actual time spent. It will help you for future projects, as well as colleagues and the management, if you indicate the reasons for any overspend in any section or extra time incurred.

It is easy to forget the causes of problems on a project but they will help you become better at predicting time and costs on other projects and to make sharper decisions about risk factors. Some of the factors may point towards organizational issues that should be resolved by management to help all projects run more smoothly, as well as some showing where you yourself might improve.

Closing the project

Once all the archiving is in place, all assets have been returned if required, and your work area is probably the tidiest it has been since you started the project, then the project is properly finished. If you don't take the responsibility to do all this at the end, you will find that the project can haunt you as the small requests from all quarters become harder to implement. You will have lost interest in the project and your own understanding of the files will fade quickly.

Many organizations do not pay enough attention to archiving. You may need to fight for the time as legitimate time to build into the schedule at the beginning, but it is in your interest. You need to bear in mind that by the end of the project you'll probably hate it, and just want to finish at all costs. It takes mental stamina to persevere with archiving, particularly when your other team members have moved on to more interesting things.

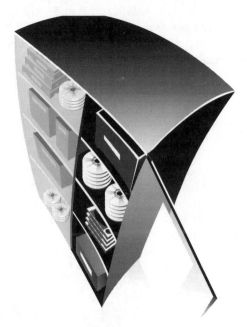

Successful archiving.

Summary

- Spending a few days archiving at the end of a project has good payback even in the short term. Fight for time in the schedule if necessary.
- Archiving is a neglected area. Employ the company's policy if one exists or define and use one yourself.
- A systematic approach to archiving projects will benefit both you and the company.
- File and index all formal documents together.

- Sort out the final versions of all scripts. Return all assets, list and date the returns.
- Trace, list and store all internal assets – video masters, audio tapes, and so on.
- Gather all relevant budget data together. Write a report on the project management aspects of the project and learn from it for future projects.

Recommended reading

This chapter was based on experience and there are no reading references.

General recommended reading

Bowen D. (1994). *Multimedia Now And Down The Line*. London: Bowerdean Publishing Company Ltd

Burger J. (1995). *Multimedia for Decision Makers. A Business Primer*. Reading, MA: Addison-Wesley

Vaughan T. (1994). *Multimedia: Making It Work*. Berkeley, CA: Osborne McGraw-Hill

GLOSSARY

8-, 16- or 24-bit image The more bits a colour image has, the more colours can be shown in it. An 8-bit image can have 256 colours because eight bits can be used for numbers from zero (00000000 in binary arithmetic) to 255 (11111111 in binary arithmetic). However, these colours can usually be chosen from a larger palette of perhaps millions of colours. If the 256 colours are all shades of grey then a photographic quality monochrome image can be reproduced. A 16-bit image will have thousands of colours, and can look photographic in many circumstances. For a truly photographic colour image the millions of colours available in 24 bits is necessary (or even more). Note that on the Apple Macintosh, an 8-bit matte or alpha channel can be added to the 24 bits, and the image can be referred to as being 32 bits.

3-D Three-dimensional, appearing to have depth.

above-the-line cost A cost that you would not be paying as part of the overhead of running the company. The cost of your in-house resources and/or staff are a below-the-line cost whereas a freelancer hired for a particular job is an above-the-line cost. These two kinds of cost are both real, since somebody has to pay them, but your attitude to them is likely to be different.

ADPCM Adaptive delta (or difference) pulse code modulation. Delta PCM is a sound encoding method that reduces the data rate by only storing changes in the size of samples rather than the absolute value of the sample. The adaptive part is where the encoding of the difference values adapts so as to more accurately follow large changes between samples.

aliasing Aliasing occurs when the way something is recorded produces errors that look or sound as if they should be parts of the real thing. The wheels of racing covered wagons in a Western movie, which often seem to be going backwards, do so because of aliasing. In this case the 24 frames per second of the film is not fast enough to accurately record the motion of the wheel. In digital audio it is possible to produce false sounds if the rate at which the sound is sampled is not fast enough to accurately represent the waveform. See **anti-aliasing**.

alpha test The first, internal, test of a complete or near-complete application. The term originates from computing and may not be used by multimedia companies originating from other disciplines.

alpha channel Besides the red, green and blue channels of an image which determine the colour of each pixel, there can be another channel which sets how transparent the pixel is. This is known as the alpha channel. The effect is similar to a matte except that a matte is usually only one bit deep so that the transparency is either full (so the background shows through) or opaque. In television this is known as keying.

alpha disc The disc on which an alpha version of an application is distributed.

analog Strictly speaking an analog is any kind of representation or similarity. However, analog is used in multimedia (and in audio and video and electronics in general) to differentiate from digital. In digital, a signal is turned into a series of numbers and the numbers are stored or transmitted. In analog the signal itself is either stored or transmitted directly or is converted into another medium that can follow its variations and itself be stored or transmitted. Whereas analog systems are prone to distortion and noise, digital systems are much less susceptible.

animatic An application that demonstrates and prototypes the final application.

animation Simulated movement of objects using computer or video effects. A simulation of a building rising from its outline foundations to completion is an example of an animation.

anti-aliasing In graphics it is possible for edges of objects to look jagged because the resolution of the screen display is unable to accurately represent the object itself. To alleviate this problem the colours of the pixels around the edge of the object are mixed gradually between the object and its background. In this way the colour resolution compensates for the lack of spatial resolution that causes the jagged edges. By definition, this technique cannot be used where only pure black and white pixels are available. Some computer displays will now automatically anti-alias text to make it look cleaner on the screen.

application A general term for a multimedia title or project.

application-based programming A program that is either self-contained or which runs entirely within one environment, such as an authoring package.

artefacts Disturbances and defects to an image or sound which are not supposed to be there, but which are the results of errors in digitization or display.

assets The media components of an application – audio, video, graphics, animations – that combine to form the content.

authoring tool A computer program designed to be simple to use when building an application. Supposedly no programming knowledge is needed, but usually common sense and an understanding of basic logic are necessary.

bandwidth The amount of data passed along a cable or communications channel of any kind. Sometimes the data channel, or pipe, is described as fat if it has a high bandwidth and can carry a lot of data quickly, or described as thin if it cannot. Bandwidth is usually expressed in bits per second or bytes per second. Because of this confusion you should be clear whether bandwidth is being expressed in bits or bytes to understand how fast the data can be transmitted.

beta If your application has 'gone beta' then it should be finished but needs testing. This testing may be carried out by people outside the production team and even outside the production company.

beta disc A disc carrying the beta version of software. If your application has 'gone beta' then it should be finished but needs testing. This testing may be carried out by people outside the production team and even outside the production company.

beta test If your application has 'gone beta' then it should be finished but needs testing. This testing may be carried out by people outside the production team and even outside the production company.

bit depth The more bits a colour image has, the more colours can be used in it. An 8-bit image can have 256 colours, but you can usually choose those colours from a larger palette of perhaps millions of colours. If your 256 colours are all shades of grey then a photographic quality monochrome image can be reproduced. A 16-bit image will have thousands of colours, and can look photographic in many circumstances. However, for a truly photographic colour image the millions of colours available in 24 bits is necessary (or even more). Note that on the Apple Macintosh, an 8-bit matte or alpha channel can be associated with the 24 bits, making 32 bits.

bitmap A graphic image which represents the image by a matrix of every pixel, usually going from top to bottom, left to right. Bitmap images usually have a resolution in pixels per inch and a size in pixels.

bookmark A function of an application whereby users can store their place so that they can quickly go back there later, even saving the bookmark for retrieval many days later. The electronic equivalent of a piece of paper between pages of a book.

browser A piece of software that allows the user to look through a number of resources, usually held in a variety of formats. A Web browser is designed for viewing World Wide Web pages on the Internet. Netscape and Mosaic are examples of Web browsers.

build The process of taking all the component parts of a multimedia application (or indeed any piece of software) and making the finished version.

bump mapping In computer graphics, a technique for giving a surface texture to objects by slightly distorting the shape.

buy-out Paying for all the necessary rights in one go rather than paying royalties.

cartogram A term for a style of illustration where a map shows statistical information in a diagrammatic way.

CD burner A machine which can write compact discs, including CD-ROMs. The discs are called WORMS (Write Once Read Many) and so sometimes the machines are called WORM burners.

CD-i Compact Disc-Interactive is an interactive multimedia platform which uses a television monitor with a CD-i player as the delivery system. Primarily developed by Philips, it allows use of all media on the system. It has its own set of authoring tools and conforms to the Green Book technical specification standards.

CD-ROM Compact Disc – Read Only Memory has progressed from allowing only text and data onto the disc to now include audio, graphics, animations and video. It conforms to the Yellow Book and ISO 9660 technical specifications. The CD-ROM drives vary in the speed for transferring data. Quad-speed drives are the best for multimedia delivery.

change control See **change management**.

change management A system set up by developers to monitor and control the number and type of changes made during development, whether the changes originate in-house or from the clients.

character generator A piece of software or hardware designed to make captions for video and superimpose them on the picture.

clearances The portmanteau term for copyright permissions.

coincident needles A stereo meter for showing volume of sound where the two needles of the meter, representing left and right signals, revolve around the same point.

competencies The definition of skills evident from practices carried out in the workplace. This term has become prominent in training circles through the link to NVQs (National Vocational Qualifications). These are new style qualifications which are concerned with accrediting people for the skills they employ naturally as they carry out their work.

compile Taking the source code of a computer program and turning it into machine code using a compiler. The source code is written by the programmer. Extra code from programming libraries is incorporated at this time.

component A video image where the colour information is kept separate from the luminance or brightness information. Usually two signals are used to represent the colour information. This is similar to RGB and the RGB signals can be extracted from the three components. The components are also specified to take into account the eye's response to different colours.

composite A video image where colour and brightness are encoded together in the same signal. PAL and NTSC are composite television systems.

composite image In video, an image where colour and brightness are encoded together in the same signal; in graphics, an image made up of several other images, blended together.

compressed but lossless A compressed signal whereby the original signal can be retrieved without any changes or errors.

compressed with loss A compressed signal where retrieving the original signal is impossible but where a version of the original is retrieved which is satisfactory for its intended purpose.

compression Reducing the amount of data needed to carry something.

computer-based training Often referred to as CBT, computer-based training is a method where some or all of the training content of a course is turned into an interactive computer program.

concept testing   Used to test out ideas on an audience chosen from a sample market. The aim is to check the feasibility of the ideas for the market before incurring expense implementing them. The method for implementation can but may not involve interactive methods. Concept testing originated with marketing and may be called Focus Groups.

contingency   In project management this means predicting the need and reserving funds, time and/or resources to cope with unforeseen circumstances that affect the project schedule. Multimedia project management needs more contingency than many other forms of projects because it is a volatile environment.

contouring   An artefact in graphics reproduction whereby smooth changes of brightness or colour become changed so that discrete steps are seen.

copyright   The right of a creator of a work of art, literature, music, and so on to have control over the use of the work.

credit   The linking of people to the tasks they performed. This is normally done by listing the name and function performed as in credits at the end of a television programme.

critical path   The identification of the optimum sequence to carry out tasks to achieve a project on time and within budget. See also task analysis and network analysis.

cross platform   The development of applications which will run on more than one delivery platform.

custom palette   A palette of colours chosen specifically to represent an image.

DAT   Digital Audio Tape, a format using 4 mm tape in cassettes originally designed for digital audio (48 KHz sampling 16 bit) but also used to store data when it operates as a streamer tape format.

debug   To study an application to remove errors.

decompile   To take the machine code version of a program and change it back into something a human can understand.

decryption   To remove the encryption from something so that the original is produced.

delivery medium   The system used to distribute an application.

delivery platform   The multimedia system or systems that people will use to interact with the application. The total specification of the platform is important so that the application is developed within the capabilities.

development platform   The multimedia system that is used to develop the application. This may not be the same as the delivery platform. It is important that the final application is tested on the delivery system to check that it will perform on the specified platform.

diaphragm   In a microphone, the membrane that is vibrated by sound and so causes the production of an electrical signal that represents the sound.

digital   In a digital system, the signal (including such things as sounds and pictures) is turned into a series of numbers and it is these numbers that are stored or transmitted. In an analog system the signal itself is either stored or transmitted directly, or is converted into another medium that can follow its variations and itself be stored or transmitted. Whereas analog systems are prone to distortion and noise, digital systems are much less susceptible.

discovery learning A learning situation that is structured to allow the learner to explore and find answers rather than be told the information.

distance learning A learning situation where the student studies a course away from the accrediting institution using any medium that is provided. This may include interactive programs. See also **Open Learning Centres**.

dither Small, seemingly random perturbations to a signal or image designed to fool the eye or ear into thinking it has greater quality than it really does. In graphics a dither is a seemingly random pattern of dots of a limited range of colours which, when viewed from a distance, appear to have a greater range of colour. When digitizing a signal a dither is used to reduce the effect of digitizing errors because our eyes and ears are less distressed by noise (which dither looks like) than by the sharp changes in a signal that the dither disguises.

document-based programming Programming where the format of the document is standardized and one or more applications can be used in concert to read or display it. The World Wide Web is an example of this.

Dolby A system for reducing noise in an audio recording.

dot pitch The density of dots of phosphor on a colour television or monitor tube. Figures of .23 to .28 millimetres are common.

dpi The density of dots in an image or on a computer screen. Most computer screen displays are 72 or 75 dpi (dots per inch).

draw objects In graphics, an image that is defined in terms of simple graphics 'primitives' such as lines, arcs and fills.

dub To copy something, usually an audio or video tape recording. A dub is the copy itself. In digital terminology a direct digital copy is often called a clone since it will be indistinguishable from the original.

dumb terminal A computer terminal with a keyboard and screen which does nothing other than show a display generated at a distant computer and send back your typed input.

educational technology The study of the ways in which the use of media and structured approaches to organizing material can aid teaching and learning.

edutainment A term derived from the words education and entertainment coined to describe a category of interactive titles. These are designed to be used in the home to inform and motivate through the use of media.

electrostatic A system for microphones, and less commonly, loudspeakers and headphones, where electrostatic charge is used to detect or cause the movement of the diaphragm.

emulator A system that pretends to be something it is not, such as a software system that pretends to be a piece of hardware.

encryption Changing a data file so that it is unrecognizable but can be turned back into its original form on receipt – if the receiver has the key to decode it.

environment mapping In computer graphics, a method of reproducing reflections on the surface of an object by determining what the object 'sees' from its position.

evaluation   Often confused with the term testing and used interchangeably, when used in a strict technical sense, there are differences. Evaluation of an application is the broad appraisal of any factors that influence the development, delivery and reaction to it. See also **testing**.

Exabyte   A type of computer streamer tape using 8 mm cassette tape in the same format as Video-8. This is a brand name of Exabyte Corporation who are the only company making such drives. Streamer tapes are usually used for backup and archiving but sometimes for software and assets (such as MPEG-compressed movies).

exclusive assigned rights   Passing your copyright on to someone else so that you no longer have rights in the material.

fair dealing   In copyright law this is an exception to infringement under certain limited circumstances because your usage of the material is very slight and/or under circumstances where free usage is seen as reasonable. Examples of this include use of extracts from books in a review.

field trials   The use of the product in situ with the intended users prior to release to identify problems for correction.

fixed-term contract   A contract that cannot be extended beyond its original term.

force majeure   A condition in a contract where neither party has control over the circumstances. This might include war, loss of electrical power and acts of God.

formative   A term used to describe evaluation processes carried out during the development cycle. These are contrasted with summative evaluation processes which occur at the end of development. In this context, team review meetings that occur during the project could be called a formative evaluation process. See **summative**.

functional specification   The document that says how an application works. The application will be written by reference to this document.

gallows arm   A kind of microphone stand with a vertical part to which is connected a horizontal extension. This is like the arm of a gallows and it is used to extend across a table (for example). The mic is fixed to the end of the arm.

golden master   The final version of an application. The one that will be distributed.

grabber board   A piece of hardware that takes in an analog signal, usually audio or video, and digitizes it for storage in the computer.

graduated mask   In graphics, a mask which determines how much of a second image shows through the first. It is graduated because it has values such that a mix of the two images is seen.

graphical structure editor   In programming, a programming environment whereby the author can lay out the relationship between sections of the application in a graphical way, like a flow chart.

hacker   A person who uses considerable computing skill in deviant ways, including introducing computer viruses into a computing community. The term is also used less often, and informally, to denote a skilled computer programmer with no malicious intent.

half-toning In graphics, a method for reproducing shades of grey by using black dots of varying sizes.

hardware A piece of equipment, as distinct from software.

high-level design A term for the first attempt to define the interactive structure and content of a program. The term comes from software engineering. See also **outline design**.

host machine The computer on which a program runs.

hot-spot A section of an image on the screen which, when the pointer enters or clicks in it, instigates an action.

hypertext Non-linear text which is read by following jumps and links in the text itself.

icon A pictorial symbol or representation used on the screen to denote an active area. It will allow access to further data or trigger an interactive reaction of some type. It has become common for a text explanation to appear when the user positions the cursor over the icon to help the user understand its significance. See also **picon** and **micon**.

indemnity A guarantee that if any cost is incurred as a result of your action, you will cover it.

instructional design The study of methods of teaching and learning with particular reference to the selection and use of media to aid instruction. The term is widely used in the USA. Europe tends to use the term Educational Technology.

instructional designer A person who applies the principles of instructional design to convey information using a variety of media and methods.

insubstantial portions In copyright, a qualitatively small proportion of a literary work which can be reproduced without infringing copyright.

integrity (of moral rights) The author's right for the work not to be changed.

intellectual property A general term for rights such as copyright and patents.

interactive design The definition of how to structure the content and interactive paths through the material for an interactive application.

interactive video Also denoted by IV. This is an interactive system which uses an interactive videodisc to deliver sound and pictures and combines them with text, sound and graphics from a computer source. More a system of the 1980s, used by large corporations for training, its use is in decline.

interface The way an application is designed for people to use. This includes the screen designs, the use of icons or menus, the way interactivity is set up and the overall structure of the application.

interlaced A television picture is made of two halves which interlace with each other like the lines of a comb and the spaces between.

ionising The process of electrically charging something by removing or adding electrons.

jaggies See **staircasing**.

JPEG A standardized method for compressing still photographic images so that little is lost from the image with high rates of compression. The acronym JPEG stands for Joint Photographic Experts Group.

layer (of graphics) Several layers of images can be combined together in graphics to make a new single image. The relationship between the layers is controlled by their alpha channels.

leadership The employment of appropriate management styles to ensure and maintain progress of a team towards common goals.

learning styles Part of the theory of learning that indicates that people develop preferred ways of learning. This has implications for designing learning materials so that people can process the information in ways appropriate for their preferred style.

letters patent The document that defines a patent.

limiters In audio, an electronic circuit that automatically controls volume to stop short peaks of volume exceeding a certain amount.

look and feel Common name for the interface of an application. See **interface**.

luminance The brightness on a television screen or any other monitor.

machine code Zeros and ones in a program that a computer can execute directly.

magneto-optical disk A type of disk used for data storage where both a laser and a magnetic field are required to write data.

mainframe A very large computer.

master tape The definitive and original recording of something.

mechanical right The right to record a piece of music.

menu A screen that has options for the user to select.

micon An icon that has moving images. Few make the distinction between icon and micon and generally icon is used to cover all selection images. See also **icon**.

milestones Defined key points of the project's development. Milestones are often linked to the end of a phase of development and can be linked to phased payment stages of the project as well.

modelling In 3-D graphics, building a scene by defining objects in the scene and arranging them and their environment.

montage A single graphic made from several sources.

moral rights Rights, related to copyright, which protect a work from unauthorized changes or misattribution without the author's permission.

morph To change one shape into another in a smooth transitional movement.

MPEG Motion Picture Expert Group, an ISO standard for compression of video.

MPEG audio The MPEG standard includes three levels of audio, of which level 2 is the most common. Level 1 is used for DCC (Digital Compact Cassette) and level 3 gives better compression but is more complex.

MPEG-1 The version of MPEG which compresses video to a data rate of around one megabit per second. The quality is similar to S-VHS.

multi-scan Referring to a computer monitor which can work with a range of displays.

multi-session disc A CD-ROM which can be/is written to more than once.

needs analysis The primary stage of a training project where the definition of the criteria for success takes place. The competence level of the target audience and the gap between this and the proficiency needed is analysed.

network analysis   Also referred to as critical path analysis. This is the definition of the core tasks and the dependent tasks needed to complete the project. These are mapped out in a network diagram to show their relationship to each other. See **critical path**.

non-exclusive rights   A licensing of rights which still allows licensing to other people.

NTSC   The television system used in North America and Japan with 525 lines in a frame and 30 frames per second.

object-oriented programming   Programming as interaction between self-contained mini-programs or objects.

objective   A precise definition of a result that is wanted in terms that will allow the result to be measured. Objectives are used particularly in education and training applications where the results of learning need to be stated, and ultimately measured, to demonstrate the effectiveness of the materials. Objectives are often confused with aims. Aims are more general statements of direction rather than measurable statements.

objective evaluation   Evaluation carried out with preset criteria which give a measurable indication of the results. See **subjective evaluation**, **qualitative evaluation** and **quantitative evaluation**.

offline editing   Video editing with working copies of the 'real' tapes and low quality equipment in order to prepare for online editing.

online editing   Video editing with the 'real' tapes on high quality equipment.

Open Learning Centres   These are centres usually set up in the workplace where a variety of learning and training materials are gathered for people to use. They can have access to the materials as and when they want. Many use interactive materials as well as videos and books. This approach to learning reflects the need for quick access to training in organizations that are changing faster than ever before.

open plan   An office arrangement that assigns space according to changing need. There are no or few permanent partitions between desks so that the space can be reorganized efficiently when needed.

operating system   The lowest level of computer software in a computer.

option bars   Part of a graphic on the screen which provides hot-spots, buttons or icons grouped together for the user to make a choice.

OS   Operating System.

outline design   A term for the first attempt to define the interactive structure and content of a program. The term comes from interactive training design. The later stage from this discipline is called the detailed design. See also **high-level design**.

palette   The colours available for use in a graphic.

pan   Moving the viewpoint of a camera from side to side by swivelling it and not actually moving the camera.

patent   The right to exclusive implementation of a process as defined in the patent document.

patent agent   A lawyer who drafts letters patent.

paternity The moral right whereby you have a right to be identified as author.

peer review Appraisal by colleagues or people performing similar jobs where the sharing of experience and insights is used to adjust, in this case, the design and functionality of the application.

performance monitoring A management process where people agree criteria of acceptable achievements for a period and review performance according to the criteria at the end of the time. The performance agreement might be linked to bonus payments. Any shortfall of performance accredited to lack of skill might prompt training initiatives.

performing right The right to perform a piece of music to an audience.

picon An icon that shows a realistic image or picture rather than a representation or symbolic image. Few make the distinction between picon and icon and generally icon is used to denote all selection images. See also **icon** and **micon**.

pilot projects Experimental projects designed as a run-up to a full-blown development.

pixels Picture elements, the basic building blocks of a picture.

port (to and a) Moving a computer program from one machine/platform to another.

posterization Reducing the smooth variation in colours in an image to a series of discrete steps. Also known as quantization. Although this is usually seen as an error, posterization is sometimes used for artistic effect.

pre-alpha A very incomplete version of a program.

primitives Basic building blocks of a computer system.

prior art In patents, a patent can be invalidated or refused if the idea has been publicized before – the prior art.

programming language Since computers can only work with zeros and ones it is rather difficult for mere mortals to program them. To alleviate this problem, programming languages have been developed which understand almost real English.

project management The specification, planning and control of time, cost, quality and resource issues to complete a project on time and within budget.

project manager A person who carries out project management. Used here to describe the leader of a multimedia team.

proposal The document where the developers outline the application content, development schedule and cost for the commissioners.

prototype A limited working version of the application used early in the project to get reaction to the general design and interface so adjustments can be made.

psycho-acoustics The science of hearing, taking into account the psychological aspects of the way the brain interprets sounds as well as the pure acoustics and physics.

psychometric tests Psychological tests which use measurable factors to attribute a score for the person being tested. The tests are used in recruitment and career management decisions, particularly in large organizations.

pushing the envelope Trying something new, usually without sufficient experience.

qualitative evaluation Takes into account a wide variety of factors that might influence the results being analysed. The attitudes of the users, the culture of the institution or country and the general environment would be examples of qualitative factors. See also **quantitative evaluation**.

quantizing Inaccuracies in the digitizing of a signal caused by the integer distance between levels of sampling.

quantitative evaluation Is concerned with measuring the results against predetermined criteria to assess if they have been achieved. The number of times help is used might be used as an indicator of how effective the interface of an application is, and the percentage of correct responses after taking help might be used to indicate the effectiveness of the help messages. These would be examples of quantitative measures of evaluation for multimedia packages. See also **qualitative evaluation**.

RAM Random Access Memory, basically the memory in a computer.

ray tracing A technique used in computer graphics to produce realistic images.

refractive index The amount by which light changes velocity when it passes between media, usually between air and glass or water. The refractive index is different at different frequencies and therefore colours, hence a prism breaking white light into its constituent colours.

render In computer graphics, to build an image.

residuals Extra rights in a licence which are not involved in the primary use but which may be applied later.

RGB Red, green, blue – the three primary colours from which virtually all colours can be built. Also refers to an image which stores the three primary colour components separately.

rights Permission to reproduce and/or sell something.

role play A technique used in teaching and psychology where a person acts out a situation, perhaps from different perspectives, to get insight into decision making and reactions.

royalties Payments based on the number of copies sold or distributed.

run-length encoding A form of compression which stores the colour of a pixel followed by how many subsequent pixels are of the same colour. This works best with images made up of large areas of flat colour such as a cartoon.

sample rate The frequency with which an analog signal is sampled on digitization. For accurate representation the sample rate must be at least twice the highest frequency in the signal.

scan To convert a flat image such as a photographic print into a digital form by measuring the relevant parameters of sections of the image in an ordered fashion, usually left to right, top to bottom.

scanner A device which converts a flat image such as a photographic print into a digital form by scanning across it.

screen resolutions The number of pixels on a screen. The most common in multimedia is 640 pixels by 480.

scripting languages   Computer languages that are designed to be used without detailed knowledge of programming. They are specialized to particular tasks.

server   In a local area network, a server is the hard disk that is not on your own computer but elsewhere and you can use it to store your files. In a wide area network or video-on-demand system, the server is the centralized repository for data.

session fee   A payment for performing in a music recording as a session musician. A principal performer would probably take royalties on sales, not a session fee.

set-top box   A computer-based system that is designed to be like a piece of home entertainment hardware (for example, a VCR or CD player) and may actually sit on top of the television set. Satellite receivers and decoders for video on demand are usually referred to in this way.

severance   In employment, the terms under which the employment is ended.

sibilance   Exaggeration of 's' sounds in a voice, sometimes natural but sometimes caused by poor acoustics or microphone placing.

sign-off   The signature of a person given the authority to agree that a phase of work has been completed satisfactorily. Sign-offs are often linked to milestones in the project which can coincide with staged payments.

simulation   A technique used to reproduce a situation as realistically as possible to allow people to develop the skills needed to handle the situation. This is used in management training quite often. The easiest example to quote is that of a flight simulator used to train pilots.

slippage   The amount of time that has been lost according to the agreed schedule and the present project position.

software   A computer program or computer programs in general. Usually used to differentiate from the equipment or hardware.

source code   The human-readable version of a computer program before it is compiled into machine or object code.

staircasing   Under some circumstances, lines on a screen that are almost, but not quite horizontal will appear jaggy. This is sometimes referred to as staircasing or jaggies.

standards conversion   In television, to convert a video signal between the PAL and NTSC standards.

standing waves   In sound, when a sound wave is reflected back on itself by a wall or end of a tube such that the wave reinforces itself. Between two walls this will reinforce certain frequencies and so colour the sound.

storyboards   A scripting convention which includes mock-up visuals used in video production originally and now sometimes used in multimedia projects.

streamer tapes   Magnetic tape, usually in cartridges or cassettes, onto which computer data is recorded or streamed for archiving and backup purposes. The most common are DAT and Exabyte.

stylus In computer graphics, a special pen without ink which is moved across a special tablet in order to draw a line or shape on the computer screen. In audio, the tip, usually diamond, on a gramophone pick-up which actually makes contact with the disc groove.

subcarrier A secondary frequency added to a signal in order to carry extra information, such as colour in a TV signal.

subjective evaluation Subjective evaluation is based on observation and analysis of non-quantifiable factors and is affected by the experience and bias of the evaluator. See also **objective evaluation**.

summative A term used to describe evaluation processes used at the end of development. This can include testing but could also include such practices as the end of project review, or debriefing procedures. See also **formative** and **evaluation**.

synchronization licence A licence to take music and juxtapose it with pictures in a film or video.

synchronization pulses Part of a video or digital signal that identifies a position in the signal, such as where a frame of video starts.

take (as in a take, a recording) An attempt to record something. If you have to try again, then you do another take.

task analysis Identification of all the processes and sub-processes needed to complete the project.

technical specification A document describing a task to be undertaken in terms of the equipment and techniques required.

teletype A teleprinter or telex machine, used to communicate with computers before monitors, or VDUs, were available.

testing The use of methods and procedures to check the performance of an application according to predefined criteria. Testing is often confused with evaluation. It can form part of evaluation which has a wider remit. See also **evaluation**.

texture mapping In computer graphics, adding a texture to the 'surface' of an object drawn in 3-D.

time and materials contract A contract for work where the cost is directly related to the time spent and the materials used. It is the opposite of a fixed-price contract.

time code Standardized signal added to video and to audio for video, to uniquely identify the individual frames. This is a great help when editing.

time lapse photography Where a camera remains in position and records events in detail over a period of time. The film is then speeded up when shown to allow people to see the changes take place in seconds rather than days. An example would be the change of a flower from bud to bloom to death.

time-based media Media that change over time such as audio and video.

uncompressed The original form of an image, sound or other data.

UNIX A computer operating system used extensively in tertiary education and industry.

usability laboratories Specially constructed rooms where people are observed using applications and where their actions are recorded on video, through the computer and on paper by the observers. The information is analysed to indicate the efficiency of the program and to make recommendations for improvements.

usability testing The use of usability testing techniques to evaluate an application. See **usability laboratories**.

user requirements A study of the needs of the users to determine how the application should be structured and how it should operate.

validation Used with slight variations of meaning according to the disciplines that use it, validation refers to an appraisal of the methods that have been used to check that they are consistent with the results. It is used sometimes with the sense of evaluation but strictly it is part of an evaluation process. Also used sometimes with the meaning of field trial as validation exercise. See also **field trials**.

version tracking In software development, keeping track of changes to the software so that development is coordinated. This is especially important where more than one person is writing code.

vertical blanking interval The part of a television signal between the bottom of one picture and the top of the next. Used for teletext, time code and test signals. In computing the VBI is useful because it provides time to change a displayed image.

video CD A compact disc, actually a Mode 2 CD-ROM, which contains MPEG-1 video and audio which can be played on a television or PC screen like a videocassette.

video on demand A system whereby a home subscriber can access television material stored remotely on a server. Some systems use high bandwidth cable and others use ordinary telephone wires for the link between the server and the consumer's television. See also **set-top box**.

video-conferencing Basically the combination of a telephone conference call and television or a video telephone. Recent video-conferencing systems operate using personal computers allowing both ends of the conference to work together on documents that each can see.

videodisc See **interactive video**.

virtual machine In computer software, the program usually controls the computer directly and is said to run on the platform or machine. To run on a different machine, the software will need to be changed. It is, however, possible to put a layer of software between a computer program and the machine such that the interface between the program and this software is standard no matter what actual machine is used. The new software exists in different versions for different machines. This software is usually referred to as a virtual machine.

voice-over An audio commentary that accompanies video or graphics. Hence voice-over artist, a person who reads the commentary.

waveform A visual representation of a signal, usually electronic in nature, that changes over time, such as recorded sound.

Web browsers The World Wide Web is an information system on the Internet devised at CERN in Europe. It uses documents, addressing and linking in standardized formats which can be read, and browsed by a Web browser. The original browser was Mosaic and the most common is Netscape Navigator.

wide area networks Computer networks that extend beyond your own home or office building or complex. Often consisting of linked local area networks as in the Internet.

wide latitude Of film – being able to record a wide range of brightness levels in a scene or cope with under- and/or over-exposure.

worm In data storage – Write Once Read Many, a type of computer disc that can be written to but not changed. Often used to denote a CD-ROM which has been written rather than pressed or replicated. The process is known as burning a WORM.

zoom Increasing the focal length of a lens in video or photography. It magnifies the scene and looks similar, but not exactly the same as, moving closer to the subject.

INDEX

Notes:
(1) Glossary page references are shown in **bold**
(2) Most references are to multimedia, which is therefore largely omitted as a qualifier

A
Abekas 236
above-the-line cost **312**
abstract concepts and icons 138
acceptance testing 295–6, 297–9, 301, 303
    defined 295
achievements 41–2, 50, 65, 68
acoustics
    psycho-acoustics **322**
    see also audio
acquisition of copyright 283
actual cost 22
adaptive delta (difference) pulse code
        modulation 208, 213, 214, **312**
adaptive palette 255
administration
    lack of 176
    see also general support
Adobe
    PhotoShop 248
ADPCM *see* adaptive delta (difference) pulse
        code modulation
advertising 36, 120
agencies
    patents 289, **321**
    team selection 163, 173
agreements
    non-disclosure 289
    rights 275, 276, 283, 308
    time limit on 157
    verbal 86
    see also contract *and under* content
aims/objectives 30–3, **321**
aliasing 213–14, **312**
    anti-aliasing 252–3, **313**
all rights agreement 283
alpha
    channels 249, 312, **313**
    disc 62, **313**

pre-alpha **322**
    test 82, 267, 296, **313**
alternatives, offering 53
ambience 203
Ampex 232, 233
analog 114, **313**, 316–17
    analogical graphics 126
    sample rate 323
analysis
    needs 32, 140, **320–1**
    risk 20
    systems 166
    training 32, 90, 178
    see also critical path
animatics 266, **313**
animation 125, 127, **313**
anti-aliasing 252–3, **313**
Apple Macintosh
    graphics production 248, 250, 257, 312
    interface design 142
    platform 103, 104, 109, 110
    rights 276
    team selection 165, 166, 168
    video production 223, 240
application **313**
    -based programming **313**
    see also project
appraisal of interface design 147
appropriate use 120
archiving 7, 306–9
    budget information 309
    formal documents 308
    scripts and assets 308–9
    streaming 107–8, 318, **324**
    time 307, 308, 310
art director 169
artefacts **313**
ASCAP 279
assertion of copyright 276

The CD-ROM can be read by any computer able to read ISO9660 or Macintosh HFS discs. This includes PCs and Macintoshes, and also most other desktop computers. You need a web browser to explore the disc, and we provide Microsoft Internet Explorer 2.0. This works with MacOS and Windows 95 (but not Windows 3.1). If you already have a different browser which supports HTML Tables (such as Netscape) then this can be used as an alternative, although the pages are optimized for Internet Explorer.